HOUSE OF SHIVAJI

HOUSE OF SHIVAJI

(Studies and documents of Maratha History : Royal Period)

By

SIR JADUNATH SARKAR, Kt., C.I.E.

GYAN

Published by

Gyan Publishing House
5, Ansari Road
Daryaganj, New Delhi-110002
Phone: 011-47034999, 9811692060
E-mail: books@gyanbooks.com

Distribution Network
gyanbooks.com
India, USA, Canada, UK, Australia, France

ISBN : 978-81-212-6808-0 (PB)
First Published, 1940

2nd Impression 2022

Printed at: Gyan Press, Delhi.

HOUSE OF SHIVAJI
Author: SIR JADUNATH SARKAR

HOUSE OF SHIVAJI

(Studies and documents of Maratha History :
Royal Period)

SIR JADUNATH SARKAR, Kt., C.I.E.,

Hony. M.R.A.S. (London), F.R.A.S.B. (Calcutta), D.Litt., (Hon. Causa, Dacca), Corr. Member, R. Hist. Soc. (Eng.) and Italian Institute of Middle and Extreme Orient (Rome)

1940

Sir Jadunath Sarkar's Works

		Rs.	As.
1.	*History of Aurangzib*		
	Vols. 1 & 2 together, 2nd ed., ..	5	0
	Vol. 3, 3rd ed., ...	3	8
	Vol. 4, 2nd ed., (rewritten) ..	4	0
	Vol. 5	4	0
2.	*Shivaji and his Times, 3rd ed.,* (rewritten)..	5	0
3.	*House of Shivaji* (studies & documents) ..	2	8
4.	*A Short History of Aurangzib,* 511 pages ..	5	0
5.	*Mughal Administration,* 3rd ed.,	3	0
6.	*Studies in Aurangzib's Reign,* 18 essays ..	2	8
7.	*Anecdotes of Aurangzib* (Eng. tr.), 2nd ed.	1	0
8.	*Ahkam-i-Alamgiri,* (Persian text of 7), 2nd ed.	1	0
9.	*India through the Ages,* six lectures ..	1	8
10.	*Fall of the Mughal Empire*		
	Vol. 1 (1739-1754), 560 pp. ..	5	0
	Vol. 2 (1754-1771), 572 pp. ..	5	0
	Vol. 3 (1771-1788), 482 pp. ..	5	0
	Vol. 4 (1788-1803) ..	*in prep.*	
11.	*Chaitanya : his life and teachings,* 3rd ed.	2	0
12.	*Bihar & Orissa during fall of Mughal Empire*	2	0
13.	*Abridged Bengali trans. of Shivaji* (4 pictures)	2	4
14.	,, *Marathi trans. of Shivaji* ,, ..	2	4
15.	,, *Hindi trans. of Shivaji* ,, ..	1	8

CONTENTS

PREFACE

For the convenience of students of Maratha history, I have collected together in one place in this volume all my writings on the "Royal Period" (1626-1700), as distinguished from the "Peshwa Period," together with critical biographies of the four eminent Marathi historical research-pioneers, Sane, Rajwade, Parasnis and Khare. My life of Malik Ambar published in the *Indian Historical Quarterly* in September 1933, has been left out for treatment on a much ampler scale subsequently.

Of the seventeen papers in this volume three (namely 8, 10 and 12) are entirely new, six (*viz.* 4, 6, 7, 11, 14 and 17) have been greatly modified and added to, and eight (*viz.* 1, 2, 3, 5, 9, 13, 15 and 16) have undergone a small amount of revision or none at all. But all of them have been minutely corrected and in several the matter has been rearranged, so as to incorporate the result of my acquisition of original documents and maturer study since the first of these papers was printed in a periodical 34 years ago. In consequence of it, some of the papers (notably 4, 6, 7 and 17) have now practically assumed a new form.

My materials have come from Persian manuscript sources (patiently gathered during a life-time), newly discovered Rajasthani despatches, French books, English Factory Records, and Marathi works discovered only in the 20th century,—besides my notes of what I have observed and heard during my score of visits to Maratha lands since 1907. Thus intimate personal information about Rajwade was secured at Dhulia where he died, and similarly about Parasnis at Satara.

CALCUTTA
May 1940

JADUNATH SARKAR

I

NORTH AND SOUTH IN INDO-MUSLIM CULTURE

It is little known, except to serious students of our country's history, that Muslim civilization in India developed in two independent centres, Delhi and the Deccan, and on two broadly different lines. This difference was due to race, creed and language no less than to geography and history. If a rough generalization is permissible, we can say that the dominant ethnic element in Northern India in the Muslim age was the Turks, in administration and war alike, with valuable assistance from the Persians in the civil business (and occasionally in warfare also), while the India-born Muhammadans (*Hindustan-zai*) were nowhere, and the Abyssinians were mere slaves, rising at the best no higher than the prefect-ship of the city police. The one form of Islam here was Sunnism, the sprinkling of Shias being compelled (except in a few localities of their own) to hide their faith by practising *takia* unless the country had a strong and liberal ruler like Akbar or Shah Jahan. In North India, the language of culture continued to be Persian almost to the end, while Urdu was a despised tongue, not generally accepted by polished society for literary purposes till a century and a half after its triumph in the Deccan, *i.e.*, after 1720, when the downfall of the Mughal empire had already begun.

In the Deccan, on the other hand, when the early years of the local sultanates were over, Abyssinians and Persians rose to supreme places in the State, with the country-born Muhammadans forming a good third. The flow of Turkish recruits from the cradle-land of Central Asia was cut off from the Deccan by the establishment of a Chaghtai-Turki empire at Delhi in 1526 the occupation of Afghanistan by the owner of Delhi and probably also by the wide spread of Shiaism in the Deccan. But, as if to compensate for this loss, increasing numbers of spirited and adventurous Afghans were pushed into the Deccan by the loss of the Delhi throne by their kinsfolk, the Lodis and the Surs. The Deccan became so welcome a refuge for Afghans that here, in the seventeenth century, their armed bands often turned the scale in dynastic contests and their generals rose to be provincial rulers. The Abyssinian emigrants here gained opportunities unequalled elsewhere for displaying their rare capacity for sea-faring, land warfare, management of men, and civil administration. They were no longer household slaves and palace eunuchs as in the North, but regents of kingdoms, generalissimos of armies, admirals of fleets, viceroys of provinces. The Deccani Muslims, some of them converts from the bravest and brainiest Marathas and Kanarese, rose to eminence in war and diplomacy, finance and government alike, and exercised no small weight in shaping the policy of the Court and in conducting war.

In the South, the Muslim population was like a drop

in the ocean of the surrounding Hindu millions. Hence, the isolation between the conquerors and the conquered, which was jealously maintained by the more numerous Muslim body of Northern India from the earliest times, broke down in the Deccan from the stress of circumstances. Hindus rose to high offices in war and diplomacy, revenue and local government, from the days of the Bahmani empire. Hindu influence permeated the Deccani sultanates long before Akbar's liberal synthesis of the two cultures in Northern India began to bear fruit in the golden age of Shah Jahan. And the local Hindu dialect invaded the speech of Deccani royalty, and the mixed product, called Rekhta or Deccani Urdu, became the literary language of kings and nobles, ministers and poets in the South-Indian Muhammadan States in a triumphant manner in the sixteenth century.

Next came religion. For causes not fully explored by historians, the Deccani Sultans embraced the Shia form of Islam, gave it recognition and power as the State-religion, and helped it by these secular advantages to become the prevailing religion, in respect of the number of its votaries in the Court circle, the official world, and the population of the capital, though not in the army. I am doubtful if the Shias ever formed a majority among the dumb masses of Muslim villagers in any Deccani kingdom, but these people did not count. The Shia religion naturally made Persian culture and Persian racial characteristics the ideal of these Southern States,—as distinct from Turkish and even Khurasani models, which ruled at Delhi (except during the latter years of Akbar). The Shia religion influenced Deccani poetry by turning the thoughts of the local poets into the channels of the lives of the Imams and the tragedy of Karbala. Lament for the murdered Husain and his progeny (*marsia*) became the universal poetical type, and under Ali Adil Shah II one poet even bore the title of Mirza *Marsiakhwan* or 'the Chanter of Elegies'. [*Busatin-us-salatin*, litho. ed., p. 434.] The anniversary of the massacre at Karbala in the month of Muharram was celebrated with fulness of ceremony and show by the Court and the people alike and called forth uncontrollable fervour. The occasion supplied the Rekhta poets with inspiration and reward, as the Olympic games did to the ancient Athenian dramatists.

Hindu metres and Hindu poetical *motifs* very early entered into the Muslim vernacular literature produced in the Deccan, and an Adil Shah wrote *dhrupads*, a Qutb Shah acted in his palace the antics of Krishna with the milkmaids of Vrindaban. *Marsia* and *ras-lila* and Spring Carnival (*Vasant*) were equally popular as themes of poetry and equally yielded a prolific crop of verses in Rekhta.

Hence, Rekhta poetry affords, apart from Muslim architecture in the South, the only key now surviving for entering into the magic garden of Deccani Muslim culture. Happily a large mass of this literature has been preserved in anthologies. We notice one in particular, India Office Library No. 3522 (Ethe's Catalogue 701) which Dr. Hermann Ethe thus describes,—*Makhzan-i-Nikat*, the most valuable anthology of the earlier Rekhta poets, by Muhammad Qiyam-ud-din Ali, compiled in 1754 A. D. Dr. Sayyid Muhi-ud-din Qadiri, Ph.D. (London), has analysed a manuscript in the Edinburgh University Library in two volumes, catalogued as "*Marsias of Hashim Ali.*" But only the first volume of it contains some 250 elegies written by Hashim Ali (a Bijapuri poet of Ali Adil Shah II's time, noticed in the *Busatin*) and entitled by him *Diwan-i Husaini*, while the second volume is a *Biyaz* or collection of elegies written by nearly 80 other poets, (lacking some leaves at each end).

II

RUIN OF THE HINDUS OF THE MADRAS KARNATAK

PARTITION OF EASTERN KARNATAK, 1636-48

I have secured manuscripts of the contemporary Persian official histories of the two Bijapuri Sultans Muhammad Adil Shah (reigned 1627-1656) and Ali Adil Shah II (reigned 1656-1672), by Zahur bin Zahuri and Nurullah respectively and of a longer and slightly earlier history, *Futuhat-i-Adilshahi* by Fuzuni Astarabad. These original authorities for the period were not available to Ibrahim Zubairi, whose Persian history of Bijapur named *Busatin-us-salatin*, written in 1824, had hitherto been our only source of information on this dynasty for that half century.

In the light of these first-rate materials and the annual Jesuit letters from Madura, it is now possible to trace step by step and in clear detail the story of how the Muhammadans seized the heritage of the recently shattered empire of Vijaynagar and crushed its numberless disunited, mutually jealous and warring Hindu feudatories, across the entire Indian peninsula from Goa to Madras. The Adil Shah of Bijapur conquered what are called in his Persian history "Malnad and Karnatak," *i. e.*, first the Kanara country of Bednur, then Mysore, starting from the

Ikeri or Nagar district in the west, on to Sera and Bangalore in the centre and the north and the Salem district in the south-east corner, and finally descending the Eastern Ghats the Madras plains up to Vellore Jinji and Valikandapuram within sight of Tanjore. The Qutb Shah of Golkonda seized the Hindu principalities due south and south-east of his capital, *i. e.*, the country beyond the Krishna, lying north-east of these new Bijapuri acquisitions.

Between these two streams of invasion, Sri Ranga Rayal, the last representative of Vijaynagar royalty, was completely crushed out. He offered a long and desperate resistance. But his worst enemies were his own people. The insane pride, blind selfishness, disloyalty and mutual dissensions of his Hindu feudatories rendered all his efforts at self-defence futile, and the Muslims conquered Hindu Deccan piecemeal with the greatest ease and rapidity. As the Jesuit missionary Antoine de Proenza wrote from Trichinopoly (1659): "The old kings of this country appear, by their jealousies and imprudent action, to invite the conquest of entire India by the Muslims." [*Mission du Madure*, iii. 42].

METHOD OF MUSLIM ADVANCE

The process of the Muslim conquest of Trans-Krishna Deccan in the 17th century affords an exact parallel to the method of the foreign subjugation of Northern India at the end of the 12th. The invaders' expeditions started every year in autumn from the settled Muslim territory to the nearest Hindu States across the frontier. These were easily defeated, often with the help of neighbouring Hindu princes, and the victors returned to their capital before the commencement of the rainy season, laden with the plunder of the forts and the promise of tribute. Next year, the raid was repeated to a more distant quarter, the Hindu chief humbled last year, as in duty bound, aiding his new masters in the attack on the independence and wealth of his brother Hindus. Or, if he proved recalcitrant or irregular in the payment of his tribute, he was crushed and his State annexed in the second expedition and made the seat of a Muslim viceroy. Thus the map of the Deccan was "coloured green" and the Muslim boundary advanced very methodically from point to point by regular stages, in a succession of ripples arising from one centre of power.

There could be no central authority for the defence of the Hindus as the imperial prestige and military strength of the Vijaynagar dynasty was now gone, and their local Rajahs (*samantas*), blinded by folly and greed, were bent solely upon enhancing their own glory by throwing off their former suzerain's authority and enlarging their petty States by fratricidal attacks upon the neighbouring Hindu territories.

On the other hand, the Muslim forces were united under one recognized central authority, which marshalled them under a regular gradation of officers and co-ordinated the movements of the columns invading different parts of the enemy country, so that every hard-pressed division was promptly reinforced by troops from other quarters, or a repulse to Muslim arms in one place was avenged next year by an overwhelming concentration of forces there. The proud Hindu kings acted each for himself and perished piecemeal in self-sought isolation.

The Muslim raiders seized the accumulated treasures of the Hindu kings of the Kanarese country,—famous from the earliest times for its fertility of soil and richness in minerals and elephants,—and thus made "war pay for war." The Hindus being always on the defensive, could only lose, and each year they grew poorer and weaker, till the final stage of complete annexation was reached by an inevitable natural process. The Vijaynagar empire broke into pieces under the shock of the crushing defeat of 1565,—in spite of some revival during the next fifty years, —and the antagonism between the Kanarese and Telugu elements, which had been the latent bane of the empire in the 16th century. openly asserted itself in the 17th and completed the disunion and ruin of the Hindus.

The numerous Hindu States of the Mysore plateau were conquered or reduced to vassalage by the Sultan of Bijapur during the years 1636-1648. The same ruin, but on a vaster scale, next befell the infinitely richer and more populous plains lying between the Eastern Ghats and the sea-coast of Madras, known in Indian geography as the Eastern Karnatak (lowlands). The whole of this tract in theory still belonged to the empire of Vijaynagar. The last representative of that dynasty, named Sri Ranga the Sixth in the English genealogical lists and Sri Ranga

Rayal (or simply the Rayal) in the Muslim histories, now had the seat of his government at Vellore at the north end of the Karnatak plain. The steady pressure of Muslim arms had, ever since the fatal day of Talikota (1565), been driving the fallen Vijaynagar Emperors further and still further south-east, to a safe distance from that centre of Muslim power the Bijapur State. Anagundi, Penukonda, Chandragiri, Vellore,—all in succession had been the refuge of these fallen monarchs, who still bore the historic title of Narasinha, ("le Narzingue" and "Narsinga") in the Jesuit and Portuguese accounts.

Proceeding southwards from Vellore, along the Karnatak plain, the next principality was that of Jinji (the ruler of which is named Rajah Rup Nayak in *Busatin-us-Salatin*), and further south, across the many branches of the Kaveri river, lay the State of Tanjore, the Nayak of which was Vijay Raghav. Adjoining Tanjore on the south was the kingdom of Madura, then under the famous ruler Tirumal Nayak (reigned 1623-1659), whose successor Chokka-nath was to reverse Tirumal's policy by shifting his capital from Madura to Trichinopoly once again.

Ruinous Policy of the Hindu Rajahs

All these three Nayaks were hereditary feudatories of the Vijaynagar empire, and their realms had enjoyed peace and prosperity and the limited but actually substantial independence of mediatized States under suzerains of their own race and creed. Only a strong and large Central Government, loyally supported by its vassal

States and provinces, can defend national liberty against foreign aggression in a vast plain like India, which has no difficult natural barrier to oppose to an invader. Swiss cantons, happy in their isolated freedom, are possible only in the poor and obscure nooks of the frowning Himalayas. On the other hand, in the Indian plains or easy plateaux, as soon as the central bond of union is dissolved or even weakened in its authority, and provincial autonomy asserts itself, our national liberty and garnered wealth become an easy prey to any compact body of invaders. In trying to be fully sovereign in our own locality and to throw off the legal dependence on a distant suzerain, we have again and again lost even the semi-sovereignty of the component parts of an empire. That passion for absolute local autonomy and unwillingness to form compact federations for the greater end of national self-preservation by sacrificing some of the smaller rights of full sovereignty, which ruined the republics of ancient Greece, was ever present in Hindu India. The evil was aggravated by the insane personal pride and territorial ambition of the vassal kings.

Every one of them considered the distress or decline of his Hindu suzerain as a golden opportunity for gaining "complete freedom" (*purna swaraj*) and "enlarging his territory" (*rajya-vistar.*) Blind to the ultimate consequences of their selfishness, the feudatories of Vijaynagar not only refused to rally round their overlord when hard-pressed by the Muslims, but openly renounced their allegiance, declared themselves fully sovereign each within his narrow bounds, and began to plunder their fellow vassals, among whom the strong arm of Vijaynagar had once kept peace and promoted the growth of wealth and culture. For the attainment of this noble ambition, they invited the arms of the Muslim sovereigns of Bijapur and Golkonda, dreaming that the latter would march back after overthrowing their former Hindu overlord.* Nor did their delusion end here; instead of doing their own work themselves, these Hindu provincial Rajahs—with a folly equalled only by their military weakness,—hoped to ensure their independence and territorial aggrandizement by setting the different Muslim Powers (invited by them) against each other! This was the very game that Rana Sanga had played, with fatal consequences to himself a century earlier, when he invited the Turk from Kabul to oust the Pathan of Delhi.

The following sections will illustrate how Indian history repeats itself and how the insane ambition of grasping all ends only in the loss of everything, even local sovereignty under light tribute.

First Stage of Muslim Conquest

The partition treaties between Shah Jahan, Adil Shah, and Qutb Shah (May-June 1636) having clearly defined

*This mentality seems to have survived to our own days. In 1919 one of our nationalist orators by letter invited the Amir of Afghanistan to invade India and drive away the present sovereign power. Thereafter, this disinterested helper of Indian Swaraj was expected by our Indian patriot to retire peacefully to his sterile mountains.

their boundaries and set an inviolable barrier to the ambition of the two Deccani Sultans in the north, they could now expand only in the southern and eastern directions, *i.e.*, across the Krishna and Tungabhadra, into Mysore and the Madras Karnatak. This extinction of Hindu rule in the south occupied the years 1637-1664 and is exactly covered by the life of Shahji as a servant of Bijapur. But the popular Maratha tradition that he was the leading general or conqueror of Mysore and Tanjore finds a complete refutation in the authentic historical sources, which prove that Shahji was not the supreme army chief, *nor even the commander of an independent division*, but only one of the many Bijapuri generals serving under the eyes and orders of the Muslim generalissimo, throughout the conquest of Mysore, and it was only very late in his life, in the invasion of Tanjore in 1660-62 (which was, however, followed not by annexation but by withdrawal), that he rose to be second in command.

The part played by Shahji in Bijapuri service will be described below in its natural setting of the general progress of the Adil-shahi arms, so that the reader may not lose a proper sense of proportion.

Campaign of 1638—Randaula Khan is given the title of Rustam-i-zaman and is sent to conquer Malnad, which he effects in the course of the next three years. Virabhadra (Rajah of Ikeri) and Keng Nayak (Rajah of Basavapatan) are humbled and heavily fined.

1639—Rustam sends Afzal Khan, original name Abdullah Bhatari, to attack the fort of Sera (held by Kasturi Ranga). The Rajah comes out to offer submission but is murdered by Afzal Khan during an interview, and the fort is taken. Rustam advances to Bangalore, which is yielded up by Kemp Gonda, who enters Bijapuri service.

Rustam places Shahji in the fort of Bangalore for the purpose of administering and guarding the district, and advances against Srirangapatan. Its Rajah, Kanti Rai, submits after one month of fighting and saves his kingdom by paying 5 lakhs of *hun*.

When Rustam-i-zaman returned from Mysore at the approach of the rainy season, Keng Nayak rebelled, and there was a general rising of the Hindu Rajahs throughout the Kanarese country against Bijapur. So, the war was renewed.

Keng Nayak defended Basavapatan, the fortifications of which he had strengthened, and also posted 70,000 foot musketeers in the broken country around it. The full armed strength of Bijapur was sent under Rustam-i-zaman to quell the rebellion. The general took his post on a hillock about two miles from Basavapatan, and sent Afzal Khan, Shahji, Medaji (MS. reads Badaji) and other officers to assault the main gate of the fort, Siddi Raihan Sholapuri and Husaini (or Habshi) Ambar Khan the second gate, and some other generals the third gate.

The garrison kept up a tremendous fire; but Afzal,

fighting most heroically, advanced, made a lodgement in the *peth* below the main gate, and beat back three sorties of the garrison. The other Bijapuri generals made a simultaneous advance, and after four hours' fighting captured the entire *peth*, slaying 3,700 of the enemy. Keng Nayak now submitted, giving up the fort and 40 lakhs of of *hun*.

While Rustam halted in Basavapatan, he sent Afzal Khan in advance, who conquered Chik-Nayakan-halli (30 m. s. w. of Sera) and Bellur(50 m.s. of Shimoga). Venkatapati, the Rajah of Bellur, was given the fort of Sakrapatan (22 m. s. of it) in exchange for Bellur. Next, Afzal captured Tamkur (nearly midway between Bangalore and Sera.)

Rustam next conquered Balapur and Kulihal (? Kunigal, 40 m. w. of Bangalore.)

The war was renewed in 1644. The fort of Ikeri, situated in the midst of almost inaccessible hills and forests, had been surprised by Rustam-i-zaman, but Shivapa Nayak (of Bednur) wrested it from its careless indolent pleasure-loving Adil-shahi commandant. So, Adil Shah sent Khan Muhammad to recover the fort. He took both Ikeri and Sagar (4 m. north of it.)

In the autumn of 1645 Khan Muhammad again marched into the Karnatak (uplands) and gained a rapid succession of victories. Early in 1646 he reported the capture of Nandiyal (Karnul district) and eight other strong forts of that region.

In all these wars Shahji did not take any part beyond what has been mentioned above. His achievements, if any, did not deserve to be "mentioned in the despatches."

Mustafa Khan's Victorious Progress

In June 1646, the prime minister Mustafa Khan was despatched from the capital to subdue the Kanarese country. By way of Bakargunda he reached the fort of Gumti (or Kumti) on the Malprava river, which he took. Thence marching *via* Gadag and Lakmishwar to Honhalli [12 m. w. of Basavapatan], he met (3 Oct.) Asad Khan and Shahji, who had gone ahead, by order of Adil Shah, for the defence of the Karnatak frontier. The next stage was to Sakrapatan (near the southern end of the Kudur district). At this time Shivapa Nayak, Dad (or Dodda?) Nayak (Rajah of Harpanhalli), Jhujjar and Abaji Rao Ghatge, Keng Nayak's brother, the desais of Lakmishwar and Kopal, and Balaji Haibat Rao joined the Khan with their contingents.

Thence in successive marches he reached Shivaganga,* a famous holy place of the Hindus. Soon afterwards Venkayya (?) Somaji, the Brahman *guru* and envoy of Sri Ranga Rayal of Vellore, waited on Mustafa Khan, with peace offerings, to induce him to turn back from the

* Shivagangapetta, a sacred hill in the north-west of the Nela-mangala taluq of the Bangalore district, 13.10 N. 77.17 E. *Venkayya* may also be read as *Yenganna.*

invasion of the Rayal's country. In the meantime, the Rajahs of Jinji, Madura and Tanjore, who had once been vassals of the Rayal and had now rebelled against him,—had sent their envoys to Mustafa Khan to offer their submission to the Bijapur Government. The Rayal had immediately set out with 12,000 cavalry and 3 lakhs of infantry against the rebels. But the Rajahs of Tanjore and Madura persisted in their war of rebellion.

Mustafa Khan refused to be dissuaded from his purpose by "the deceitful words of the Rayal's envoy" and hastened towards the Kanavi or pass near Vellore. He agreed to stop wherever he would hear that the Rayal had withdrawn from the war with the three Rajahs and agreed to make peace with them. Somaji promised to induce the Rayal to return to Vellore in one week. He took leave of Mustafa Khan and was accompanied by Mulla Ahmad on behalf of Bijapur to settle the terms with the Rayal and induce him to visit Mustafa Khan near Mallipatan in the uplands of Mysore. For the Mulla's return Mustafa halted before a difficult pass 28 miles from Vellore. At first he had wished to detain Somaji in his camp and send Mulla Ahmad alone on his peace mission, but Shahji assured him that he had taken from Somaji solemn oaths of fidelity to his pledge and himself undertook entire responsibility for Somaji carrying out his promise.

Immediately on his arrival at Vellore, Somaji advised the Rayal to prepare for war and block the pass. On hearing of this breach of faith, the Bijapuri wazir decided to make a detour and first enter the kingdom of Jagdev Rao by the Kanavi or pass. This country consisted of the northern corner of the Salem district (the Kaveripatan or Krishnagiri taluq) and the adjacent part of the N. Arcot district. The Rayal hastened to defend the Kanavi or pass. The wazir, who was at Masti [30 m. e. of Bangalore], advanced and on 29 December 1646 sent Asad Khan ahead of himself with a strong force. These men forced their way into Jagdev's country slaying the defenders of the pass, and then halted at a tank five leagues from Masti, for 20 days to level the path through the hills.

The Rayal advanced with a vast army, by the way of Gudiatam and Krishnadurg, to attack the division left at the tank under Shahji and Asad's diwan, (Asad Khan having gone back to Masti on account of illness). The wazir hurried up reinforcements, but while he himself was still six leagues behind, Jagdev Rao, at the head of the Rayal's numerous troops, attacked the Bijapuris under Shahji. After a bloody fight the enemy were routed and Jagdev's mother was killed. The wazir soon afterwards arrived, rewarded his victorious subordinates, and then advancing, halted at the Kanavi or pass, in order to ensure the safe crossing of it by his army.

Then by way of the tank where Asad had halted before, and the fort of Ankusgiri [40 m. s. e. of Bangalore], he reached Krishnadurg on 30 January 1647. After a siege Krishnadurg surrendered. Then the wazir sent a detachment to capture Virabhadra-durg, the capital of Jagdev, [25 m. s. of Ankusgiri]. It was taken after a severe fight and Balaji Haibat Rao left in it as commandant. Then the wazir resumed his march on 7 February. Next Dev-durg was surrendered by Jagdev's minister.

DEFEATED AT VELLORE, SRIRANGA SUBMITS

The Bijapuri army marched by way of Anandbar, Amaravati, and Gudiatam (the last fort being stormed after slaying 1,700 of the enemy), and reached Uranjpur, four leagues from Gudiatam. This place, vacated by its Rajah, was plundered.

Then, after a halt to rest the troops, Mustafa Khan arrived before Vellore, the stronghold of the Rayal. Here a severe battle was fought on the plain between the Bijapuris and Vili Vayuar, the general of the Rayal. In this battle Shahji was posted with the other Hindu officers in command of the Right wing of the Bijapuri army, which faced the enemy's Left wing (under Dilawwar Khan and Raghu Brahman, formerly of Nizam-shahi service). Asad Khan supported Shahji with a division from behind.

This was the decisive battle of the war; the Rayal's general fled wounded, leaving 5,800 of his men dead on the field. Vellore was besieged, the Rayal submitted, promising 50 lakhs of *hun* and 150 elephants as war indemnity. (*c.* April 1647.)

After a halt of one month at Vellore, the wazir set out for further conquests. Turning back from Vellore, by way of Gudiatam, he proceeded conquering Ambur, Kankuti, Tirupatur, Kaveripatan, Hasan Raicotta, Raidurg, Kanakgiri, Ratangiri, Melgiri, Arjunkot, and Dhalinkot (?) —all in Jagdev Rao's country.*

At the end of this brilliantly successful campaign, he returned to Court, leaving Asad Khan and Shahji with many other officers to hold the conquered country. He was welcomed by his royal master, who advanced to the bank of the Krishna to meet and honour him !

How the Muslim came to the Karnatak Plains

Tirumal, the Nayak of Madura, wanted to free himself from the yoke of Vijaynagar, of which he was a tributary. Indeed, the founder of this Nayak dynasty had been a general of that empire posted to Madura (1558). Tirumal formed a league with the Nayaks of Tanjore and Jinji against their common sovereign Sri Ranga. But the Nayak of Tanjore betrayed his allies. Sri Ranga struck the first blow and marched with a large force against the nearest rebel, the ruler of Jinji. Then Tirumal sent a secret letter praying to the Golkonda viceroy on the frontier to invade Vellore. Sri Ranga had, therefore, to turn back from the way to Jinji and expel the Muslim force that had

* Uranjpur—*Erinjeveram*, midway between Gudiatam and Vellore. Kankuti—*Congoondy*, 20 m. west of Ambur. Melgiri—*Soolgiri*. Dhalinkot—*Denkani-colla*. Jagdev Rao's country—*Kaveripatan*. There is a *Raudurg*, on the Pennar river, south west by west of Jinji fort.

entered the Vellore district. Then the three rebels sent their agents to Mustafa Khan, the Bijapuri general, who had reached Bangalore, invoking his protection. The Khan, as we have seen, after long fighting, took tribute from Vellore, about April 1647. Sri Ranga, after an attempt to recover his possessions in that district with secret Qutbshahi help, finally in 1653 lost this last capital and fled to the forests of the robber tribes situated north of Tanjore [Akal Nayak's wood ?] He lived there in great poverty and hardship, abandoned by his courtiers, and finally took refuge with the ruler of Mysore, who had once been his vassal.

[The Jesuit missionary Antoine de Proenza, in his letter from Trichinopoly dated 1659, records the rumour that Sri Ranga was expelled from Vellore by a second and stronger Golkonda force. But the authentic Persian history *Muhammadnamah* and the Dutch factors state that the conquest was achieved by Adil Shah.]

The Golkonda forces advanced from the north conquering towards Jinji, and the Tanjore Nayak made a treaty with them, throwing himself on their mercy. Tirumal had once before been betrayed by the Nayak of Tanjore and had thus become his mortal enemy ; he now appealed to Adil Shah, who sent 17,000 horse under Mustafa Khan to invade Jinji. Tirumal joined this force with his 30,000 soldiers of the ill-armed militia type. The only hope of salvation of the Jinji Nayak lay in a quarrel between the two bodies of Muslim invaders. But as we shall see, they made a mutual agreement by which Hindu Karnatak was to be amicably partitioned between Bijapur and Golkonda in the proportion of two to one. Mir Jumla, the Qutb-shahi viceroy, retreated from the neighbourhood of Jinji, leaving it to fall to the Bijapuri besiegers, while he resumed his career of conquest further north, in the Kadapa distict.

SHAHJI ARRESTED BUT RELEASED BY ADIL SHAH

On 10th January 1648, Mustafa Khan was sent on his last and greatest campaign, the siege of Jinji. The siege was protracted for a year, amidst great famine, and Mustafa Khan, who was now an old man stricken with an incurable disease, was greatly disturbed by the open disobedience of his chief subordinates like Siddi Raihan and Shahji. He had at last to place Shahji under arrest on 25th July, under circumstances which I have described in detail in my *Shivaji* (3rd ed., 35-38.) Mustafa himself died on the 9th November following, and the command of the Bijapuri siege army devolved on Khan Muhammad, the new wazir, who by a vigorous combined assault succeeded in capturing this almost impregnable fort (28th Dec. 1648.)*

A letter from Abdullah Qutb Shah to Haji Nasira (his envoy at Bijapur) tells us that he had received on

* The lithographed *B. S.* gives the date in figures and words as 22 Zihijja 1058 (28 Dec. 1648), while two MSS give the year *in figures and words* as 1059 (-17 Dec. 1649), which is an error.

6th Zihijja [probably in 1057 A. H.=23 Dec. 1647] a petition from Shahji Bhonsle, begging to be taken under his protection, but that Qutb Shah had then and repeatedly before this rejected Shahji's prayer and told him to serve Adil Shah loyally. Another Hindu Rajah,—whose name reads in the Persian MS. as D-h-r-v-y-a-n (?)—had similarly offered to desert Adil-shahi for Qutb-shahi service. [Folio 29 *b*.]

The arrest of Shahji at Jinji was clearly due to these disloyal intrigues. He was coquetting with both the Rayal and Qutb Shah, and the latter sovereign divulged the fact to Adil Shah. We have seen how Shahji had been won over by the Rayal's Brahman agent Venkayya Somaji, during Mustafa Khan's first march towards Vellore, in November 1646.

How Shahji was restored to liberty and his high position is described below on the authority of *Muhammadnamah* (pp. 386-393 of my MS.) :—

After the capture of Jinji, Khan Muhammad sent Afzal Khan in charge of property beyond calculation and 89 elephants for the king. He sent with this force Shahji loaded with fetters on his feet, some of the tricks of which deceiver have been previously described....The Sultan received Afzal Khan in the Kalian Mahal which had been decorated for the *nauroz* festival....Shahji, whom Afzal Khan had escorted with every caution, was sent to the prison of warning. The nobles and gentry of the city were astonished at the graciousness of the king and began to say, 'Shahji Rajah deserves to be put to death and not to be kept under guard. Now that he has been ordered to be imprisoned [instead af being immediately beheaded], it is clear that he would [in time] be granted his life and liberty.' Some councillors did not at all like that Shahji should be set free, because 'if that faithless man were released, he would play the fox again. Many others held the view that to liberate this traitor and ruined wretch would be like treading on the tail of a snake or straightening the coiled sting of a scorpion with one's own fingers knowingly and with open eyes; no wise man would rest his head on a hornet's nest as on a pillow....

"The Sultan, who was prepared to forgive the faults of a whole universe, placed Shahji in charge of Ahmad Khan, *sar sar-i-naubat*, and declared that he would be pardoned and restored to his former honours, if he gave up to the king the forts of Kondana (which he had seized during the dissolution of the Nizam-shahi monarchy), Bangalore, and Kandarpi [40 m. e. of Chittaldurg and the same distance s. w. of Handi Anantpur, in the Kaliandurg sub-division of the Bellary district.]

"Ahmad Khan, by the king's order, conveyed Shahji to his own house, kept him confined, imparted to him the happy news of the royal favour, and did his utmost to compose his mind. Shahji....decided to obey, and wrote to his two sons, who were residing in the above forts, to deliver them to the Sultan's officers immediately on the receipt of his letters. They obeyed promptly."

"Thus, all the numerous misdeeds of Shahji were washed away by the stream of royal mercy. The Sultan summoned Shahji to his presence, gave him the robe of a minister, and settled his former lands on him again."*

After this we have no further mention of Shahji in *Muhammadnamah*, which stops abruptly with the capture of Vellore and the humbling of the Rajah of Mysore into a tributary vassal by Khan Muhammad, about 1653. There is thus a gap in our knowledge of Shahji's doings from 1649 onwards, which is partly filled by the brief notices occurring in Aurangzib's correspondence and the Jesuit letters from 1659 onwards; but these letters deal solely with the history of Jinji and Tanjore and tell us nothing of what happened in Kanara proper or Mysore.

The letters of Abdullah Qutb Shah, drafted by Abdul Ali Tabrezi (British Museum, Persian MS. Addl. 6600) give some extremely valuable information on Karnatak history of this time. We learn fron them that it was agreed between Bijapur and Golkonda that Sir Ranga Rayal's territory and treasures were to be conquered and divided between the two in the proportion of two to one, —two-thirds of them falling to Adil Shah and one-third to Qutb Shah. Then Abdullah writes whimpering to Shah Jahan that Adil Shah had broken his promise and was

* A son was born to Muhammad Adil Shah on 5th May 1649, and the Court rejoicing that followed was utilised to release the political prisoner Shahji eleven days later. [*Md-namah* and *Jedhe Shakavali.*]

forcibly taking away Qutb Shah's portion. On the other hand, the Bijapuri panegyrist Zahur complains, in his *Muhammadnamah*, that the ungrateful Abdullah,—whose forces had been defeated by the Rayal and who could not have won an inch of the Karnatak without Bijapuri support,—had formed a secret alliance with the infidel (*i. e.*, the Rayal) and sent his general Mir Jumla to assist the Hindus in the defence of Jinji, but that Mir Jumla arrived too late, and was subsequently defeated in another quarter, by the Bijapuri general Baji Ghorpare.

The Bijapuri siege of Jinji was prolonged for nearly one year (1648). But the arrival of the new wazir Muzaffar-ud-din Khan-i-Khanan Khan Muhammad (shortly after Mustafa's death on 9 Nov. 1648,) infused an unwonted vigour among the besiegers and struck dismay into the hearts of the garrison. He made a most heroic attack, with his full force, on the defences. After a bloody fight on the first day, the soldiers of Jinji lost heart, killed their women, and took to flight. The Bijapuris gave chase, slew many of the fugitives, and captured the fort, while the Nayak took refuge in the citadel, perched on the highest rock. [For a description of the forts, see *History of Aurangzib*, vol. 5]. This he held for one entire day, but admitted defeat at night, begged for mercy, waited on Khan Muhammad, and made his submission. (28 Dec. 1648.)

This is the account given by the Bijapur official historian Zahur bin Zahuri. The Jesuit letter says nearly the same thing: "The Adil-shahi forces continued the siege of Jinji...A revolt broke out among the garrison. In the midst of the confusion, the gates of the citadel were opened to the enemy." [*Mission du Madure*, iii. 46.] *Busatin-us-salatin*, p. 328, gives a different version of the event: "Rajah Rup Nayak, the ruler of Jinji, whose family had owned the place for seven hundred years past and made the country famous for its cultivation and population,—was, unlike his predecessors, too fond of youthful pleasures and intoxication to attend to the administration; his affairs were neglected and delayed. All the zamindars of that tract and neighbouring rulers, like the Rajah of Tanjore, turned their faces away from him and gave him no aid during the siege. At last owing to the length of the siege, his provisions were exhausted, and losing all hope of help from outside, he surrendered his fort to the Muslim heroes.... The spoils taken by the Government amounted to four *kror* of *hun* (16 *kror* of Rupees), besides what the soldiers plundered for themselves."

Hindu Disunion: Further Muslim Progress

After the fall Jinji the Bijapuri army marched against the Nayaks of Tanjore and Madura, plundering and devastating their realms. These Hindu princes made submission, offering to pay tribute. As the Jesuit missionary writes, "The Adil-shahi forces returned to Bijapur after conquering a vast country, subjugating two powerful kings, and gathering treasure beyond calculation, without having had to fight one battle and almost without losing a single soldier." [*Mission*, iii. 47.] This was evidently in 1649-50.

But while Khan Muhammad, who had grown sick of long campaigning and wished to enjoy himself at the capital, was absent from the Karnatak, Sri Ranga with the help of Mysore recovered a part of his former dominions and repulsed a Golkonda army that had advanced to fight him.* [Proenza supported by *Muhammadnamah*]. But Hindu disunion and mutual bad faith prevented him from freeing the whole of the Karnatak from the foreign invaders.

Tirumal Nayak, instead of helping to restore Sri Ranga, appealed to the Muslims, opened the mountain passes to them and thus enabled them to carry the war into Mysore. Thus Sri Ranga, losing his last ally, fell finally. Khan Muhammad left the country after levying enormous contributions from Tanjore and Madura!

* In 1651 Qutb Shah was worsted in a war with Adil Shah over the division of the conquered country and had to pay the latter 6 lakhs of *hun* for being left in possession of his conquests. Then Mir Jumla (the Golkonda general) instigated the Mysore Rajah and Sri Ranga to oppose the Adil shahi generals. The Rayal tried to reconquer the Vellore district, but was finally (1653) deprived of Vellore fort by a Bijapuri army after a long siege and forced to content himself with Chandragiri, which now formed the sole remnant of the great empire of Vijaynagar. The Rayal's futile appeals to Prince Aurangzib, then Viceroy of Mughal Deccan, to compel the two Deccani sultans to restore his family dominions to him have been described fully in my *History of Aurangzib*, I. ch. 10.

The war was renewed. The king of Mysore attacked the ever faithless Nayak of Madura. But Tirumal died in 1658 at the age of 65 after 36 years of reign. His son and successor, Muttu Virappa, refused tribute, and Adil Shah, therefore, sent an army of chastisement, which suddenly turning from the east to the south, fell upon Tanjore by surprise, on 19th March 1659. The commandant of the capital, on being struck by an arrow, which made a slight wound, disgracefully capitulated! The victorious Muslims marched against Manarcoil and Vallankota, south-west of Tanjore. They found the latter fort deserted, and put a small garrison in it. Then they sat down, enjoying the fertile and beautiful kingdom. [*Mission*, iii. 47—53.]

BIJAPURI OCCUPATION OF TANJORE

The Jesuit letter for 1662 written from Trichinopoly informs us: "The Muslims under the command of Shahji and Moula [? Mulla Ahmad Navaiyat], generals of Adil Shah, have occupied the realms of Jinji and Tanjore for the last two years, and seem to wish to fix their domination there. The people have submitted to the yoke of a conqueror from whom they get less cruelty and more justice than from their own sovereigns." [*Mission*, iii. 119.] From the same source we learn that a famine, due to the disorder and devastation attendant on war, was raging in all that country, in an extremely severe form, so that all the inhabitants who could had fled to Madura and Satya-mangalam (in the centre of the

Coimbator district). The "Muslims were the first victims of pestilence, having been themselves the cause of it, their horses and men perished of famine in such large numbers that the corpses could not be buried or burnt, but were flung in the midst of the field, which imprudent act bred diseases and increased the mortality. Finally, disunion broke out among the generals and officers of the Bijapuri army. Moula, alarmed at the sad condition of his troops, ...was forced by famine and pestilence to abandon Tanjore. He advanced to besiege Trichinopoly, 'the key to the kingdom of Madura'; but it was ably defended by Lingama Nayak, and Moula was forced to accept a small sum as the price of peace and to retire beyond the hills." [*Ibid.*, 120.]

THE TROUBLES OF THE MADURA KINGDOM.

Muttu Virappa died shortly after this peace and was succeeded by his son Chokkanath (or Chokka Linga), aged six years. The government was conducted by a very able Brahman regent, who with his secretary monopolized all power and sent the other nobles and generals into banishment from the Court. These two deputed Lingama Nayak with 40,000 troops to attack Shahji and capture Jinji, but Lingama was bribed by the Bijapuri general to waste the royal treasure in a long and fruitless campaign. This failure reacted on the situation at Court. The Brahman regent and his secretary were overthrown by the Rajah with the help of two loyal generals. Chokkanath afterwards tried to seize Lingama but the latter escaped to Shahji and returned with 12,000 foot and 7,000 horse to besiege Trichinopoly (to which the capital of Madura had been transferred.)

Chokkanath had more than 50,000 men to defend his capital with, but the faithlessness of his new Brahman minister caused division and trouble among his troops. He, however, made a personal appeal to his army and with such good effect that Lingama and Shahji were foiled and fled for refuge to Tanjore, the Nayak of which had favoured this traitorous invasion.

The Madura Nayak, at the head of 70,000 "well-disciplined warriors," now marched upon Tanjore. The two generals, Shahji and Lingama, took to flight and were pursued towards Jinji. The Tanjore Nayak made a humble submission to the lord of Madura.

The usual horrors of war were intensified by famine. The Muslims, during their temporary occupation, were terribly oppressive, and the Tanjore Christian converts had to flee to Trichi for refuge, returning to their homes only after the invaders had left. [*Ibid.*, 121—123.]

Maratha Conquest of Tanjore Kingdom

In 1663 the Bijapuri army repeated its invasion of Madura under a general whose name is spelt as Vanamian [Bahlol Khan Miana ?] in the Jesuit letter. He laid siege to Trichinopoly, but was stopped by the bombardment from the fort-walls, and plundered all that he could. At last he was bribed to retire on the payment of a large sum by the Nayak under the name of war contribution.

Then Chokkanath turned upon the faithless Tanjore Nayak who had, in violation of their recent treaty, joined the Muslim invaders. He took Vallam, a citadel eight miles south-west of Tanjore city, and on the Nayak submitting left a garrison to hold it for him. [*Ibid.*, 151—160.]

Shahji died on 23rd January 1664, and was succeeded by his son Vyankoji in his post as one of the three Adilshahi generals among whom the province of Jinji was partitioned. [*Mission*, iii. 201.]

At last, in April 1674, the Nayak of Madura attacked Tanjore, defeated and killed its Nayak Vijay Raghav, and seized the kingdom. The son of the vanquished king appealed to Adil Shah, who sent Vyankoji Bhonsle with an army to restore him to the throne. Vyankoji, in concert with Sher Khan Lodi, began the siege of Tanjore in January 1675, but had to encamp at a great distance from its walls and merely attempt a blockade of the fort. The elder brother of Chokkanath, who had been left to govern the new conquest, ably checked Vyankoji, who was forced to halt for one year on the frontier of Tanjore.

Then a quarrel broke out between Chokkanath and his brother. Vyankoji profited by this disunion and took Tanjore at the first assault on 12th January, 1676, and soon occupied all its territory, crowning himself with grand ceremonies as king of Tanjore on 5th March 1676. [*Mission*, 247—248; Martin's *Memoires*, i. 603, ii. 9 and 25; *Bhosal-vamsham* for dates.]

The first effects of the conquest were deplorable. A famine broke out. "The Tanjore kingdom was despoiled by Vyankoji from one side and by the Mysore king from the other." But after usurping the throne, Vyankoji assumed the title and authority of an independent king, and then sought to make himself beloved by the people. The justice and wisdom of his government began to close the wounds of the preceding reign and to develop the natural resources of the country. By repairing the canals and tanks, he gave fertility to the vast fields which had been left untilled for many years, and "the last harvest [*i.e.*, in 1676] has surpassed all that was seen before." [*Mission*, iii. 248-249.]

The new king was threatened by attacks from a fresh Adil-shahi army, all the forces of the Madura Nayak, and a third body of troops assembled by the ruler of Mysore on his frontier "in alarm at the establishment of an audacious people (*i.e.*, Marathas) on his border." But these war clouds rolled away and Vyankoji remained safe in Tanjore while retaining possession of one-third of the province of Jinji, *i.e.*, the southern extremity of it immediately north of the Kolerun river, which his father had acquired long ago.

The popular Maratha story, given in the *Chitnis Bakhar*, i. 22, that Shahji conquered Tanjore at the invitation of the Nayak of Madura who gave him five lakhs of Rupees, must be rejected in the light of the contemporary information quoted above. Shahji had merely plundered the Tanjore territory twice but never *annexed* it.

III

EARLY LIFE OF SHAHJI

1. During the regency of Malik Ambar, 1608-1626

The rise of the Bhonsla family is closely connected with the dissolution of the Ahmadnagar kingdom, within whose territory lay their homes, Ellora, Chamargunda, and finally Poona, and to whose service belonged Shahji, his father-in-law Lakhji Jadav, and many of their relatives. The declining fortunes of the dynasty greatly added to the value of able and enterprising leaders of mercenary bands and gave them splendid opportunities of winning wealth, power, and large estates for themselves.

In August 1600 Akbar had captured the capital Ahmadnagar and sent its king Bahadur Nizam Shah (a nephew of the famous Chand Bibi) to a State-prison. But the entire kingdom was far from being conquered or even normally occupied. That task required 36 years more. Soon after the fall of the capital, the Nizam Shahi nobles retired to the provinces, to which the Mughals were not yet strong enough to penetrate, and one of them set up Burhan Nizam Shah (called Murtaza II by Firishtah, ii. 165) a son of Prince Shah Ali, as king, with Parenda in the south as his capital. This was done late in 1600 or early in 1601. In a few years an Abyssinian slave, named Malik Ambar, got possession of this puppet king, defeated his rival nobles, and made himself regent and *de facto* ruler of the whole kingdom. Great in war and civil administration alike, Ambar defeated the Mughals, recovered the fort of Ahmadnagar (Oct. 1610), waged successful wars with Bijapur, and brought nearly the whole of the old Nizam Shahi kingdom under his sway. He had three long wars with the Mughals in the reign of Jahangir, in the second of which (1617) he was defeated and forced to restore Ahmadnagar, and after the third agreed to live on terms of peace with Delhi. In the meantime he had transferred the capital and the puppet king to Daulatabad.

Lakhji Jadav of Sindkhed was originally an important general of Malik Ambar, and Shahji first saw service probably as the commander of the small contingent of his family under the banners of Malik Ambar. He must have been a petty captain during the regency of Malik Ambar, who died on 14 May 1626, when Shahji was about 31 years old. Shahji's name is not mentioned even once in the autobiography of Jahangir and the other Persian histories of the Mughal wars in the Deccan during that monarch's reign (1605-1627), though many other Maratha captains are noticed. Even the Bijapur historian Fuzuni Astarabadi is silent about him in the body of his book, though some one has added the word *Shahji* in the *margin* of the British Museum manuscript of this work in relating the battle of Bhatvadi (1624.) There is contemporary official record that even four years after Malik Ambar's death Shahji could muster only 2,000 horse of his own and possessed no territory beyond his paternal villages.

(November 1630, in Abdul Hamid, I.A., p. 327.) He first rose to independent and high command under Fath Khan (the son of Ambar), who was evidently his first patron. From 1620 to 1629, Lakhji Jadav was on the side of the Mughals, and therefore Shahji could not have fought as a member of his father-in-law's force.

Malik Ambar died at the ripe old age of eighty, on 14th May 1626, and was succeeded in the wazirship by his son Fath Khan, an extremely haughty, incompetent and blood-thirsty man. He made the mistake of alienating his friends by an invasion of Bijāpur, shortly after the death of Ibrahim Adil Shah (on 12th Sept. 1627) and the succession of his son Muhammad Adil Shah, a boy, domineered over by his minister Khawas Khan. Khan-i-Jahan Lodi, the Mughal governor of the Deccan, was heavily bribed by Hamid Khan, (the new Abyssinian favourite of Nizam Shah) and treacherously "gave back to him all the territory that Akbar and Jahangir had wrested from the dynasty with so much loss of men and money." Only the commandant of Ahmadnagar fort refused to obey the traitor's order and loyally held the fort for the Mughal Emperor.

This happened at the troubled close of Jahangir's reign. On the death of that royal voluptuary (29th Oct. 1627), Shah Jahan succeeded and in a few months firmly seated himself on the throne, and then turned to restore his authority in the Deccan. Nizam Shah was called upon to give back what Khan-i-Jahan had without proper authority ceded to him.

The Nizam Shahi *wazir* tried to play a double game. He professed willingness to restore the disputed territory, but secretly instructed his officers to resist the Mughals. The result was disastrous. Vast Mughal armies, under able generals, entered the Deccan; Shah Jahan secured the neutrality of Bijapur by offering its king a slice of the Nizam Shahi territory. In November 1628, when the Mughal viceroy of the Deccan advanced to take possession of the fort of Bir, Fath Khan treacherously sent Shahji and a party of other *siladars* with 6,000 cavalry to make a raid on East Khandesh and create a diversion in the rear of the Mughals. But an imperial officer, Dariya Khan Ruhela, who held a large jagir in Banswara, attacked the raiders, slew many of them, and expelled the whole party from the Doab between the Tapti and the Purna. (*Padishahnamah*, I. A. 251.)

The war with the Mughals went against Fath Khan, and all the misfortunes of the kingdom were ascribed to his incompetence and ill-luck. His master seized the odium excited by the minister's administrative failure to get rid of him. The whole Court had been alienated by Fath Khan's overweening pride and jealous monopoly of power. Besides, Fath Khan's rival, Hamid Khan (another Abyssinian noble) had wormed his way into Nizam Shah's heart by presenting him with his own wife, a woman of marvellous craft and fascinating power. (*Tuzuk*, 415.) Hamid Khan signalised his accession to the wazirship by sending an expedition against Bijapur, which was commanded by his wife. (*Tuzuk*, 416.)

At the instigation of Hamid Khan, Nizam Shah treacherously arrested Fath Khan and threw him into prison at Daulatabad. (*Basatin-i-salatin*, 286.) This event took place probably early in 1630.

2. Massacre of Jadav Rao by Nizam Shah

The imprisonment of Fath Khan threw Nizam Shahi affairs into worse confusion than before: all the other nobles took alarm and began to devise plans for safeguarding their own lives and family honour. Lakhji Jadav Rao, who was one of the chief nobles and highest officers of the State, for self-preservation began to think of fleeing and taking refuge with the Mughals. Nizam Shah got scent of the matter and took counsel with Ikhlas Khan and Hamid Khan, saying "Jadav Rao is old and experienced and knows all the secrets of our State. If he joins the Mughals, he will cause us harm beyond repair." They advised him to imprison the Rao. Nizam Shah ordered Farhad Khan, Safdar Khan and Moti Khan Khattala to arrest him. Shortly after, when Jadav Rao came to the Audience Hall, Nizam Shah after a few minutes withdrew from it. The three Khans all together fell upon Jadav Rao and his son Achalji and snatched away their swords. Jadav Rao and Achalji then drew daggers from their belts, faced the enemy, and fought desperately. At last Jadav Rao was slain by Safdar Khan and Achalji, and some of their comrades also fell in the struggle. Lakhji's brother Bithoji (or Nathuji), who had dismounted at the cistern of Qutlugh Khan, immediately after the affair fled to the Mughals. Lakhji's son-in-law Shahji, who was then stationed near Parenda, on hearing the news, hastened towards Sangamner, and thence reached Puna, plundering on the way. (*Basatin-i-salatin*, 286-287.)

The Mughal official history briefly tells us that Lakhji Jadav Rao had at first been a high mansabdar of the Empire, having deserted Malik Ambar for the Mughal service in 1620, and received for himself and his kinsfolk *mansabs* totalling 24,000 cavalry, and had next (about April 1630) gone over to Nizam Shah, who during an audience at Daulatabad murdered him with his two sons, Achla and Raghu, and his son's son Yeshwant Rao. But his brother Jagdev and the latter's son Bahadurji fled to their home at Sindhkhed near Jalna. And so also did his heroic wife Girija (Bai), who, on hearing of her husband's death, did not lose time by shedding womanly tears, but quickly gathered together her property and the remnant of her family, and with great skill and daring made her way to safety. (*Pad.* i. 308-310.)

From Sindhkhed they sent petitions to the Emperor Shah Jahan, who received them into his protection and favour. Lakhji's brother and two grandsons were given *mansabs* in the Mughal army, with jagirs, (Aug. 1630.) The murder seems to have taken place on 12th Aug. 1630. (*Jedhe corrected.*)

From his home at Puna, Shahji petitioned the Emperor for permission to enter his service. On receiving a favourable reply, he came over to the Mughal viceroy's camp (November 1630), with 2000 cavalry, and was created a Commander of 5000 with two lakhs of Rupees as his bounty; his brother Minaji became a 3-hazari and his son Shambhuji a 2-hazari. (*Pad.* I. A. 327-28.) After a short time he was deputed by the Mughal viceroy from Talangi (near Parenda) to occupy the districts of Junnar and Sangamner, (which had been given to him as *jagir*) and Bezapur (*Ibid.*, 331, 357.) A little later he was ordered to stay at Nasik, which was in the *jagir* of Khawjah Abul Hasan, a Mughal officer. (*Ibid.*, 367.) About May 1632, the mahals of Fath Khan's jagir which had been granted to Shahji, were transferred to Fath Khan by order of the Emperor, and Shahji at once left the Mughals. (497.)

We now turn to the history of Shahji during 1631. Retiring to Puna he raised a great disturbance, plundered and took forcible possession of the Nizam Shahi country around and some Adil Shahi territory in the neighbourhood. Khawas Khan, the *wazir* of Bijapur, on hearing of these disorders and acts af usurpation, appointed Murari (Pandit) from Bijapur with a large army to chastise and extirpate him. When Shahji found danger threatening him from all sides, he made friends with Srinivas Rao, the *sar-nayak* and governor of Junnar, and took refuge with him. Murari burnt and plundered Puna, Indapur, and other villages and abodes of Shahji, totally desolated them, and founded a fort name *Daulat Mangal* on the hill of Bhilsar 32 miles from Puna, posting Raya

(? Rama) Rao with 2,000 troopers there. He then detached Chandra Rao, Dalve and other captains of his army with their own contingents to conquer Tal Konkan, sending them towards Dabul, and himself returning to Bijapur. (*B.S.* 287.)

As Shahji was now living under the protection of Srinivas Rao in Junnar, and had no strong place of his own for a home, he built a new fort, named *Shahgarh* on the site of Bhimgarh, which had been lying ruined and deserted for a long time past. Making it his stronghold, he assembled five or six thousand troopers and set to conquering the country and forts in the neighbourhood.

3. Extinction of Nizam-Shahi Monarchy

At this time many nobles urged Nizam Shah to restore Fath Khan to the wazirship and thus strengthen his Government, as the dreaded Mughal enemy was only waiting for an opportunity to crush him and his State was in utter confusion. He agreed, released Fath Khan from prison (18th January, 1631) and made him *wazir* again, saying to him "Guard my life and kingdom like your great father." The change was followed by a reform of the administration for a time, and people hoped for the best. But a few months afterwards, Burhan Nizam Shah was seized with insanity. Fath Khan brought him (at the end of July) out of the palace to his own house (formerly the mansion of Salabat Khan) for treatment. But the king died in two months, and Fath Khan was universally suspected of having poisoned him. (*B.S.* 288-290, 296; *Pad.* I. A. 442.) This happened about February 1632.

With the murder of Burhan Nizam Shah began the last stage of the fall of the once glorious Ahmadnagar kingdom. Fath Khan set up a puppet on the throne, Husain III, the son of the murdered king, a boy of seven only. (*B.S.* 296.) At once the provincial governors and commandants of forts refused obedience to the king-maker and his crowned prisoner. Shahji seized this opportunity of making himself great by imitating the example of Fath Khan. He deserted the Mughal service (about June 1632), and seized the districts of Nasik, Trimbak, Sangamner, and Junnar, as well as parts of Northern Konkan, (*Pad.* I. A. 442; *B.S.* 304.)

The Nizam Shahi *qiladar* of Galna (in W. Khandesh) rebelled against Fath Khan's government and negotiated with Shahji for the sale of the fort to him. But the Mughal viceroy of the Deccan heard of the matter, and by heavily bribing the *qiladar* induced him to sell the fort to the imperialists instead. It was delivered to them on 7th Oct. 1632, after Shahji's agents had been sent back in disappoinment. (*Pad.* I.A. 443.)

We shall here conclude the story of the death agony of the Nizam Shahi monarchy. The Mughals had got possession of most of its strong places—Bir in 1628, Dharur on 17th June 1631, Galna on 7th Oct. 1632. But their military career had been chequered. A Mughal advance under Asaf Khan against Bijapur in Dec. 1631-

June 1632 had ended in failure, retreat, and a patched up peace. Their siege of Parenda, under Azam Khan, was unsuccessful; the Bijapuris sent a contingent under Murari Pandit to assist the garrison, the fort was provisioned, and Azam Khan, finding that no fodder was available for 40 miles round the fort, abandoned the siege and retired to Dharur (about March, 1631.) A terrible famine desolated the Deccan throughout 1631, causing indescribable suffering and loss of life. (*Pad.* I. A. 362-364; *B. S.* 296.)

Fath Khan after the murder of Burhan Nizam Shah (about Feb. 1632) was universally detested by all parties in the Deccan, and saw that the only means or saving himself was to seek Mughal protection. For this he petitioned Shah Jahan (about the middle of 1632.) The Emperor took him under his wing, and restored to him that portion of his old *jagir* which had been bestowed on Shahji during the Maratha's temporary submission to the Mughals. (*Pad.*, 497.) Shahji at once went over to Bijapur, and Adil Shah sent an army to aid the Maratha chief in wresting Daulatabad from Fath Khan's hands. Fath Khan wrote to the Mughal viceroy, Khan-i-Khanan Mahabat Khan, "Shahji is coming against me; there is no provision in the fort and it cannot hold out for a day. Come quickly and take it and save me: I shall become a servant of the Emperor." Mahabat sent an advanced force by rapid marches, and himself set out for the place (on 1 January 1633) with 40,000 troops. Meantime the treacherous Fath Khan had repented of his offer to the

Mughals and made terms with the Bijapuris. Muhammad Adil Shah decided to aid Nizam Shah in his last hours against their common enemy, the insatiably ambitious Emperor of Delhi, and sent a vast army under Randaula Khan to reinforce the Nizam Shahis. The allies barred the path of the Mughals near the village of Khirki (now Aurangabad,) and the Adil Shahis introduced into the fort 3 lakhs of *hun* and provisions. Fighting took place round Daulatabad and in the neighbouring district for five months, and in it Shahji, acting as a lieutenant of the Bijapuris, took a conspicuous part on many occasions.

Khani-i-zaman, the son of Mahabat, drove Shahji away from Nizampur (February). (*Pad.* I. A. 496-520; *B. S.* 287-289.) But the latter and other Bijapuri officers continued to hover round the Mughal camp and cause constant harassment and loss to them. Khan-i-Khanan Mahabat Khan himself arrived on the scene on 1st March and after severe struggles invested the fort closely. Fath Khan made a despairing appeal to Adil Shah to send him food and reinforcements, promising to yield the fort to him. Adil Shah sent a large army and vast quantities of provisions and other needments to the fort under Murari Pandit, about May. (*Pad.* I. A. 496-520, *B. S.* 297-299.)

But the Muslim nobles of Bijapur were jealous of Murari, whose overweening pride and power were solely due to the favour of the dictatorial *wazir* Khawas Khan. They all decided not to fight or exert themselves so long as Murari was there, because in the event of their gaining success all the credit of the victory would go to Murari. The Brahman general also very unwisely refused to deliver the grain he had brought for the besieged. When Fath Khan in the extremity of starvation begged him to send the provisions in, Murari replied by calling upon him to cede the fort to him first. Fath Khan had no help but to make terms with the Mughals, and at last on 17th June 1633 surrendered the impregnable fort of Daulatabad with all its treasure and war material to Mahabat Khan. Husain, the last of the Nizam Shahi kings, thus fell into the hands of the Mughals and was sent to Gwalior to end his days in the State-prison there. (*B.S.* 300-301 ; *Pad.* I. A. 528-540.)

The Adil Shahi troops now left the environs of Daulatabad, covered with failure and humiliated in their master's eyes. Murari was severely censured by Khawas Khan, as the blame for this miserable result was laid entirely on him. (*B.S.* 302.)

4. Shahji as King-maker

The Nizam Shahi dynasty was now extinguished. Its local officers set up for themselves: Srinivas Rao at Junnar, Siddi Saba Saif Khan in Konkan, Siddi Ambar at Janjira-Rajpuri, Siddi Raihan at Sholapur. (*B.S.* 303.) Shahji Bhonsla retired from the walls of Daulatabad to Bhimgarh (July 1633), and seized all the Nizam Shahi dominion from Puna and Chakan to Balaghat and the environs of Junnar, Ahmadnagar, Sangamner, Trimbak, and Nasik, and collected a force of seven or eight thousand cavalry, with which he plundered all sides. The new Mughal commandant of Daulatabad, Iradat Khan, wrote to Shahji through Maloji Bhonsla to join the Emperor's side, promising him very high *mansabs* for himself and his sons and the granting of every one of his demands. He knew that if Shahji could be enlisted in the imperial service and the Nizam Shahi territory could be occupied by the Mughals through Shahji's help, it would greatly enhance his own credit with the Emperor. But Shahji "who was one of the cleverest, most far-sighted and most ambitious of men," intrigued with Khawas Khan through Murari, saying, "What does it matter if out of the 84 forts of Nizam Shah the one fort of Daulatabad has been lost? [Other strongholds] like Junnar still remain. If you help me I can uplift the Nizam Shahi banner again with all my energy." This was also the desire of Khawas Khan and of all the other Adil Shahi nobles (except Mustafa Khan, the rival of Khawas.) The policy was adopted; Khawas Khan sent a large army under Murari Pandit to assist Shahji. The Maratha chief took out of fort Jivdhan, on the top of the Nana Ghat, some 30 miles west of Junnar [or fort Anjaneri, acc. to *Pad.* I.B. 36] a Nizam Shahi prince named Murtaza. aged 10 or 11 years, who had been kept there as a State-prisoner, and crowned him at Shahgarh (formerly Bhimgarh) with the assistance of Murari, September 1632. (Jedhe, *B. S.* 306. *Pad.* I. A. 402, I.B. 36.)

In the name of Murtaza Nizam Shah II., Shahji carried on the government for three years, seized districts and forts, and levied troops. He and Murari wrote to Siddi Saba Saif Khan, who had got possession of Tal-Konkan and was residing at Kalian, to come and pay his respects to the new king, and co-operate with Shahji. The Siddi declined and decided to live at the Court of Bijapur, ceding the province to Shahji,—so that the whole of Tal-Konkan from Mahad to the frontier of Jawhar, with the exception of the forts, fell into Shahji's hands. Murari left Shahji as regent and virtual ruler of Murtaza Nizam Shah, with a contingent of 5 or 6 thousand Bijapuri troops under Ambar Khan for his assistance, and himself returned to Bijapur. On the way he halted at Pabal, near the point of junction of the Bhima and the Indrayani, (now called Tulapur, north of Poona) for a holy bath on 23 Sept. 1633, and *tula* (weighing one's self against gold &c., to be given away in charity). Shahji, who hated Saif Khan for his refusal to co-operate with him, attacked him while he was coming to Murari with his 2,000 cavalry with a view to accompanying him to Bijapur. [Shahji's plea was that Saif Khan had seized the Nizam Shahi elephants in fort Kohaj.] A bloody battle was fought between the two near Khed (12 miles due west of Pabal); many were slain and wounded on both sides; Siddi Ambar Atish Khani, the commander of Saif Khan, was wounded and taken prisoner by Shahji's men, while the Khan himself was invested at Khed for two days. Murari relieved him and took him to Bijapur in safety. (*B.S.* 306.)

After this Shahji proposed a marriage between his

eldest son Shambhuji and the daughter of Srinivas Rao, the governor of Junnar, treacherously imprisoned the Rao, and thus made himself master of the forts of Junnar, Jivdhan, Sunda [? Sudha], Bhor, Parasgarh, Harshagarh, Mahuli and Kohaj.

He next removed the puppet king Murtaza from Bhimgarh to Junnar, and himself lived there in great wealth (seized from the property of Srinivas Rao and other rich men of the place). Some twelve thousand of the dispersed former troops of the Nizam Shahi kingdom now gathered under him. Mahabat Khan found that the capture of Husain Nizam Shah III and his capital had not finished the business, but Shahji had revived the trouble. So war was declared against Shahji and Adil Shah. A large Mughal army was sent under Prince Shuja to besiege Parenda (24 Feb. 1634), which Adil Shah had gained by paying its Nizam Shahi *qiladar* three lakhs of *hun*. But Murari brought relief to the fort, and the siege was abandoned by the Mughals in May. (*B.S.* 307; *Pad.* I. B. 36—45.)

Meantime, that is late in 1633, Shahji having assembled his troops near Ahmadnagar, had been looting the environs of Daulatabad and Bidar, and closing the roads to grain-dealers and other wayfarers. A Mughal detachment was therefore sent to ravage Chamargunda, the home of the Bhonslas, and then take post at Sangamner, about December 1633 or the next month. (*Pad.* I. B. 36.) The Mughal failure was due to quarrels among their generals.

5. Mughal armies crush Shahji

Next, Shahji seized the opportunity of the death of Mahabat Khan, the viceroy of the Deccan (26 Oct., 1634), to lay hands on the villages near Daulatabad and collect the revenue. But as soon as Khan-i-Dauran, the new acting viceroy, arrived near the scene of the disturbances, (middle of January, 1635), Shahji and other troublers of the public peace, at the news of it, fled away from the neighbourhood of Daulatabad towards Ramduda. Khan-i-Dauran himself arrived at Ramduda on 28th January, and then pursued the enemy through Shiwgaon, Amarapur (2 miles east of Junnar), and the pass of Muhri. Meantime, the fugitive Shahji had sent his baggage by the pass of Manikduda towards Junnar, but it was intercepted by the Mughals and its guards were defeated and dispersed with slaughter. On this occasion the Mughals took all the property of Shahji's camp, 8,000 oxen loaded with grain, some other oxen carrying arms and rockets, and about 3,000 men as prisoners. The victorious Khan-i-Dauran returned to Ahmadnagar. (February. *Pad.* I. B. 68-69.)

Next year, Shah Jahan himself arrived at Daulatabad (21 Feb. 1636), and launched a vast force of 50,000 troopers, to overawe Golkonda, invade Bijapur (if necessary) and crush Shahji. One division of the army, under Khan-i-Zaman, was to ravage the home of Shahji at Chamargunda and then wrest the Konkan from him. Another, 8,000 strong, commanded by Shaista Khan, was to conquer Junnar fort, Sangamner, Nasik, and Trimbak. (*Pad.* I. B. 135-137.)

The division under Khan-i-Zaman, starting from Ahmadnagar carried on a successful campaign against Shahji during March, chasing him through Pargaon to Lauhgarh, in the pargana of Puna, then belonging to Adil Shah, and situated across the Bhima. Shah Jahan's orders having been not to pursue Shahji if he entered Bijapur territory, the Khan stopped there. One of his officers captured the walled village of Chamargunda. At this time Khan-i-Zaman was recalled to join the invasion of Bijapur. (*Ibid.* 160-162). Shaista Khan arrived at Sangamner on 8th March 1636, and wrested the parganas of the country from the hands of Shahji's son and other owners, expelling the enemy from the district. Leaving Shaikh Farid as *thanahdar* there, he went in pursuit of the enemy to Nasik. The Marathas fled from Nasik to the Konkan. Shaista Khan detached 1500 men to occupy the Junnar region and punish the enemy. At this time an imperial order recalled the general to the defence of Ahmadnagar. A detachment from his army had taken the town of Junnar from Shahji's servants, and another had gone towards Mahuli where the enemy was reported to be present. At this time Shahji's son [Shambhu ?] joined him near Chamargunda, and then with a party as escort set off for the *fort* of Junnar, where his family was living. When [Shambhu] arrived near Junnar, the Mughals sallied forth from the city and attacked him, many being slain on both sides.

Immediately after hearing the news, Shaista Khan sent 700 men from his side to reinforce the Mughals at Junnar. These men cut their way through the Marathas who barred their path, entered Junnar city and strengthened its defence. In fact, the Mughal force in Junnar was closely besieged and driven to sore straits by shortness of provisions and fodder. Shaista Khan at one hastened to Junnar, and beat and chased the enemy back to the bank of the Bhima river. Baqar Khan was recalled from the Konkan to the defence of the city of Junnar, and Shaista Khan set out on his return on 21st March to meet the Emperor at Daulatabad. (*Pad.* I. B. 148-151.)

The campaign against Shahji was thus brought to a premature close, because Bijapur had defied the Emperor and the main Mughal forces had to be diverted against that kingdom. However, in May next Adil Shah made peace with the Emperor, one of the terms being that Shahji was not to be admitted to office under Bijapur unless he ceded to Shah Jahan the forts of Junnar, Trimbak and some others still in his hands. (My *History of Aurangzib*, I. ch. 3 $ 3.)

The Emperor was now free to turn his forces against Shahji. The campaign was reopened in July and proved a complete success, as I have described in detail in my *History of Aurangzib*, Vol. I. ch. 3 $6. Shahji capitulated in fort Mahuli (which he had some eight months before secured from its *qiladar* Manaji Bhonsla); he entered Bijapur service, gave up to the Mughals the shadowy king Murtaza Nizam Shah, together with Junnar and six other forts* still held by his men. (*Pad.* I. B, 225-230.)

6. Khawas Khan and Murari Jagdev as patrons of Shahji

From the above facts of Shahji's early history it will be clear that he received a crushing blow to his fortunes in the fall of his patron Fath Khan and the murder of his father-in-law Lakhji Jadav Rao in 1630, and that though he afterwards asserted himself in the Puna-Nasik region, it was only as a petty plunderer, and his rise to power and prestige, as a king-maker and wielder of the legal authority of the Nizam Shahi State, was due mainly to the support of Khawas Khan and the resources of the Bijapuri kingdom. Murari Pandit, the favourite and right-hand-man of that Bijapuri *wazir*, played a most important part in the early life of Shahji. He had first met Shahji as an enemy (Aug. 1630), but soon came to cherish a personal affection for the young Maratha chief and a high opinion of his ability and intelligence. The story of Shahji having taught Murari (23rd Sep., 1633) how to weigh an elephant, is well known. The history of the rise and fall of Khawas Khan (and of Murari along with him) is therefore an inseparable part of the life-story of Shahji.

Sultan Ibrahim Adil Shah had a favourite slave of the

*Forts Trimbak, Tringalvadi, Harshagarh, Jivdhan, Chawand and Hadsar.

Maratha race named Daulatyar (created Daulat Khan and commandant of the capital), whom he instructed, just before his death to place the crown on the head of his second son, Muhammad Adil Shah. Daulat Khan effected this change of succession (12 Sep. 1627), blinded the eldest Prince, Darvish, and mutilated his two youngest brothers. (*B.S.* 284; *Pad.* I.B. 219). Thereafter Daulat Khan, now entitled Khawas Khan, ruled Bijapur as regent and virtual king. His policy (like that of his old master) was to prop up the Nizam Shahi kingdom as the only barrier between the dreaded Mughals and themselves. For this reason Adil Shah and his *wazir* forgave a thousand acts of ingratitude and wanton aggression on the part of Nizam Shah and helped him with men, money and provisions every time he was attacked by the Mughals. Mustafa Khan, the rival of Khawas, was the only noble of Bijapur who advocated a policy of alliance with the Mughals for dividing the heritage of Nizam Shah. (*B.S.* 291-293.) At last, after seven years of virtual dictatorship, Khawas Khan provoked a civil war in the State by his haughtiness, greed of power and incapacity. He suddenly imprisoned his rival Mustafa Khan in Belgaum. All the other nobles who were smarting under the ill-treatment of Khawas and his creature Murari, were instigated by the king to overthrow him. They wrote to Khawas to dismiss Murari, who was universally unpopular. Khawas refused. Immediately a civil war broke out. Khawas intrigued with Shah Jahan for help, sending his envoy Shaikh Muhiuddin

Dabir to Agra. His enemies gathered together at Gulbarga under Randaula Khan, who was soon joined by Raihan from Sholapur. The main army of Khawas was sent under Murari to suppress Raghu Pandit, but after attacking Raghu at Dewalgaon it was routed, and Murari took refuge with the Naikwar of Dharur. Adil Shah instructed his petition-bearer, an Abyssinian named Siddi Raihan (not Malik Raihan, the governor of Sholapur), to put an end to Khawas. When the hated minister was coming out of the Court, the conspirators fell on him and stabbed him (late in 1635). The wounded man was conveyed to his home, but his doors were broken open and his head cut off. Mustafa Khan was now released and restored to the premiership. (He had been the *titular wazir* even during Khawas's usurpation of power. *B.S.* 307-312.)

Murari lost all his power after the death of his patron. He was arrested by the local officer of Halihal, and sent to Court in chains. There he opened his mouth in foul abuse of the Sultan, who ordered his tongue to be cut out, the prisoner to be paraded in a cart through the city, and then his joints to be hacked off one after another. This happened one month after the murder of Khawas Khan. (*B.S.* 314.)

The history of Shahji after he had entered Bijapur service and the part he played in the conquest of the Karnatak for his new master (from 1646 onwards), have been treated in Chapter II.

IV

THE LEADING NOBLES OF BIJAPUR 1627-1686

The kingdom of Bijapur attained to its greatest extent and prosperity in the reign of Muhammad Adil Shah (1627-56). But from the year 1646, when this king was attacked by a prolonged illness, its decline commenced, which ended in the annexation of Bijapur to the Mughal Empire in 1686. The popular history of the Muslim Sultans of Bijapur, the *Busatin-us-salatin* of Mirza Ibrahim Zubairi, though written in 1824, is a very useful and accurate compilation. But as I possess manuscripts of original seventeenth century sources like Zahur bin Zahuri's *Muhammadnamah*, Fuzuni Astarabadi's *Futuhat-i-Adil Shahi*, and Nurullah's *Tarikh-i-Ali-Adil Shah Sani*, besides the printed histories of the Mughal Empire and the letters of Jai Singh (in Ms.), I have followed the *Busatin-us- salatin* only where the earlier authorities are silent.

WAZIRS OF BIJAPUR *

1. Mustafa Khan, Khan Baba (name Mirza Muhammad Amin Lari), 12 Sep. 1627—9 Nov. 1648 (when died).

* In Bijapur, as in the Ottoman empire the term *Wazir* was not reserved for the prime minister but was conferred on every high official [*Encyclo. Islam*, iv, 1135] But I shall use it in that restricted sense.

2 Khawas Khan (name Daulat-Yar), usurped power and virtually ruled the State (but without the title of prime minister) till his murder in 1635, when No. 1 was restored to authority.

3. Khan Muhammad, Muzaffar-ud-din Khan-i-Khanan, (name Siddi Raihan, first title Ikhlas Khan), 1648—1657; murdered on 11 Nov. 1657.

4. Ibrahim Khan (son of Ibrahim Bakhtar Khan), 11 Nov. 1657—24 Dec. 1660 (when he left for Mecca with the dowager queen Bari Sahiba).

5. Abdul Muhammad (son of No. 4), Jan. 1661—24 Nov. 1672, when he resigned.

6. Khawas Khan (second son of No. 3), 24 Nov. 1672—11 Nov. 1675 (when deposed), murdered on 20 Jan. 1676.

7. Bahlol Khan (name Abdul Karim Miana), 11 Nov. 1675—23 Dec. 1677 (when died).

8, Siddi Masaud, 21 Feb. 1678—21 Nov. 1683 (when resigned).

9. Aqa Khusrau, 19 March—12 Oct. 1684 (when died).

Notes.—Ibrahim Adil Shah on his death-bed (1627) wished to place his second son Muhammad on the throne, setting aside his eldest son named Darvish. He found that Muhammad Amin Lari was the only noble capable of carrying out this *coup*; but the latter asked that he should be given as his assistant a slave named Daulat-Yar, a

Maratha by race, who was remarkably skilful in the conduct of affairs. This Daulat had been previously thrown into prison, but released at the entreaty of Muhammad Amin and reinstated in the post of commander of Bijapur fort. Ibrahim Adil Shah agreed to the request, but warned Muhammad Amin that Daulat would prove faithless to him. When Muhammad Adil Shah was crowned, he gave Muhammad Amin Lari the title of Mustafa Khan Khan Baba, and Daulat that of Khawas Khan. Mustafa was an indolent ease-loving noble, and all real power was wielded by Khawas, whose right hand man was a Brahman named Murari Jagdev, originally his private secretary but now created commander-in-chief. Shahji Bhonsle, the father of the famous Shivaji, was a great favourite of this Murari, and rose through his help. [*M*. 63, 126; *B.S*. 281-283.]

Khawas Khan fulfilled Ibrahim Adil Shah's prophecy by attacking and imprisoning his patron Mustafa Khan in the fort of Belgaon (1633). But Adil Shah sent an army under Rustam-i-Zaman against Khawas, who was later stabbed when on a visit to the Court and beheaded by order of the king (1635). Mustafa Khan was then restored to the wazirate, though he was subsequently (1645) cast into prison for a short time by his master. Mustafa's daughter, Taj-i-Jahan, was married to Muhammad Adil Shah in 1632. [*M*. 132-139, 201, 207, 145; *B.S*. 307-314; Abdul Hamid Lahori's *Padishahnamah* I.A. 360, 404.]

Siddi Raihan, an Abyssinian slave, was originally employed by Muhammad Adil Shah as *Ruqa-rasan* or officer charged with the presentation of petitions to the king in his private chamber. He was a very able and energetic general and greatly distinguished himself in the conquest of Mysore and the Eastern Karnatak, being entitled first as Ikhlas Khan and later as Khan-i-Khanan Khan Muhammad. The circumstances under which he was murdered (11 Nov, 1657) are narrated in my *History of Aurangzib*, Vol. I. Ch. XI. He should be distinguished from another Siddi Raihan (usually called *Malik* Raihan), who gave up Sholapur fort to Adil Shah, entered the Bijapuri service as a general, and frequently quarrelled with Mustafa Khan in the Eastern Karnatak expeditions of 1647-48. [*M.* 137, 174; *B.S.* 312, 340.] In *Muhammadnamah* Khan Muhammad is often styled Muzaffar-ud-din.

The father of Ibrahim Khan (No. 4) is called *Bichittar* Khan in *Alamgir-namah* 993, but the *Tuzuk-i-Jahangiri* speaks of a Bijapuri envoy at Jahangir's Court named *Bakhtar* Khan, [p. 197.]

Khawas Khan (No. 6) distinguished himself in the Adilshahi wars with Shivaji (1664) and Jai Singh (1665-1666). He was the leader of the Deccani party and enemy of the Afghan faction at the capital. How he ousted Abdul Muhammad and seized the supreme power at the accession of Sikandar Adil Shah (24 Nov. 1672), how he was himself overthrown by Bahlol Khan in. 1675. and how the Afghan faction misgoverned Bijapur are described in my *Aurangzib*, Vol. IV. Ch. 42. Khawas. was an idolent pleasure-seeker and grossly incompetent for administering a State. His wife Habiba Sultan conducted all affairs for him with marked ability. [J. Sarkar's *Shivaji*, 3rd ed., 234-236; *B.S.* 436-447.]

How Siddi Masaud got possession of Bijapur fort and the office of regent is described in my *Shivaji*, 3rd ed., p. 317. He left his post in disgust on 21 Nov. 1683. [*Aurangzib*, Vol. IV. Ch. 45.]

FAMILY OF KHAN MUHAMMAD.

Four of his sons are known in history, namely.

(*a*) Muhammad Iklilas, commander of the *Khasa-khel* [*H. A.* 86 *b*; Nurullah 165; *B. S.* 410; *F.R.*, Gyfford to Surat, 20 July 1663; Carwar to Surat, 29 Aug. 1665].

(*b*) Khawas Khan (No. 6), married a daughter of Rustam-i-Zaman; died 1676. [Nurullah.]

(*c*) Sher Khan, died in 1665. [*F.R.* Carwar to Surat, 29 Aug. 1665; *Shivaji*, 3rd ed., 239.]

(*d*) Nasir Muhammad, who sold the fort of Jinji to Shivaji in 1677. [*Memoires* of Francois Martin, i. 576.] Grant Duff (Ch. IX) is wrong in calling him the son of *Ambar* Khan.

BAHLOL KHAN MIANA

As Mirza Rajah Jai Singh, when campaigning against Bijapur in 1666, wrote, the Afghans formed more than one half of the army of Bijapur. They also formed the more efficient part of it, as they were the only troops that could meet on equal terms the heavy Mughal cavalry and the recklessly daring Rajput soldiery who served under the banners of the Delhi Emperors,—while the Maratha light horse were no match for these northern warriors in pitched battles, though very useful in making forays and scouting for news.

Miana is the name of one of the clans of Afghanistan. The first member of this family to enter imperial service was Hasan Miana, whom Jahangir posted to the Deccan where this soldier died. One of his sons, named Bahlol Miana rose to be a *hazari*. In 1616 Jahangir at Prince Shah Jahan's recommendation promoted him to the 1500 grade and ennobled him with the title of Khan, adding (in his autobiography, p. 201) "his exterior was as handsome as his inside was adorned with bravery." At Shah Jahan's accession, Bahlol Miana, now a commander of 4,000 (3,000 *sawar* rank) was jagirdar of Balaghat; but he fled away from the imperial dominions as soon as he heard of the flight and rebellion of his friend Khan Jahan Lodi (about Nov. 1629), and took refuge in the Deccan. Such a tried warrior was eagerly sought after by the Deccani potentates in their unceasing warfare, and Bahlol made his living as a soldier of fortune there. He is found fighting on behalf of Sri Ranga Rayal, the titular Emperor of Vijaynagar, in the defence of his capital Vellore against the Adil Shahis in 1647, and after the defeat of that Rajah he entered the service of Bijapur with his two sons, who soon afterwards rose to independent commands by their military efficiency,

These two sons, named Abdul Qadir and Abdur Rahim, succeeded one after another to the title of *Bahlol Khan* (we shall call them nos II and III.) Each of the brothers left seven sons. On the death of Abdur Rahim (*i.e.*, Bahlol Khan III) in July 1665, the Bijapur Sultan was induced (by means of costly presents, as Jai Singh reports) to confer the headship of the family and the title of Bahlol Khan (IV) on Abdul Karim, the son of the late deceased. At this, Abdul Muhammad, the son of Abdul Qadir (or Bahlol II), left Bijapur in disappointment and came over to the Mughals (Nov. 1665.) He fought under Jai Singh and other imperial generals and was created Ikhlas Khan in the Mughal peerage (to be distinguished from nobles with the same title in the Adil Shahi State), about February 1669. He was defeated and wounded by Shivaji at the battle of Dindori, on 17 Oct, 1670. This family quarrel is described in detail in the English factory letter from Carwar to Surat dated 29th August 1665.

On the death of Bahlol Khan the Fourth, who was *wazir* of Bijapur from 1675 to 1677, the affairs of this family fell into confusion; his soldiers oppressed his relatives for their arrears of pay, and next year his clansmen and troops were bought over by the Mughals. (*B.S.* 457-460, 470.) Miraj and Bankapur were the chief jagirs of this noble.

Bahlol III (*i.e.* Abdur Rahim) got Kopbal (now a jagir of the Salar Jang family in the Hyderabad State) as his fief. His younger son Abdun Nabi was granted Kadapa and some other placs. This Abdun Nabi's grandson was slain by the Marathas and that grandson's son Abdul Halim at first lost half his estate to the Marathas and finally the whole of it to Haidar Ali.

Abdul Karim (*i.e.*, the wazir Bahlol IV) had two sons, one being Abdur Rauf* who served Adil Shah till the extinction of that dynasty by Aurangzib in 1686, when he was taken into Mughal service with the title of *Dilir Khan* and the high rank of a six-*hazari*. Later he became faujdar of Savanur and Bankapur, dying about 1710. Rauf's brother Abdul Ghaffar succeeded to the title of *Dilir Khan* and the headship of the family, and this noble's son Abdul Majid (again entitled Dilir Khan) was given the title of Sitwat Jang by Nasir Jang the Nizam, and had a son named Abdul Hakim. We meet with these later Mianas in the course of Maratha history in the 18th century.

Bahlol Khan III had placed his jagir of Kopbal in charge of a fellow-clansman but no near relative, named Husain Miana. When Shivaji planned the conquest of the Karnatak, his general Hambir Rao attacked Kopbal, which is justly described in the Marathi histories as "the gate of the Karnatak"—*i.e.*, the Mysore uplands. In a battle near Yelburga fought in January 1677 Husain Miana was defeated and taken prisoner along with his brother Qasim Khan. When pressed by the Maratha king to yield the fort of Kopbal to him as the condition

* Misspelt as *Rup* by Chitnis (*Bakhar*, i. 131) and Grant Duff, and as *Rupal* by Sabhasad (*Bakhar*, p. 89.)

of his release, Husain sent his brother with a Maratha force to give delivery of it. But his son, who was in command of the garrison, refused and the irate Marathas put Qasim Khan to death. At last on 3 March 1679, the fort was ceded to Shivaji and Husain was set free. He is said to have next entered Maratha service for a living [*Jedhe*], but in 1683 went over to Aurangzib at Aurangabad and was highly welcomed and created a five-*hazari* with the title of Fath Jang Khan. He was next captured by the Marathas, but Shambhuji sent him honourably to Raigarh, where he died. [*Masir-ul-umara*, iii. 30-32. Best account in Br. Mus. Or. 1641, f. 145.] Most of his sons died in his lifetime; one named Qudrat-ullah rose to be Mughal faujdar of Talikota and later (1706) of Mehkar, another was Yasin Khan. Kukanur, a city 15 miles north of Kopbal, was the seat of Husain Miana.

Sharza Khan

Sayyid Iliyas, of the Mahdavi sect, was surnamed Sharza Khan I, and commanded the Bijapuri vanguard in the invasion of Sunda and Bednur in 1663. On 2 April 1666, during the war with Jai Singh, he suddenly fell down dead when returning from the field, after rescuing his young son Sayyid Habib, who had charged single-handed a body of Mughal troops and been hemmed round by them. *B.S.* (422) says that there was no apparent cause of his death, such as wound or shot. This suggests apoplexy or heart failure. The Mughal official history, *Alamgirnamah* (1013-14), states that

Sharza was killed by a musket-shot in his arm and a spear-thrust in his shoulder, and that his son was severely wounded.

Sharza Khan was the bravest of the brave among the warriors of the Deccan, as the English Factory Records, Jai Singh's despatches, and the Bijapur historians all agree in declaring. His eldest son Sayyid Makhdum was created Sharza Khan II. He opposed the domination of the Afghan faction at Bijapur and fought their leader, the wazir Bahlol Khan, in March 1676. Then in 1678-79 he quarrelled with Siddi Masaud, the new wazir, and finally joined the Mughal army under Dilir Khan. The Emperor gave him the title of Rustam Khan, but this officer was captured by the Marathas near Satara in May 1690 and again in Jan. 1704. Jai Singh in 1665 remarked "The Mahdavi sect are foremost in raising tumults." [*H.A.* 90 *b.*] There was another general bearing the same title at this time, but it was a member of the Qutbshahi peerage.

RUSTAM-I-ZAMAN

An Abyssinian general of Bijapur named Randaula Khan (the son of Farhad Khan and nephew of Khairiyat Khan) took the lead in organizing the armed overthrow of Khawas Khan who had usurped the supreme power in the Adilshahi Government (1635.) In 1638 he was given the title of Rustam-i-Zaman and sent by the Sultan to conquer Western Kanara, *i.e.*, Ikeri and Bednur. Among the factions that divided the Adilshahi Court, he was the friend and supporter of Shahji Bhonsle and it was probably this Rustam-i-Zaman's son who made a secret pact with Shivaji and was repulsed by the latter near Kolhapur on 28th December 1659, shortly after the death of Afzal Khan. This family held south Konkan and Kanara (*i.e.*, Karwar district) as their fief. Early in 1674 he was succeeded by his son Abu Khan, whom we may call Rustam-i-Zaman III. The history of this family is detailed in my *Shivaji*, ch. 10, and many facts about them can be gleaned from the English Factory Records, as they owned the famous port of Rajapur and much of the pepper-growing district of Kanara before the annexation of these places by Shivaji.

The Mulla Family of Kalian

They were Arab settlers in Gujrat and were called *Navaiyats*. [*Bombay Gazetteer*, 1st ed., Vol. XV, Pt. i, pp. 400-410, Pt. ii, 266, Vol. IX, Pt. ii, 14.] William Finch speaks of them as "Naites, speaking another language and for the most part seamen." Many of them were merchants also, and settled at Surat in 1225 [Barbosa, 67.] Khafi Khan (ii. 113) writes, "Mulla Ahmad's ancestors were *sharifs* newly come from Arabia, on flight from the tyranny of Hajjaj, the Umayyad. They settled in Konkan and were called Navaiyats." Jai Singh wrote in 1665, "In the parganas of Kalian and Bhivandi reside Mulla Ahmad and most of the Navaiyat clan. There are many poor men enjoying *Sayurghal* grants." [*H.A.* 80 *b.*]

When the Nizamshahi kingdom of Ahmadnagar was partitioned between the Mughal Emperor and the Sultan of Bijapur, Konkan fell to the share of the latter. Mulla Ahmad was granted much of this province by Adil Shah as his jagir, he being one of the highest nobles of the Bijapur Court. During the protracted illness of Muhammad Adil Shah (1646—1656), Mulla Ahmad came to reside at Bijapur and brought away most of his troops there, thus leaving Konkan an easy prey to Shivaji. [*A.N.* 575-576.] His younger brother Mulla Yahia joined Aurangzib in Dec. 1663, and was created a 2-*hazari* on 5 June 1664. [*A.N.* 850, 860]. Mulla Ahmad was secretly won over to the Mughal side by Jai Singh with great effort and large promises of advancement in the imperial service, but he died on his way to Delhi in Dec. 1665. [*A. N.* 906, 919, 925.] Ahmad's son was named Asadullah and his brother's son Mukhlis Khan (whose son Zainuddin Ali became faujdar of Konkan and Nasik in 1705).*

Siddis of Karnul and Adoni

Siddi Jauhar was a slave of Malik Abdul Wahab (son of Malik Raihan I, an officer of Adil Shah). After the death of Wahab, Jauhar cast his master's son, Malik Raihan II, into prison and made himself master of Karnul. [*B.S.* 524.] Ali Adil Shah II created him Salabat

Anwar-ud-din the Nawab of the Carnatic, well-known to us from the Anglo-French wars between Madras and Pondicherry, was a Navaiyat Arab, but the Indian home of his family was Gopamau in the province of Oudh.

Khan and sent him against Shivaji, [see my *Shivaji*, ch. 4]. He died in 1662.

Jauhar's son Abdul Aziz wished to imprison his sister's husband, Siddi Masaud, but the latter took shelter in Adoni fort, which he soon afterwards seized. He opposed the Afghan rule at Bijapur under Abdul Karim Bahlol Khan, and became wazir in 1678. "Masaud was a masterly defender of forts, but cherished low people and suspected his friends and even his wives and sons. ...He knew not how to cherish the soldiers and the cultivators. One of his six confidants was Venkatadri Murari, a Brahman." [*B.S.* 524-525.] Masaud's son was named Siddi Darvesh.

V

SHIVAJI'S LIFE AND WORK ANALYSED

1. His Genius

Our conception of Shivaji needs revision in the light of an exhaustive and critical study of the many original sources of his history which have been opened to the present generation. The theory that he was merely a lightly moving and indefatigable raider, a brigand of an ampler and more successful type than the ordinary, can no longer be held.

No blind fanatic, no more brigand, can found a State. That is the work of a statesman alone. And statesmanship has been well-defined by the Right Hon'ble Mr. H. A. L. Fisher as the power of correctly calculating and skilfully utilising the forces of one's age and country so as to make them contribute to the success of one's policy. The true statesman does not grumble when he cannot find the materials for his purpose ready to his hand; he does not denounce the society round himself as hopelessly bad. Nor, on the other hand, does he, like the doctrinaire reformer, court failure by insisting on a standard of abstract perfection impossible in his age—and, indeed, in any age. Statesmanly wisdom consists in taking correct stock of the available human material around us, making different appeals to different individuals or social groups, rousing the vanity of one, the cupidity of another, the idealism of a third, so as to enlist them *all* in the service of the grand aim and undertaking of the statesman. That aim must be the paramount object of his pursuit, and a statesman's genius is shown only in enlisting the greatest amount of public support to his policy while weakening that policy as little as possible by his concessions. No unprincipled opportunist, no spineless leader who tries to be everything to everybody by yielding on all points, can be a statesman. The true statesman is an unfailing judge of human character and of the social forces of his age; he has an almost superhuman acumen in knowing beforehand what is possible and what is not in that age and country. The greatest of Italian statesmen and patriots, Couut Cavour, has rightly defined statesmanship as *tact des choses possibles* or the instinctive perception of what is possible under the circumstances. Shivaji's success proves his divine gift of genius, which baffles our analysis.

2. His Environment

Let us survey the situation in Maharashtra proper at the time of Shivaji's rise. Ever since the battle of Tirauri (1193), when Prithvi Raj went down, wave after wave of foreign onset had swept over the Hindu world through five centuries without a break. After the fatal day of Talikota (1565) no Hindu, even in the more sheltered southern land, had raised his head above the flood of Muslim conquest as a sovereign with a fully independent

State under him. Thencefoth, the ablest Hindu, with all his wealth and power, had only been a feudal baron, a mercenary general under an alien master.

Every generation that had passed away in this state had naturally made the rise of a Hindu to sovereignty more and more difficult. Indeed, the very tradition of Hindu independence and Hindu maintenance of a complete and self-contained kingdom seemed to have faded into a dim distant and almost forgotten memory. Thus, when in 1659-60, a poor, friendless, humbly born youth of thirty-two set himself to face at once the might of the Mughal empire (then in its noon-day splendour) and the nearer hostility of Bijapur (which had been the "Queen of the Deccan" for nearly a century, and whose internal decay was not yet visible to any human eye),— he seemed to be the maddest of all mad men. No one could foresee in 1560 what the Mughal empire would sink to in 1707; as yet it was resplendent with all the prestige of Shah Jahan's victorious and magnificent reign. Shivaji had no brother Hindu chieftain to help him, nor even a Muhammadan Court which could have ventured to give him an asylum from Mughal vengeance, in case of defeat. In embarking on war in 1660 he, therefore, as the English saying is, "burnt his boats" and made retreat impossible for himself.

The result in fourteen years was that he founded a State, he did make himself a fully independent sovereign (*Chhatrapati*). Therefore, there can be no denying the fact that he was, as the ancient Greeks would have called him, "a king among men,"—one endowed with the divine instinct or genius.

3. No Nation created in Maharashtra

Shivaji founded and maintained a sovereign *State* in the face of unparallelled difficulties and the opposition of the three greatest Powers of India in that age,—the Mughals, the Bijapuris, and the Portuguese. But did he succeed in creating a *nation*? Let us appeal to history for the answer.

A century and a half after Shivaji the Maratha State fell before the impact of England. Its political condition is graphically described by an exceptionally talented and shrewd Scotch contemporary. Sir Thomas Munro writes:

> 18 Dec. 1817.—"I have already got possession of a considerable number of places in this district, entirely by the assistance *of the inhabitants* of whom *nine-tenths* at least are in our favour. All that the inhabitants had requested was that they should not be transferred to any [Maratha] jagirdar." [Gleig, iii. 221.]

> 19 May, 1818.—"No army was ever more completely destroyed than the Peshwa's infantry. Of the few who escaped [after the fall of Sholapur] with their arms, the greater part were disarmed or *killed by the country people*." [Gleig, iii. 256.]

Let us try to imagine a parallel case in Europe. The Germans, provoked to war by the imbecile French Emperor Napoleon III, have invaded France. The French soldiers, after a disastrous defeat at Worth or Mars-La-Tour, are escaping to their homes before the enemy, and they are "disarmed or killed by the country people."

Is such an event conceivable? If not, then the conclusion is irresistible that the French are a nation, but the Marathas were not even after a century and a half of *Hindupat Padshahi*, or a purely national Government without any foreign admixture or control.

What was the attitude of the higher classes, the natural leaders of the people in Maharashtra, during the national disaster of 1818? Let Munro again speak:

"Most of the Southern jagirdars would, I believe, be well pleased to find a decent pretext for getting out of it [*i.e.*, the war, in which they were standing by the side of the Peshwa."] [Gleig, iii. 301.]

"We have in our favour, with the exception of a few disbanded horsemen and the immediate servants of the late Government, almost the whole body of the people. We have all the trading, manufacturing and agricultural classes." [Gleig, ii. 270].

4. Caste as a hindrance to National Union

The Maratha failure to create a nation even among their own race and in their small corner of India, requires a searching analysis on the part of the Indian patriot and the earnest student of Indian history alike. And for such an analysis we have to go down to the roots, to the social condition of Shivaji's time.

A deep study of Maratha society, indeed of society throughout India,—reveals some facts which it is considered patriotism to ignore. We realise that the greatest obstacles to Shivaji's success were not Mughals or Adil Shahis, Siddis or Ferings, but his own countrymen.

First, we cannot blink the truth that the dominant factor in Indian life—even to-day, no less than in the 17th century,—is caste, and neither religion nor country. By caste must not be understood the four broad divisions of the Hindus,—which exist only in the text-books and the airy philosophical generalisations delivered from platforms. The caste that really counts, the division that is a living force, is the sub-division and sub-sub-division into innumerable small groups called *shakhas* or branches (more correctly twigs or I should say, *leaves*,—they are so many !)—into which each caste is split up and within which alone marrying and giving in marriage, eating and drinking together take place. The more minute and parochial a caste subdivision, the more it is of a reality in society, while a generic caste name like *Brahman*, or even a provincial section of it like *Dakshina Brahman*, does not connote any united body or homogeneous group. Apart from every caste being divided into mutually exclusive sections by provincial differences, there are still further sub-divisions (among the members of the same caste in each province) due to differences of district, and even the two sides of the same hill or river! And each of these smallest subdivisions of the Brahman caste is separated from the other sub-divisions as completely as it is from an altogether different caste like the Vaishya or Shudra. *E.g.*, the Kanyakubja and Sarayu-pari Brahmans of Nothern India, the Konkanastha and Deshastha of Maharashtra.

These are live issues of Indian society. Where three

Karhare Brahmans (to take only one example) meet together, they begin to whisper about their disabilities under the Chitpavans. A Prabhu stranger in a far off town would at once be welcomed by the local Prabhu society of the town, ignoring the other members of visiting party if they belong to another caste.

5. Kulinism aggravates Caste differences

The evil penetrates deeper. For the purposes of marrying and dining together,—which are the only *real* bonds of social union,—even Sarayu-pari Kanyakubja North Indian Brahman cannot be safely taken as the last indivisible unit. Within this seemingly ultimate subdivision there is a force of still minuter cleavage, due to blood,—or what is called *Kulin*-ism.

Thus Shahji Bhonsle and Chandra Rao More both belonged to the same small social group as regards caste province and local subdivision, but More could not give his daughter to Shahji's son without a lowering of his social status or defilement of his blood, because he was a *kulin* (blue blood), while Shahji was a *non-kulin* or plebeian. And why so? Was More descended from an ancestor of a higher caste, sanctity or learning than Shahji? No. Both families had gained wealth power and social prestige by serving the same Muhammadan dynasty, but the Mores had been eight generations earlier in the field than the Bhonsles.* It was exactly as if the

* Another example is Jadav Rao's reluctance to marry his daughter Jija Bai to Shahji.

grandson of a Rao Bahadur created by Lord Canning were to sneer at a Rao Bahadur created by Lord Reading as an upstart.

Thus, even the smallest sub-division of a caste was further subdivided, and a united nation was made one degree still less possible. The same forces, the same beliefs, the same false pride in blood, are operating among us today. Without the completest freedom of marriage within a population—and not the much advertised Aryan Brotherhood Intercaste dinners (on vegetables !)—that population can never form a nation. Englishmen of today do not consider their blood as defiled when they say in the words of their late poet laureate:

"Saxon and Norman and Dane are we."

Where caste and kulinism reign, merit cannot have full and free recognition and the community cannot rise to its highest possible capacity of greatness. Democracy is inconceivable there, because the root principle of democracy is the absolute equality of every member of the *demos*—the belief that

The rank is but the guinea's stamp.
A man's the gold for all that.

Without the abolition of all distinctions of caste, creed and kulinism, a nation cannot come into being. And further, without eternal vigilance in national education and moral uplift, no nation can continue on the face of the earth.

This duty the Maratha State never attempted to perform, nor did any voluntary agency undertake it.

6. Personal jealousy hindering Shivaji

Shivaji was not contented with all his conquests of territory and vaults full of looted treasure, so long as he was not recognised as a Kshatriya entitled to wear the sacred thread and to have the Vedic hymns chanted at his domestic rites. The Brahmans alone could give him such a recognition, and though they swallowed the sacred thread they boggled at the *Vedokta*! The result was a rupture. So, too, his favourite secretary Balaji Avji (of the Prabhu caste) invested his son with the sacred thread, for which he was excommunicated by the Brahmans. Whichever side had the rights of the case, one thing is certain, namely, that this internally torn community had not the *sine qua non* of a nation.

Nor did Maharashtra acquire that *sine qua non* ever after. The Peshwas were Brahmans from Konkan, and the Brahmans of the upland (Desh) despised them as less pure in blood. The result was that the State policy of Maharashtra under the Peshwas, instead of being directed to national ends, was now degraded into upholding the prestige of one family or social sub-division.

Shivaji had, besides, almost to the end of his days, to struggle against the jealousy, scorn, indifference and even opposition of certain Maratha families, his equals in caste sub-division and once in fortune and social position,—whom he had now outdistanced. The Bhonsle Savants of Vadi.

the Jadavs of Sindhkhed, the Mores of Javli, and (to a lesser extent) the Nimbalkars, despised and kept aloof from the upstart grandson of that Maloji whom some old men still living remembered to have seen tilling his fields like a *Kunbi*! Shivaji's own brother Vyankoji fought against him during the Mughal invasion of Bijapur in 1666.

7. Why the Peshwas' State lost public support

Thirdly, there was no national spirit, no patriotism in the true sense of the term, among the Maratha people, to assist Shivaji and hasten his success. Not to speak of the common people, who patiently and blindly tilled a grudging soil all their lives,—many of the higher and middle class Maratha families were content to serve Muslim rulers as mercenaries throughout the Chhatrapati or royal period of their history, as their descendants did the English aliens by deserting Baji Rao II. And why? Because in that troubled divided society, with century after century of the clash of rival dynasties and the rapid dissolution of kingdoms, land was the only unchangeable thing in an ever-changing world. The ownership of land,—or what amounted to nearly the same thing, the legal right to a village headman's dues,—was the only form of wealth that could not be quickly robbed or squandered away, but could be left as a provision for unborn generations of descendants. Dynasties did change, but the conqueror usually respected the grants of his fallen predecessor.

It has been well said of the Scottish Highlanders that, after the Jacobite risings of the 18th century, they could forgive to the Hanoverian Government the hanging of their fathers but not the taking away of their lands.

Such being the economic bed-rock on which Maratha society rested, it naturally followed that fief (*watan*) was dearer than patria (*swa-desh*)' and a foreign Power which assured to the *watan-dar* the possesssion of his land was preferred to a grasping national king who threatened to take away the *watan* or enhance his demand for revenue. As Munro writes :—

"The Patwardhans and the Desai of Kittoor will be secured in the enjoyment of their possessions [by the British conquerors], instead of being exposed to constant attempts to diminish them, as when under the dominion of the Peshwa." [ii. 267]

Even Sindur [of the Ghorpare family] was in danger of treacherous seizure by Baji Rao II during his pilgrimages to the river. [iii. 235.]

The same clinging to land, which was quite natural and justifiable in that age,—drew many Deccani families to the Mughal standard against Shivaji and Shambhuji, and kept them faithful to the alien so long as the Mughal Empire did not turn hopelessly bankrupt and weak, as it did after 1707. There could, therefore, be no united Maharashtra under Shivaji, as there was a united Scotland under Robert the Bruce. Shivaji had to build on a loose sandy soil.

8. SHIVAJI'S REAL ACHIEVEMENTS

But the indispensable bases of a sovereign State he did lay down, and the fact would have been established beyond question if his life had not been cut short only six years after his coronation. He gave to his own dominions in Maharashtra peace and order, at least for a time. Now, order is the beginning of all good things, as disorder is the enemy of civilisation, progress and popular happiness.

But order is only a means to an end. The next duty of the State is to throw careers open to talent (the motto of the French Revolution of 1789), to give employment to the people by creating and expanding through State effort the various fields for the exercise of their ability and energy—economic, administrative, diplomatic, military, financial, and even mechanical. In proportion as a State can *educate* the people and carry out this policy, it will endure. Competition with the prize for the worthiest,—modified partly by the inexorable rules of caste and status and the natural handicap of the mediæval conditions of the then society,—was introduced into Shivaji's State.

The third feature of a good State, *viz.*, freedom in the exercise of religion, was realized in Shivaji's kingdom. He went further, and though himself a pious Hindu he gave his State bounty to Muslim saints and Hindu sadhus without distinction, and respected the *Quran* no less than this own Scriptures.

But his reign was too brief and his dynasty too short-lived, for the world to see the full development of his constructive statesmanship and political ideals. Thus it happened that on the downfall of the Hindu Swaraj in Maharashtra, a very acute foreign observer could remark (evidently about its outlying parts and not the home-land):—

> "The Mahratta Government, from its foundation has been one of devastation. It never relinquished the predatory habits of its founder. It was continually destroying all within its reach, and never repairing". [Munro's letter, 11 Sep. 1818. Gleig, iii 276].

For this result Shivaji's blind successors at Satara and Puna were to blame, and not he. In that early epoch and in his short span of life, he could not humanly be expected to have done otherwise.

Today, after the lapse of three centuries from his birth, a historian taking a broad survey of the diversified but ceaseless flow of Indian history, is bound to admit that though Shivaji's dynasty is extinct and his State has crumbled into dust, yet he set an example of innate Hindu capacity (superior to Ranjit Singh's in its range) and left a name which would continue to fire the spirit of man and shine forth as an ideal for him for ages yet unborn.

9. His Religious toleration and equal treatment of all subjects

He stands on a lofty pedestal in the hall of the worthies of history, not because he was a Hindu champion, but because he was an ideal householder, an ideal king, and an unrivalled nation-builder. He was devoted to his mother, loving to his children, true to his wives, and scrupulously pure in his relations with other women. Even the most beautiful female captive of war was addressed by him as his mother. Free from all vices and indolence in his private life, he displayed the highest genius as a king and as an organiser. In that age of religious bigotry, he followed a policy of the most liberal toleration for all creeds. The letter which he wrote to Aurangzib, protesting against the imposition of the poll-tax on the Hindus, is a masterpiece of clear logic, calm persuasion, and political wisdom. Though he was himself a devout Hindu, he could recognise true sanctity in a Musalman, and therefore he endowed a Muhammadan holy man named Baba Yaqut with land and money and installed him at Keleshi. All creeds had equal opportunities in his service and he employed a Muslim secretary named Qazi Haidar, who, after Shivaji's death, went over to Delhi and rose to be Chief Justice of the Mughal Empire. There were many Muhammadan captains in Shivaji's army and his Chief Admiral was an Abyssinian named Siddi Misri. His Maratha soldiers had strict orders not to molest any woman or rob any Muhammadan saint's tomb or hermitage. Copies of the *Quran* which were seized in the course of their campaigns were ordered to be carefully preserved and then handed over respectfully to some Muhammadan.

Among his Hindu servants there were Brahmans and Non-Brahmans enjoying the highest civil and military offices;—Brahmans, Prabhus (*i.e.*, Kayasthas), Marathas, Kunbis and the trading caste all found recognition from him.

Before his rise, the Maratha race was scattered through many foreign kingdoms and lived as servants and subjects and not as their own masters. Shivaji united them into one people by giving them a national State with a national king of their own. This was true "Hindavi Swaraj." His infant kingdom became a centre of learning and piety, of trade and wealth, of new literary creation and social improvement.

10. Shivaji's Political Ideals

Shivaji's political ideals were such that we can almost accept them even today without any change. He aimed at giving his subjects peace, universal toleration, equal opportunities for all castes and creeds, a beneficent, active and pure system of administration, a navy for promoting trade, and a trained militia for guarding the homeland. Above all, he sought for national development through action, and not by lonely meditation nor by straining the throat on platforms. Every worthy man,—not only the natives of Maharashtra, but also recruits from other provinces of India,—who came to Shivaji, was sure of being given some task which would call forth his inner capacity and pave the way for his own rise to distinction, while serving the interests of the State. The activities of Shivaji's Government spread in many directions and this enabled his people to aspire to a happy and varied development, such as all modern civilised States aim at.

All this national expansion proceeded from the initial energy of one man. Shivaji was the central power-house of the new Maharashtra. He had, I admit, the supreme royal gift of quickly judging every man's character and capacity and choosing the best instrument for every task that he wanted to get done. But he was a self-taught man, he never lived at any great capital, court or camp. His administrative and military systems—perfectly suited to his country and age—were his own creation. Unlike Ranjit Singh or Mahadji Sindhia, he had no French adviser or lieutenant. Everything proceeded from his own heart and brain. Therefore, the historian of Shivaji, at the end of a careful study of all the records about him in eight different languages, is bound to admit that Shivaji was not only the maker of the Maratha nation, but also the greatest constructive genius of medieval India. States fall, empires break up, dynasties become extinct, but the memory of a true "hero as king" like Shivaji remains an imperishable historical legacy for the entire human race—

The pillar of a people's hope,
The centre of a world's desire,

—to animate the heart, to kindle the imagination and to inspire the brain of succeeding ages to the highest endeavours. Therefore, as the saint Ramadas truly said :—

"Shivarajas athavaven. .kirti-rupen."

VI

HISTORICAL LETTERS RELATING TO SHIVAJI

INTRODUCTION

In the Persian language many letters relating to Shivaji have been traced by me. Some of them were written to him or to his father Shahji, some written by their secretaries to their dictation, others though addressed to local officers by Muslim sovereigns, throw much light on the affairs of these two Maratha kings. It is difficult to overestimate the importance of these letters for the historian of Shivaji. First of all, unlike most Marathi letters, these are exactly dated and thus enable us to get fixed points for reconstructing the correct chronology of Shivaji's and Shahji's careers. Secondly, they have been mostly preserved in the original and therefore cannot be said to have been tampered with by later fabricators, as many title-deeds and legal decisions about heritage in the Marathi and Persian languages, fondly cherished by private families in Maharashtra, admittedly are. In the term *letters* I include news-letters or manuscript reports of proceedings and speeches at the royal Court or camp, called *akhbarat*, which are invaluable raw materials for the history of mediæval India.

Finally, these historical letters are really State-papers in the true sense of the term and therefore the most valuable original sources for the historian, while the thousands of "Letters of Shivaji's times" in the Marathi language printed by Rajwade and others are merely petty land grants or "succession certificates" or partition awards, *i.e.*, purely private legal documents, whose only connection with Shivaji is that they were written when he was on the throne!

In this section I shall give translations of the more important earlier letters about Shivaji, faithfully preserving the sense but pruning away the ornate verbiage of the Persian epistolary style. The letters that relate to the Purandar Campaign and his visit to Agra will be given in separate sections.

1. Bijapur Sultan and Shahji and Shivaji

Sultan Muhammad Adil Shah to Kanhoji Nayak Jedhe. 1st August, 1644.

This royal letter is issued to Kanhoji Nayak Jedhe in *Shahur San* 1044. As Shahji Bhonsla has become a rebel against this august Court, and Dadaji Kond-dev, his supreme agent (*mutliq*), is [campaigning] in the Kondana district,—therefore, with a view to putting a stop to his activity and gaining possession of that country, Khandoji Khopde and Baji Khopde have been appointed to accompany our grand ministers. It is proper that he [*i.e.*, Kanhoji Jedhe] also with his contingent should join the aforesaid persons and under their guidance punish Dadaji Kond-dev and the associates of that base fellow and bring them to annihilation, and take possession of that district, so that it may result in his [*i. e.*, Jedhe's] being exalted. Know this to be urgent. Written on 7th Jamadi-us-sani, year 1054 of the Hijera (=1 August 1644.)

Explanatory Notes.

Kanhoji Jedhe, deshmukh of Bhor, in the Puna district, came over to Shivaji's side during the latter's contest with Afzal Khan (1659) and with his own contingent fought the Maratha king's battles right manfully in various places for many years afterwards. The chronology (*shakavali*)*kept by this family is one of the most valuable sources of early Maratha history. Their home is the village of Kari some ten miles from the town of Bhor, in the territory of the Sachiv, one of the *sardars* of the Puna district. During a visit to the place in January 1930, I discovered the following *farman* of Muhammad 'Adil Shah, Sultan of Bijapur, issued to Kanhoji Jedhe on 7th Jamadi-us-sani 1054 A. H. (=1 August 1644.)

Kari is situated in the heart of the Maval country. This tract was in one sense a frontier of the Nizam-shahi kingdom of Ahmadnagar. When that dynasty was extinguished, it passed into the hands of Adil Shah of Bijapur (about 1636), but it was long before the new sovereign's authority was fully recognised there. The Jedhes had been originally retainers of Randaula Khan,

*Tr. by me in *Shivaji Souvenir*, ed. by G. S. Sardesai (1927), pp. 1—44.

and continued to find in him their master and protector after the district came under Adil-shahi sway. At first the new sovereign gave the fief of the Jedhes to a Muhammadan female (of Kalian?), but on appeal the Jedhes got it back, evidently through the mediation of Randaula Khan (about 1637-38.) From Randaula's service they were transferred to the contingent of Shahji Bhonsla, who was a lifelong friend of Randaula.

The present *farman* is of the greatest importance as fixing the exact date of the Maratha acquisition of Kondana (Singh-garh) and Shahji's first rupture with the Adil-shahi Government.

Ali Adil Shah II to Shahji Bhonsla. 26th May, 1658.

To Maharaj Farzand (= son) Shahji Bhonsla.—Be honoured with our royal favours and know that:—

At this time it has been reported to His Majesty that owing to the disloyalty and audacity of Shivaji Bhonsla you are alarmed lest his faults should be laid on your head. Be it known to this loyal subject that the improper conduct and acts of Shivaji are evident to His Majesty. Therefore, the faults of Shivaji will not be laid upon you, but his offences are being imputed to him only.

Hence, keep your mind composed regarding all matters, and the grace and favours which you had enjoyed from His late Majesty [Muhammad Adil Shah], in the same measure,—nay more than that,—are confirmed to you by me. There will be no change or deprivation in your rank and fiefs.

I restore to you the territory around the fort of Bangalore which you used to enjoy before. Should any one allege anything against you, I shall consider it as utter falsehood and give it no place in my mind. Compose your heart in all ways, because this is [confirmed by my] oath and prayer to God.

Written on 4th Ramzan, 1068 A.H. = 26 May 1658. [Hyderabad ms.]

Ali Adil Shah II to Yekoji Bhonsla. 3rd March, 1660.

This auspicious *farman* is issued to the following effect:—

Yekoji Bhonsla, be exalted by our royal favour and know that, as the constant aim of His Majesty is to spread the faith of the Sayyid among Prophets [Muhammad], therefore the breeze of victory has always blown upon the banners of my generals. The proof of it is that at this time the infidel wretch and rebel Shiva had raised his head in tumult and shown the utmost audacity. Therefore,....[Siddi] Jauhar Salabat Khan was sent by us with an army and officers to root out that infidel rebel. When this general marched out for uprooting that impure *kafir*, the wretch feeling himself unable to confront the Islamic army, turned his face towards flight, and the army of unbelievers that had gathered round him like wild dogs, dispersed in different directions. The army of Islam is in pursuit of him, and by the grace of God will in a short time either make him a captive or destroy him.

You should, on hearing this glad news, offer thanks to the undiminished fortune of His Majesty.

Written on 1st Rajab, 1070 A.H. (=3 March 1660.)

Notes.—Siddi Jauhar, an Abyssinian slave who had usurped Karnul, was given the title of Salabat Khan by Ali Adil Shah II and sent against Shivaji who had killed Afzal Khan (on 10th November before) and captured the fort of Panhala and many other places in South Konkan. Jauhar easily swept away the Maratha resistance in the open and drove Shivaji into Panhala fort (2nd March 1660) which he besieged with a force of 15,000 men. *See* my *Shivaji*, 3rd ed., ch. IV. § 1.

2. Prince Murad Bakhsh and Shivaji

Prince Murad Bakhsh to Shivaji. 14th March, 1649.

Shivaji Bhonsla......hope for our princely favours and know that the letter professing extreme devotion that you had sent me has been placed before me. In the matter of your coming to my presence, you have begged for a letter from me summoning you and giving you assurances of safety. It is the practice of true loyalty that you should first of all send to me a high envoy of yours,—who may be relied upon—so that I may learn of your intentions and demands, and send you [in return] a princely letter of conciliation stamped with the impression of my palm, and accompanied by many favours. Keep your mind composed in all respects and send your envoy quickly.....Written on 10th Rabi-ul-awwal, year 22 of His Majesty's reign, corresponding to 1059 A.H. (= 14 March 1649.)

This letter is issued through the agency of Abdul Latif, the humblest of the devoted slaves [of Shah Jahan.]

Prince Murad Bakhsh to Shivaji. 14th August, 1649.

Shivaji Bhonsla....be glorified with our boundless princely favours and know that, as with extreme graciousness the pen of forgiveness has been drawn through the offences of your father and the doors of favour and pardon have been thrown open to his loyalty and devotion, now is the time for you to come to my presence along with your father and your clansmen, for the purpose of saluting the Emperor's threshold, so that after attaining to that happiness you may be exalted among your peers by the grant of a *mansab* of 5-hazari *zat* with 5,000 *sawar*-rank and suitable rewards, and your father may have his former *mansab* (rank) in the imperial service restored. Your brethren and clansmen who may come along with you will be enrolled among the servants of the Emperor. Keep your mind composed in all matters and take to your heart this gracious princely letter which is adorned with the impression of my palm....Written on 15th Shaban, regnal year 23, corresponding to 1059 A.H. (= 14 August 1649.)

Through the mediation of Abdul Latif.

Prince Murad Bakhsh to Shahji. 31st October, 1649.

Be honoured with our boundless princely favours and know that the petition which your son Shivaji had sent to me has passed under my eyes. As it professes loyalty and service, it has increased my graciousness [to him.] He has prayed for the pardoning and release of his father. As I am starting on a journey to the imperial Court, I assure you of my princely favour and inform you that you should keep your mind composed in all matters, as after my arrival at the 'imperial Court, I shall report all your prayers and get them granted. But it is the way of true devotion and loyalty that you should send your trusted envoy so that the imperial *farman* giving you safe-assurances and adorned with His Majesty's hand-impression may be despatched through him. Shambhaji and other sons of you, also, by favour of the Emperor will get their release (*nejat*) and be honoured with their former *mansabs* and many kinds of favours....I am sending you a gracious robe (*khilat.*)

Written on 5th Zilqada, regnal year 23rd (= 31 Oct. 1649.)

Through the mediation of Abdul Latif.

Prince Murad Bakhsh to Shivaji. 30th November, 1649.

The petition that you had sent with Raghu Pandit has been placed before me. You have applied for the post of *desh-mukh* of parganas Junnar and Ahmadnagar. Rest assured that when I arrive at the imperial Court your desire will be gratified. It is proper that you should speedily send your *wakil* (envoy), so that I can ask him about your desires and report them to the Emperor, and thus prevent delay in the transaction of your business.

Written on 5th Zihijja, regnal year 23, corresponding to 1059 A.H. (= 30 November 1649.)

Through the mediation of Abdul Latif.

Notes.—Prince Murad was appointed by Shah Jahan viceroy of the Deccan on 15 July 1648 and ordered to be replaced by Shaista Khan on 4 Sep. 1649. He arrived in and departed from his province about two months later than the dates of these "Gazette" orders. It is evident that Shahji, after his captivity by Adil Shah (25 July 1648—16 May 1649) was eager to leave this ungrateful master's service and gain greater safety by going over to the Mughals.

All this correspondence of Shivaji and Shahji during the captivity and after was held with Prince Murad and never with Shah Jahan directly. Rajwade did not know that the terms *Sultani* and *Shahi* in these letters mean 'pertaining to the prince' and not 'imperial', also that *nishan* means a prince's letter to an inferior, while *farman* means an Emperor's letter.

3. Aurangzib and Shivaji down to 1664

Prince Aurangzib to Multafat Khan (written "by order" by Secretary Qabil Khan), c. September, 1656.

Received your letter....enclosing the letter of Shahji's son to you and a copy of your reply to him. The Prince orders that in future you should keep the same path of correspondence with Shiva open and continue to write to him words of reassurance and conciliation, which may be the cause of inciting him to loyalty to this Court, so that he may exert himself in that path even more than before.

Notes.—Multafat Khan was governor of Ahmadnagar, in whose jurisdiction the lands of Shivaji were situated. [This letter is from *Adab-i-Alamgiri*, A.S.B. ms, f. 144*b*.]

Prince Aurangzib to Multafat Khan (per Secretary Qabil Khan), c. 15th March, 1657.

Received your letter with its annexure, a letter from Shivaji Bhonsla to you. The Prince orders me to inform you that some days before this, his vakil also arrived here with a letter from him and submitted his demands and desires to the Prince. Very soon a gracious *nishan* (*i.e.*, a letter from a Prince to any inferior person or equal) will be issued to him in reply. After you have received a copy of that *nishan*, you will draft your reply to Shivaji's letter in accordance with it....Our siege-trenches have reached the edge of the moat [of Bidar fort] and we are filling the ditch up. [*Adab*, f. 146*a*.]

Prince Aurangzib to Shivaji, 22nd April, 1657.

The petition which you had sent after the receipt of my letter to you, has been placed before me and made your demands known to me. I tell you that what I had to say on every matter has been already communicated to Sonaji your envoy. He has surely reported them to you and reassured your mind.

In fact, all the forts and *mahals* pertaining to Bijapur that are in your possession have been confirmed in you as before. I also leave to you the revenue of the port of Dabhol and its dependencies, as desired by you.

After you have displayed the marks of loyalty and devoted service,—the time for manifesting which is this,—in the proper manner, and you have attained to the honour of interviewing me,.......your remaining prayers will be granted and you will be comprehended in my favour and grace more than you can imagine.

I have given your envoy, who was in a hurry to go away, leave to depart, so that he may return to you and inform you of my daily increasing graciousness towards you, and in consequence you may remain firm in your loyalty and service without the smallest omission and never deviate from the path of obedience....

In this season of victory,....I have broken the back of my enemies and my victorious troops have conquered in one day the fort of Bidar with its citadel, though the fort is so strong that up to this time no Governor had even conceived the idea of conquering it, and it is the key for opening the entire realm of Deccan and Karnatak. In the course of one month of siege such a victory has been attained; it is the prelude to inconceivably more victories, and other rulers could not have achieved it in the course of years....

Written on 18 Rajab, regnal year 31 (= 22 April 1657.)

Through the mediation of Zia-ud-din Husain.

Notes.—On the succession of Ali Adil Shah II, Aurangzib with the consent of Shah Jahan invaded Bijapur under the pretext that Ali was not really a son of the late king. He first laid siege to the fort of Bidar on 2nd March 1657, and stormed its walls on the 29th of the same month. This fort had hitherto been considered as impregnable and no previous ruler had even attempted its capture for the 300 years since its foundation. Aurangzib rightly boasted of this success to his arms in many of his letters. [See my *History of Aurangzib*, vol. I ch. 11 § 5.]

Prince Aurangzib to Nasiri Khan, c. November 1657.

What you have written in reply to the letter of the defeated and disgraced Shivaji, is approved by the Prince. Although it is proper to extirpate that miscreant, and after his manifestations of crime and hostility he cannot even in his imagination hope for any safety from us,—yet, if he acts as you have written to him and sends a trusty agent to you, and if you find his demands worthy of being reported to the Prince, then you should write the nature of his desires in your letters to the Prince. Remain ever on the alert!

[*Adab*, f. 156 *b.* Nasiri Khan was the officer in command of the outpost and sub-division of Raisin, in the Ahmadnagar province.]

Prince Auranzib to Shivaji Bhonsla, 24th February 1658.

The letter which you sent with Raghunath Pandit,

your envoy, to my Court, has been placed before me along with the letter which you have addressed to Krishnaji Bhaskar Pandit. Your prayers have thus become known to me.

My reply is:—Although your offences are too many and too grave to merit pardon, yet as you are professing an intention to render loyalty and service to me and showing penitence and sense of shame for your past misdeeds, I draw the pen of pardon through the pages of your crimes, but on condition of your remaining firm in obedience and service in future. You ought now to make every effort to manifest your true devotion and obedience, which will be the means of your gaining rank and fortune.

You have written:—" If I am given the glad news of being granted all the mahals appertaining to my ancestral estate (*watan*) along with the forts and country of Konkan after the imperialists have annexed the [old] Nizam-shahi territory which now belongs to Adil Khan (*sic*)—I shall send Sonaji Pandit to your Highness. And after I have received a princely rescript granting my demands, I shall depute one of my generals to your Highness's camp with a good force, which will consist of not less than 500 expert soldiers, and I shall myself join the imperial officers, in protecting the boundaries of the imperial dominions [in the Deccan] and prevent disturbance from any source taking place there."

My reply is:—Act according to your undertaking. Immediately on the receipt of this letter send Sonaji to me with a letter stating your demands, so that these may be granted. Know this matter to be urgent. In no way deviate from the royal road of true obedience and loyalty. Written on 24 February 1658.

Postscript added about 20 April, 1658.

Know that at this time a splendid victory has fallen to my lot. It is this: Rajah Jasawant Singh and Qasim Khan, with 25,000 troopers and many pieces of artillery, were staying at Ujjain. When my army arrived within six *kos* of Ujjain, they audaciously came forward to give me battle, but were soundly beaten, and after giving up six or seven thousand of their men to slaughter, they turned their faces towards the wilderness of flight. Their camps with their treasures, guns, elephants and other property were plundered by us.

It is proper that you should exult at this happy news and remain firm in the path of obedience.

Through the agency of Murshid Quli Khan.

Emperor Aurangzib to Shivaji Bhonsla, 14th July, 1659.

Know that God has adorned my banners with victory and defeated and crushed my rivals who were enemies of the Faith......On the 24th of Ramzan (=5 June 1659), the imperial throne was made resplendent by my accession.

The letter that you had sent to me by the hand of one of your servants has reached me. Remain firm in your loyalty and service to my throne, which will be the means of realising your hopes, Amir-ul-umara Shaista Khan has been appointed subahdar of the Deccan. Act according to his orders and never deviate from his instructions. Exert yourself so that the things you have promised may be carried out in the best manner and your prayers may be granted.

I have established peace throughout the empire. Dara Shukoh has been captured with his family and followers on the frontier of Bhakkar [in Sindh.] God willing, Shuja too will be soon annihilated.

Know my favour to be turned towards you. A robe of honour is conferred on you for your exaltation. Written on 4th Zilqada 2nd regnal year [text wrongly reads *First year.*]

Notes.—The second or grand Coronation of Aurangzib took place at Delhi on 5th June 1659, the first one, a year earlier, having been a plain and hurried affair. Dara was captured at the Indian end of the Bolan pass on 9th June 1659, and Shaista Khan was given *congee* for the viceroyalty of the Deccan on 5th July of the same year.

Maharajah Shivaji, to the Officers and Counsellors of the Emperor Alamgir

Letter drafted by Nila Prabhu Munshi, *c.* 1664.

Be it not concealed from the hearts of far-sighted and thoughtful men, that, for the last three years, the able counsellors and famous generals (of the Emperor) have come to these parts. To the orders issued by the Emperor for seizing my country and forts, they reply, "These will be soon conquered." They do not know that even the steed of unimaginable exertion is too weak to gallop over this hard country, and that its conquest is difficult. It is a matter of great wonder that they do not at all expect the fruit of shame from such writings filled with fictitious statements, but (on the contrary) cast off truthfulness, which is the cause of salvation. And why so? My home, unlike the forts of Kalian and Bidar, is not situated on a spacious plain, which may enable trenches to be run (against the walls) or assault to be made. It has lofty hill-ranges, 200 leagues in length and 40 leagues in breadth; everywhere there are *nalas* hard to cross; sixty forts of extreme strength have been built, and some (of them are) on the sea-coast. Hence, Afzal Khan, an officer of Adil Shah (Ali II, king of Bijapur) came to Javli with a large army, but perished helplessly. Why do not you truly report to the Emperor what has happened (here), so that the same fate may not overtake you?

After the death of the above-mentioned Khan, the Amir-ul-umara, who was appointed against these sky-kissing hills and abysmal passes, laboured hard for three years, and (constantly) wrote to the Emperor that I was going to be defeated and my land conquered in the shortest space of time. But at last, as all false men deserve, he encountered such a terrible disaster and went away in (such) disgrace, that it is clearer than the sun. (Verses)

It is not everywhere that the charger can gallop ;
There are places where one has to fling away his shield.

It is my duty to guard my land.

Although, to save their reputation, they had written to the Emperor the opposite of the true state of things, yet, thank God, the bud of desire of no invader of the beloved country of this retired man has (yet) blossomed forth. (Verse)

The wise should beware of this river of blood,
From which no man (ever) carried away his boat (in safety.)

Notes.—In May, 1657, Shivaji first violated Mughal territory by plundering the town of Junnar. But he could not be punished, as Aurangzib, then viceroy of the Deccan, was soon called away to northern India by the fight for his father's throne. In May, 1661, the Mughals renewed hostilities. Shaista Khan, the new viceroy, entitled *Amir-ul-umara* or Premier Peer, took some of Shivaji's forts and occupied Poona. Here, in April 1663, Shivaji made the daring night-attack in which the Khan lost a son and narrowly escaped death himself. Shaista Khan in disgust secured a transfer from the ungracious service in the Deccan to Bengal (end of 1663). Shivaji had now a freer hand and merrily plundered Mughal cities, including Surat (on 6-10 Jan. 1664). The above letter was evidently written later in 1664.

VII

SHIVAJI AND MIRZA RAJAH JAI SINGH

The Story of the Discovery

The Purandar campaign of 1665 was the greatest achievement in the highly eventful career of Jai Singh I and the most signal defeat in the still more brilliant career of Shivaji. But up to 1904 the only accounts of it known to us were a fairly long narrative in the Persian official history *Alamgir-namah* (which as we now find was a faithful abstract of Jai Singh's field despatches to the Emperor) and the Marathi stories which merely represent camp-fire gossip or absurd later traditions. In 1904 I traced a Persian manuscript in the Bibliotheque Nationale of Paris which gives Aurangzib's replies to Jai Singh and Jai Singh's despatches to that Emperor during the Rajput Rajah's pursuit of Dara Shukoh in 1659 and the Purandar siege of 1665. But unfortunately the ms. ends abruptly in the midst of the latter campaign just before Shivaji's visit to Jai Singh for making his surrender.

A quarter century after that year the Jaipur State archives were explored under expert historical guidance, but these wanted despatches of Jai Singh were not found there,—not even the contents of the Paris ms. And for a very sufficient reason. The duplicate copies of Jai Singh's letters used to be kept in charge of his secretary Udiraj Munshi. This man enjoyed the Mirza Rajah's unbounded confidence and exercised unrivalled influence over him in his last years. We possess a contemporary record of a talk in Kumar Ram Singh's house at Agra in the presence of Shivaji in which the Kachhwah officer who had conducted Shivaji from the Deccan to Agra said, "The Maharajah listens to nobody, neither to his nobles (*thakurs*), nor even to Dilir Khan. He is guided solely by the advice of Udiraj." Hence the officers and relatives of Jai Singh were mortally jealous of Udiraj, and when the Mirza Rajah died during his return journey from the Deccan the cry arose that Udiraj had given him poison. The Kachhwah troops led by the Rajah's second son Kirat Singh, made a dead set against Udiraj, but the Munshi fled to the governor of the town (Burhanpur) and claimed his protection by at once turning Muslim! He thus saved his life and property,—including the official papers of his master then in his hands, which never came to be deposited in the Jaipur State archives. After this Munshi's death, his son put his drafts together in a volume entitled *Insha-i-Haft Anjuman*, intending it to serve as a model of epistolary style for students of the Persian language. But no copy of this book happened to come to the Jaipur Raj library till I discovered this work and (in 1939) lent my own ms. to the State.

My discovery of the *Haft Anjuman* happily followed only a few years after my discovery of the fragmentary despatch-book of Jai Singh in Paris. In the course of a visit of courtesy which I paid to Maulana Shibli Numani at Lucknow (in 1902 or 1903), he told me of a ms.

containing some letters of Jai Singh and Aurangzib which he had heard, was owned by a Kayastha of an old family at Benares. In 1905-'7 I paid three visits to Benares and traced this manuscript. But during centuries of neglect, the leaves of the volume had stuck together, because the gum arabic which is mixed with Indian ink in order to give a gloss to the writing had moistened in the monsoons, and then the weight of the pile of books above our volume had turned it into a sort of card-board! In forcing the leaves apart the writing was damaged in many places, but I took a transcript of it as it was. Thus the *Haft Anjuman* again became known to the world after two and a half centuries of oblivion.

Our good fortune did not end here. About twelve years after this, Professor Abdur Rahman of St. Stephen's College, Delhi, purchased a perfect copy of the *Haft Anjuman* in an old curiosity shop of his native town of Jaipur for five Rupees only! No other ms. is known to exist.

This work gives us all the letters that Udiraj wrote for his two successive masters,—Rustam Khan and Jai Singh —either directly from them or "by order" of them, besides what he wrote in his own behalf, as well as two petitions to the Emperor which he drafted for Shivaji in the correct Persian style for such letters. These last are given in this section.

After the surprise of Shaista Khan and the sack of Surat by Shivaji, Aurangzib despached the able and wise

Mirza Rajah Jai Singh and the brave Afghan general Dilir Khan, to subdue the "mountain-rat." Jai Singh arrived at Poona on the 3rd of March 1665, and so vigorously pushed on operations against Shivaji that the Maratha king came to him on 12th June to surrender. The Rajput prince then gave the following account of his success in a despatch to Aurangzib.

Mirza Rajah Jai Singh I to Emperor Aurangzib, June 1665.

May is please your Majesty! After the arrival of the imperial army near Pabal, Shiva's agents began to visit me, and again up to my arrival at Poona they twice brought letters from him. But I gave no answer, and sent them back in disappointment. I knew that unless a strong hand was laid on him, his words and stories would not contain a particle of truth.

When he sent a long Hindi letter with a trusted officer named Karmaji, and the latter repeatedly entreated me saying, "Do please listen only once to the contents of this letter and condescend to grant an answer," I listened to what Shiva had written. Its purport was, "I am a useful servant of the imperial threshold, and many services can be secured from my humble self. If the Mughal army turns to the invasion of Bijapur, such a course would be better than undergoing the many hardships (of campaigning) in this hilly region (*i.e.*, Konkan) of difficult paths and stony soil." I wrote in answer to Shiva, "The imperial army, countless like the stars, has been appointed in the South against you. Do not put your faith in your hills and stony country. God willing, it will be trodden flat with the dust by the hoofs of the wind-paced chargers of the imperial army. If you desire your own life and safety, place in your ear the ring of servitude to the slaves of the imperial Court,—which (ring) is a source of glorification and honour even to your masters,—and withdraw your heart from your hills and forts. Otherwise the fate you will meet with will be only the consequence of your own deeds." After getting this sort of reply, he repeatedly sent me (further) letters. In a less proportion than he was put to hard straits (by our military operations), he proposed to pay tribute and cede one or two places, which I did not deem valuable. My reply was the same as the one he had received (before). Eventually our troops captured the fort of Rudramal, and I divided my army, sending Daud Khan and Rajah Rai Singh to plunder Shivaji's country, and appointing one party to guard the camp and to go rounds, and another party to forage and patrol—who were to remain constantly in the saddle,—so that the soldiers in the siege-trenches in peace of mind worked their hardest to accomplish their task, and I as far as possible looked after every place.

As the result (of these arrangements) at this time Shiva declared publicly, "While Daud Khan and Rajah Rai Singh were out riding, as often as I planned to go and destroy the trenches by an attack, I found the soldiers so ready and prepared, that if I had made my way into (their lines) my return to Rajgarh would have been very difficult."

In short, as the siege of the fort was effectively conducted, five towers and one battlement (*kangura*) were captured by us, his country was plundered by our cavalry, his troops collected in such a long time were seduced by us—because I had at this time by giving passports and promises of safety summoned to myself many of his cavalry and induced them to enter the imperial service with proper *mansabs* (military rank) and stipends of 10 or 15 (rupees), and (by giving them) 10 or 20 rupees above the promised rate, in cash from the treasury.

I had also summoned 500 infantry under Khelo Bhonsla from Javli, and daily sought how to separate Shiva's army from him.

Shiva, finding the state of affairs to be such, decided to choose one of these two alternatives: first, he would submit his proposals to me and beg to be spared his life and property. If this overture were accepted, nothing could be better. If not, he would adopt the second alternative, restore a part of the Bijapuri Tal-Konkan to the Sultan of Bijapur, join the latter, and oppose the Mughals.

Trustworthy spies brought me the news that the Sultan of Bijapur, while professing that the wresting of some *mahals* of his former Tal-Konkan was a proof of his loyalty to the imperial cause, had secretly promised (to Shiva) every possible help and was posting an army of his own in that Tal-Konkan, in order that the imperial forces might not desire to march thither.

When I learnt of this, it struck me that to render Shiva hopeless would only drive him into an alliance with Bijapur. True, it is not very difficult for the victorious Emperor's fortune to conquer *both* of these wretched rulers. But if policy can accomplish a thing, why should we court delay (by resorting to force)?

Just then, about the middle of the month of *Ziqada* (say 20th May, 1655), Shiva's *guru* styled the Pandit (Raghunath Rao), arrived on a secret embassy, and stated Shiva's terms after taking the most solemn oaths possible among the Hindus. In view of what I have reported to your Majesty, I replied, "The Emperor has not at all permitted me to negotiate with Shiva. I cannot, of my own authority, hold conference with him openly. If Shiva comes unarmed, in the guise of offenders begging pardon, and makes supplication for forgiveness,-well, the Emperor is the shadow of God, the ocean of his mercy may possibly flow (towards Shiva.)" The Pandit went back and brought the message that Shiva would send his son to me in the above manner. I replied, "The coming of his son is neither proper nor acceptable." Then Shiva prayed, "Well, if you cannot publicly grant me promise and safe-conduct, make the same promise in private, that I may go to you in reliance on it."

With promise and engagement I fixed the terms of peace in his memory, thus: If after his arrival (in my camp) Shiva consents to obey the Emperor's orders, he would be pardoned and granted favours, otherwise, he would be allowed to return in safety to his home.

On 9th June 1665, the Brahman went to Shiva; and on the 11th one *prahar* of the day being past, while I was holding court, he brought the news that Shiva had arrived at hand in that manner, accompanied by six Brahmans and some *kahars* (bearers) of his palki. I sent Udiraj Munshi and Ugrasen Kachhwah to meet him on the way and tell him that if he agreed to surrender all his forts he might come, otherwise he should turn back (thence.) After hearing this message, Shiva said, "I have entered into the (imperial) service. Many (of my) forts will be added to the imperial dominions." Saying this he came on in the company of the men deputed by me. I sent Jani Beg Bakhshi to the door of the tent to conduct Shiva in.

After his arrival, Dilir Khan and my son Kirat Singh, according to a plan which I have submitted to your Majesty in another sheet (*band*), on getting a signal (or order) from me, assaulted and entirely captured the fort of Khadkala* and tried to conquer the interior of the fort (of Purandar.) The fire of fighting could be seen from my place. Shiva, immediately on his arrival and inquiry (into the matter), offered to surrender fort Purandar. I answered, "This fort has been (all but) conquered through

* The lower fort of Purandar, 400 feet below the summit which is crowned with the main fort. Sometimes written as *Khadakla*.

the exertions and valour of the imperial troops. In an hour, in a minute, the garrison of the fort would be put to our swords. If you want to make a present to the Emperor, you have many *other* forts (for the purpose.)"

He begged for the lives of the besieged garrison. So, I sent Ghazi Beg with a servant of Shiva to Dilir Khan and my son, to take possession of the fort and let off its inmates. Your Majesty will learn from the news-letter the details of how the imperialists entered the fort and how the garrison evacuated it.

Then I lodged Shiva in my audience-tent (*diwan-khana*) and came away. Through the mediation of Surat Singh Kachhwah and Udiraj Munshi negotiations were conducted. Till midnight questioning and answering, entreaty and submission on his part took place. I declined to abate a single fort. Gradually after much discussion we came to this agreement: that 23 of his forts, large and small, of which the revenue was 4 lakhs of *hun*, should be annexed to the Empire: and 12 forts, large and small,—one of which was Rajgarh,— and the standard revenue of which was one lakh of *hun*, should be held by Shiva on condition of service and loyalty (to the imperial Government.)

Besides the above-mentioned prayer, Shiva further requested, "Hitherto I had no wisdom and prudence, and have trodden the path of shortsightedness. I have not the face to wait on the Emperor. I shall send my son as his Majesty's servant and slave, and he will be honoured with the rank of a commander of 5,000 horse (the same number of troopers, each man with two horses and three horses.) Wherever the High Diwan's office assigns him a jagir on condition of payment for six months, it will be accepted by me. He will constantly attend on duty. As for me sinner, exempt me from *mansab* and service. So long as I live I shall not draw my neck back from obedience to orders of service. Wherever in your Deccan wars I am appointed to any duty, I shall without delay perform it. If, out of Bijapuri territory,—of which Bijapuri Tal-Konkan yielding 4 lakhs of *hun* is in my possession—some *mahals* of Balaghat, of which the total revenue is 9 lakhs of *hun*, be granted to this newly purchased slave (*i.e.*, myself) and an imperial *farman* be issued to the effect that 'if at any time the imperial command is sent for the conquest of Bijapur, the above *taluq* would be left to Shiva,'—then I agree to pay a tribute of 40 lakhs of *hun* to the Emperor, in instalments of three lakhs every year."

If I had first reported the above proposals to your Majesty and waited for a reply, great delay would have taken place. And Shiva, too, after discussing affairs wanted leave to return. If, in spite of my solemn promise and safe conduct I had by stratagem detained him, (there would have been two effects:) first, the chieftains of this country, Paligars and Naiks, would have lost faith in the promises and oaths of your officers, which are firm like Alexander's rampart; and secondly, trustworthy informants had reported to me that Shiva before starting on his visit to me had made such arrangements about his household and forts that in the event of his not being allowed to return from our camp his followers might give him up for lost and do their best to guard his house. In view of the above two possibilities, I considered it true policy to reassure Shiva, grant him leave to depart, and assent to his prayers. Next day I urged him to give up those forts. He sent one of his men to fort Rohira ordering it to be vacated. I wrote to Rajah Sujan Singh to send his brother Indraman with a suitable force to take possession of that fort. Shiva deputed another servant to forts Lauhgarh, Isagarh, Tanki and Tikona, all of which forts are situated on the top of the the same hill close to each other, and are very strong and lofty. I wrote to Qubad Khan to hasten to this part with 1,500 cavalry from the force posted at Poona and take possession of the above forts. Halal Khan and other men of the (Mughal) outposts also would accompany him. About fort Kondana Shiva said that after leaving me he would deliver it to my son Kirat Singh, and then proceed to Rajgarh. Sending his son he would direct the evacuation of the other forts (by his men.)

On the 13th of June, as the public did not yet know of his arrival, I mounted Shiva on an elephant and sent him with Rajah Rai Sing to Dilir Khan at the *machi* of fort Purandar. On the 14th I presented him with an elephant and two horses, and sent him away with Kirat Singh. He begged hard for the full suit of the robe of honour worn by me, and I made him wear it, and ordered that after taking him to the quarters of Daud Khan (for a farewell interview), they should set out for their destination. So it happened. At noon he reached Kondana, delivered the fort to my son, and set off for his home, taking with himself Ugrasen Kachhwah who was to bring Shiva's son away with him.

On the 15th Shiva reached Rajgarh, halted there for the 16th, and on the 17th sent his son in charge of Ugrasen. They came to Kirat Singh in the evening of that day, and on the 18th arrived in our camp with him. I lodged the son in my own quarters as I had done the father. That very day came the news of the entry of Indraman Bundela into fort Rohira, and of Qubad Khan into forts Lohgarh, Isagarh, Tanki, and Tikona. I am sending the keys of these 7 forts, and (that of) the Khadkala or Rudramal to your Majesty by the hand of Ghazi Beg. Now that his son has arrived, I shall depute men to take his other forts over, and after they have been occupied their keys also would be sent to your Majesty.

I beg to present to you, as an offering of congratulation on this victory, the money that has been spent out of the imperial treasury in the operations for the capture of Purandar,—because the conquest of this fort is the first victory of the Deccan expedition, and my life and fortune are at the service of the Emperor. I therefore, hope that your Majesty would graciously accept it, and the aforesaid amount would be credited against me.

The real facts about the humbled Shiva's proposals are as follow:—

(1) True, he has got 12 large and small forts including Rajgarh. But even while he had *all* his impregnable forts and was besides aided by the king of Bijapur, we succeeded through God's help in pressing him hard. Now that we have taken away from him the forts of Balaghat, such as Purandar, Rohira, Kondana, Lohgarh, and in Tal-Konkan Mahuli, Muranjan, Khirdurg, Takhul (?), &c., not one of which had hitherto been besieged and taken by anybody, and now that we have hemmed him-round, like the centre of a circle, (with our possessions), *if* Shiva strays by a hair's breadth from the path of obedience he can be totally annihilated by us with the slightest exertion.

(2) The rank which I have recommended for his son is not high in comparison with the ranks procured by previous viceroys (of the Deccan) for his officers. If he be granted a *jagir* in Aurangabad, it would be politic, as the resumption or continuation of the jagir would be in our power. Concerning the territories of Bijapur—of which Bijapuri Tal-Konkan is actually in his possession, and some other tracts of Bijapuri-Balaghat are desired by him,—if your Majesty is planning to punish him,—in view of his insincerity and alliance until recently with the enemies of the Emperor (*i.e.*, Bijapur), and his consent to accompany the imperial army in this very necessary expedition now that the time is favourable (to us),—what can be better than this that first we overthrow Bijapur with the help of Shiva? Your Majesty's wishes with regard to Bijapur should be communicated to me without

the knowledge of anybody else, so that I may submit proper plans for truly carrying them out. It would be impolitic to make them public.

Please state your wishes and send to me your reply to all the points of Shiva's requests. The *farman* which your Majesty would issue to Shiva should contain the statement that every promise and agreement which this old slave (*i.e.*, Jai Singh) had made to Shiva was approved by your Majesty, and that after the forts had been taken possession of by the imperial officers and another despatch had arrived at Court from Jai Singh, a *farman* giving details (of the terms granted) would be issued (to Shiva.)....

I shall now describe the manner of the capture of fort Purandar. I had reported before this the affair of two towers (or bastions) and one *khangar* (? *kangura* or battlement) of the fort of Khadkala (which is the lower half of Purandar.) Next a trench also was wrested from the enemy. This place was appointed the *malchar* of the imperial troops; the enemy retired further behind and fortified another place of shelter. In the night preceding 11th June 1665, the news reached me that Shiva professing submission would arrive at my place next day. In case he arrived, sending forth our men to fight and ordering them to make an assault did not seem good (to me), but it was necessary to give him a demonstration of the power of the imperial army, that a consideration of it might make him the more eager to tread the path of submission.

Therefore, in the night before the 11th of June I sent word to Dilir Khan and Kirat Singh that by the next dawn they should carry the *malchar* of our heroic troops to a place which bears two white marks (in the plan sent to the Emperor), in front of the trenches of the enemy. It was appointed that as soon as the *malchar* would reach them, (our men) must engage in fight. Our men, armed, pushed on their trench to the appointed place. The enemy immediately sallied forth from their shelter and began to oppose. A fight at close quarters took place. My Rajputs and Dilir Khan's men after a heroic fight beat back the enemy in front of them.

The enemy began to flee from the fort of Khad-kala,—on both sides of which were strong bastions and broad and deep ditches, and the path was so narrow that only one or two men could pass (abreast) with the greatest difficulty.

At some places, where they made a stand in the midst of their flight, they came within the reach of our arrows and swords; many of them were sent to hell, and the rest fled, till they reached the first gate of the fort. At this time my men and those of Dilir Khan, who had taken post in the *malchar* right opposite the *deorhi* of the gate and had by their artillery fire demolished the tops of the gates and bastions,–rushed out of their places and mounted (the wall). From both directions our heroes engaged the enemy with sword and dagger, and slew many of them. On our side, too, many were slain and wounded. The enemy fled towards the fort. Our men after much fighting got possession of two strong gates of the fort, and arrived before the 3rd gate which, too, had been damaged by our artillery, and tried to force their way in. Just then Shiva arrived to offer submission.....

Among the men deputed by me to different places, Muhammad, the sister's son of Qutbuddin Khan, took delivery of fort Nardurg, Sayyid Hamid that of Khaigarh (also called Ankola), Haji Alahwardi that of fort Marg-garh (also called Atra.) On the 21st of July Abdullah Shirazi entered Mahuli, one of the famous forts of this country and having much of Ahmadnagar Tal-Konkan under it. Forts Bhandardurg and Tulsi Khul, close to Mahuli, were also occupied by us. I am sending to your Majesty the keys of these six forts.

After that the imperial officers on different dates got delivery of forts Kuhaj, Basant, Muranjan, Nang, Karmala, Khirdurg, Songarh, and Mangarh. The keys of these 8 forts and two other keys—of the Khandkala near Kondana and of Rudramal,—are sent to your Majesty.

In the capture of Purandar Rs. 30,000 in cash has been spent out of the imperial treasury, The price of the ammunition, such as shot and powder, which was spent from the imperial stores, will be reported later.

THE TREATY OF PURANDAR, 1665

The terms of the agreement made between the Mughal general Mirza Rajah Jai Singh and Shivaji at Purandar on 13 June 1665, are distinctly and repeatedly given by Jai Singh in his despatches to Aurangzib, as the Emperor made particular inquiries about them. Early in August, Jai Singh wrote to the Emperor: "Your Majesty has asked—'What promises and agreements have been made by Shiva? What oaths, considered solemn by the Hindus, have been sworn by him? How did you compose your mind about his (possible) bad faith, when allowing him to go away?' My liege! when I dismissed Shiva, I took from him oaths no stronger than which a Hindu can possibly take and the violation of which is believed to make a man accursed and doomed to perdition. We agreed to the following conditions: (*a*) Shiva should be content with the 12 forts, large and small, and land yielding one lakh of *hun* (*i.e.*, 5 lakhs of Rupees) which I had left to him as a mark of imperial grace, and he should never act disobediently nor plunder the imperial dominions. (*b*) Wherever in the (*subah* of) Deccan he is ordered on a service, he should perform it. (*c*) His son Shambhuji, with the rank of a Commander of five thousand, and accompanied by Netaji, who is surnamed the Second Shivaji, should (always) attend on the *subahdar* of the Deccan. (*d*) If lands yielding 4 lakhs of *hun* in Tal-Konkan and 5 lakhs of *hun* in Bijapuri Balaghat (*i.e.*, uplands) are granted to Shiva by the Emperor and he is ensured by a *farman* the possession of these lands after the (expected) conquest of Bijapur (on which Jai Singh was about to set out), then he would in return pay the Emperor 40 lakhs of *hun* in yearly instalments of 3 lakhs. (*e*) 23 forts with territory yielding 4 lakhs of *hun* in Balaghat and Tal-Konkan Nizam-shahi (*i.e.*, the former territory of the extinct kingdom of Ahmadnagar) will be taken away from Shiva and annexed to the Mughal empire." (*Haft Anjuman*, Benares ms., 66*b*-67*a*.)

A little later Jai Singh writes:—"Your Majesty has replied, 'Bijapuri Tal-Konkan is granted to Shiva, but no order will be issued by me about Bijapuri Balaghat being given to him. If he can take it, let him wrest it from Adil Shah.' True, such a remark is equivalent to an order from your imperial grace, but Shiva, out of extreme obedience to your wishes, will not venture to undertake the conquest of the latter territory unless he gets a definite *sanad* to that effect....The standard revenue of these mahals was 9 lakhs of *hun* in former times. But it will now fall short of that sum, even after the pacification of the country and the settlement of *ryots*.....Adil Shah had offered to cede this territory to Shiva if he allowed his brother's son to enter the Bijapur service. But Shiva in reliance on the sanctity of my promises and in hopes of the Emperor's liberality, declined...I pray that Shiva's request may be granted and it may be entered in the imperial *farman* that 9 lakh *hun* worth of land in Bijapuri Tal-Konkan and Balaghat are bestowed on Shiva, on condition of his paying 40 lakhs of *hun* by fixed instalments." (*Ibid*., 70 *a* & *b*.)

Still later Jai Singh writes! "My liege! You have graciously accepted my recommendation about the demands of Shiva....He reached my camp on 27th September, 1665, and welcomed the imperial *farman*. He promised to accompany me in the Bijapur expedition with the troops of his son's *mansab*, and, in addition, 7,000 expert infantry.

"As for the land worth one lakh of *hun* annually which the Emperor has left to him out of the old Nizam-shahi dominions, he very humbly submits that he has no other source of income except this; because the ryots of Bijapuri Tal Konkan have been unsettled by the hostility of Adil Shah. As for Bijapuri Balaghat, though he (*i.e.*, Shiva) can occupy it before our march on Bijapur, yet during that expedition (in which Shiva must be present) the ryots will disperse and cultivation will cease. Shiva, therefore, prays that he may be granted villages and mahals yielding one lakh of *hun* in the Nizam-shahi territory. But after much enquiry I learn that there is an immense difference between the former (*i.e.*, theoretical) revenue and the present (*i.e.*, actual) yield of the Nizam-shahi parganas. Therefore, instead of at once ceding to Shiva villages with a theoretical revenue of one lakh *hun*, I have decided that at first the entire Nizam-shahi territory, except the 12 forts in Shiva's possession, should be administered by the crownlands department, so that the true facts about its revenue may be learnt (by our collectors). At the end of one year, mahals yielding one lakh (in actual collection) will be selected for Shiva out of this tract. In the meantime, to meet the expenses of Shiva's contingent during the coming war against Bijapur, I have agreed to pay him two lakhs of rupees in cash, as a substitute for the jagir (from which he is to be kept out for this one year).

"As for the *jagir* due to Shambhuji, I told Shiva plainly that so long as I was not assured of the payment of the annual instalments of 3 lakhs of *hun*, out of the 40 lakhs agreed upon as his fee (for the possession of Bijapuri Tal-Konkan and Balaghat), I could not grant any jagir to his son. He very loyally replied, 'Although the land for which these 40 lakhs have been promised, *has not yet been fully taken possession of* by me, and although the real income from it can be known only after taking full possession, yet I shall supply the contingent of troops which my son's *mansab* (rank in the army) makes it necessary for him to keep under his banner; and I pray that the salary of his *mansab* may be taken as an equivalent of the instalment of tribute due from me to the imperial Government.' I have agreed to these proposals, as Shiva can render very valuable help to us in the impending war (with Bijapur)." (*Ibid.*, 74*b*-75*a*.)

Comment.

It is clear from the above that the treaty was really an agreement between the Mughals and the Marathas for the partition of the Bijapuri kingdom between them. Shiva was to conquer his portion either before or during the war, and the Mughals agreed not to claim this portion after the conquest of Bijapur on the ground of their being heir to *all* the lands of Adil Shah, but to confirm Shiva in possession of it, in return for a fee of 40 lakhs of *hun*. The two robbers here agree as to how the booty should be divided, in anticipation of the territorial brigandage they are just going to commit. Not a word is said about Shiva being given the right to levy *chauth* on Bijapuri territory, as is asserted in the Marathi accounts. No promise was made by Jai Singh or his master to confer on Shiva the viceroyalty of Mughal Deccan, as the *Bakhars* allege (*Sabhasad*, 38), and the idea of such a promise appears to me to be extremely improbable.

Some account of the places mentioned in the treaty is necessary in order to assist the reader's comprehension of the real state of affairs. *Tal-Konkan* is the low land lying at the foot of the Western Ghats, *i.e.*, the coast strip, while *Balaghat* (Marathi, *Ghatmatha*) is the highland on the top of these hills. In the 16th century and a part of the 17th, these two regions had been divided between the Nizam-shahi (or Ahmadnagar) and Bijapuri kingdoms,—the former holding the northern half and the latter the southern. But the repeated shocks of Mughal invasion from 1599 to 1633 utterly shattered the Nizam-shahi kingdom and its fragments were seized by its neighbours. The treaty of 1636 made a partition of the dominions of this extinct kingdom between the Emperor of Delhi and the Sultan of Bijapur, the latter getting Nizam-shahi Tal-Konkan and Balaghat. (For details see my *History of Aurangzib*, i. Ch. 3 § 3, and *Haft Anjuman*, 67*b*.) As the result of Aurangzib's invasion of Bijapur in 1657, Adil Shah agreed to cede to the Mughals Nizam-shahi Tal-Konkan and Bijapuri Balaghat. (*History of Aurangzib*, i. Ch. 11 § 8 and *Haft Anj.*, 67*b*.) But the war of succession broke out soon afterwards and

Adil Shah refused to yield the promised territory. But this region was never effectively occupied and administered by the Bijapuris; Shiva had, long before 1665, seized several places in it. In fact, it was now a no man's land which the Mughals offered to Shiva.

Shivaji to Aurangzib, June 1665.

Most respectfully submits,—

Although this offender and sinner was deserving of all kinds of punishment, yet, through the mercy and grace of the gracious and favour-showering (imperial) Court,—which is the shadow of the mercy of the Creator and the reflection of the pity of the Nourisher, he has, by means of submission and humility, turned the face of deliverance towards the hope of life and the safety of his life and property, in the shelter of the promise and agreement of the officers of the lofty Court which resembles Heaven in splendour; he has reached the abode of safety of his desire, obtained a new life, and made his forehead of servitude auspicious with the brand of a slave (of the Emperor). He begs to represent that hereafter he will remain firmly engaged in performing the Emperor's work, as a reparation for his past life and an amendment of his uselessly spent days; he will never deviate from the position of rendering service, risking his life and carrying out the imperial mandates,—which is a means of glorification to the rulers of the seven climes of the globe, not to speak of this most abject particle and humblest of drops (*i.e.*, Shiva himself), the (worth of) whose life is well known. Hereafter he will not consent to ruining his own house and destroying the foundation of his own life (by rising in rebellion.) A detailed account of this slave will reach the imperial presence from the despatch of the chief of the Rajahs of the age, Mirza Rajah Jai Singh. He hopes that out of the store-house of (your Majesty's) grace, pardon of offences and cherishing of offenders, life to this slave may be granted, and an imperial *farman* may be issued pardoning his offences, granting security to his house and family, and bestowing life on him.

Note.—Dilir Khan, an impetuous soldier, hated diplomacy. He was hurt, too, at Shivaji submitting to his colleague Jai Singh and thus robbing him of the credit of the capture of Purandar which was impending. The following taunting letter was now written by him to Shivaji. The reader will mark how some of the boastful phrases of Shivaji's earlier letter were remembered and flung in his teeth by the victorious Mughal general.

Dilir Khan to Rajah Shivaji, June 1665.

May good Providence be your helper! My wish to see you is so strong that it baffles measuring. Now, to my object. Your letter, sent with some palace guards (*mahaldars*), has been received and its contents learnt by me. It treats of peace, and I have comprehended it. Be it not concealed from your heart that the words most appropriate for saying on this occasion are "First fight and then peace." If a man craves peace without fighting it sounds as an unbecoming proposal to the imperial generals, who have come at the bidding of their master from the garden of Hindustan in order to travel and hunt in your hilly country. They have come solely for this that you would show yourself in battle. They are guests arrived in this hilly tract with an intense desire for it; but you have not appeared (before them)! In spite of (your) many "strong forts, sky-kissing hills, abysmal ravines, and brave soldiers lying in ambush," you have not once shown any sign of yourself anywhere. And (now) you propose peace! Although you should have thought of it long ago and made the overture before this, yet even now it is welcome.

Emperor Aurangzib to Shivaji, 5th September, 1665.

I have read the petition which you have now sent me, written with extreme humility and profession of weakness and penitence, and describing how you came to Mirza Rajah Jai Singh with the desire of gaining the blessedness of entering the service of the imperial throne, and praying for the pardon of your offences from this threshold of grace and favour by means of obedience and loyalty to my Government; and the purport of your letter has become known to me.

As previous to this, from the despatch of that noble (*i.e.*, Jai Singh) it had become known to me that you, after recognising loyalty and service to my throne as the means of ensuring the advancement of your fortune and being ashamed and penitent for your past misdeeds, have sought refuge with this imperial Government, and given up twenty of your forts to my servants and have prayed for being granted twelve [other] forts and a tract of land yielding one lakh of *hun* as revenue, out of the forts and territory of the [extinct] Nizam-shahi dynasty,—

And that you have further begged that if the Emperor issues an order for granting you *mahals* worth four lakhs of *hun* annual revenue in Bijapuri Tal-Konkan, and five lakhs in Bijapuri Balaghat (uplands),—then you would undertake to pay me 40 lakhs of *hun* in annual instalments of three lakhs by way of tribute (*peshkash*).

Although the offences committed by you up to now through your thoughtlessness about the consequences of your acts, are beyond count, yet as this devoted Rajah [Jai Singh] has prayed for your pardon,—I, out of my characteristic noble habit of shutting my eyes to faults and granting the pardon of lives, do forgive your past deeds and sins and grant all your prayers, namely,

(*i*) I bestow on you twelve forts named in the annexed schedule, and the lands appertaining to them, whose revenue is one lakh of *hun*;

(*ii*) I also order that in respect of the *mahals* yielding a revenue of nine lakhs of *hun* consisting of (*a*) *mahals* worth four lakhs of *hun* in Bijapuri Tal-Konkan which are in your possession and which have been included in my empire on account of your being enrolled among my servants (*i.e.*, as a *mansabdar*) and (*b*) *mahals* yielding five lakhs of *hun* in Bijapuri Balaghat, subject to the conditions that you conquer them before my [projected] campaign against Bijapur, and whenever Jai Singh would invade Bijapur, you would, at the head of a proper contingent of your own troops, co-operate most heartily with him and give him satisfaction by the excellence of your service,—and further that, you would always remain firm in fidelity, devotion and obedience and pay the tribute you have agreed to,—you would be confirmed in these mahals, worth nine lakhs of *hun* a year.

Out of my practice of cherishing slaves, I confer the rank of 5,000 *zat* (5,000 *sawar do-aspa seh-aspa*) on your son,—and I am sending you this royal edict, stamped with the impression of my royal palm and accompanied by a splendid robe of honour, in order to exalt your head.

You ought to recognise the value of our royal favour and render thanks for the same. Always remain true and constant in loyalty and serviceableness.

Written on 5th Rabi-ul-awwal, 8th regnal year=5th Sept. 1665.

Through the mediation of Jafar Khan [the Grand Wazir of Aurangzib.]

Schedule

According to the rent-roll (*tumar*) forwarded by Mirza Rajah, the following twelve forts,—

Rajgarh, Torna, Rairi, Lingana-garh, Mahar-garh, Pali-garh, Ghosala, Asheri, Pal-garh, Bhorap, Kumari, and Udaidurg.

Notes.—Some of these names are indistinctly written in the ms. and have been doubtfully transcribed by me. *Lingana* (in Colaba district) suggests an alternative reading Malang-garh (in Thana district.) *Pali*, also known as Saras-garh is in Bhor State. *Ghosal-garh*, alias Virgarh (in Colaba district.) *Asheri* in Thana dist. *Palgarh* in Ratnagiri dist. *Bhorap* alias Sudha-garh, in Bhor State. *Kumari* in Poona district.

Shivaji to Aurangzib, September 1665.

Shiva, the meanest of life-devoting slaves,—who wears the ring of servitude in his ear and the carpet of obedience on his shoulders,—like an atom, represents the following words to those who stand at the Court of the eternal kingship and the intimate ones of the Court of the Khalifate of perpetual duration:

A high and gracious *farman* (*i. e.*, imperial letter), adorned and illuminated with the stamp of the palm of the imperial hand, has auspiciously arrived. This slave received from a letter of Mirza Rajah Jai Singh, the chief of the nobles of the age, the good news of his eternal happiness, *viz.*, (these) favours from the Emperor, and made long strides to welcome on the way this *farman*, which is as it were an amulet for protecting his life and a means of his salvation. By receiving the high and resplendent letter and gorgeous robe of honour (*khilat*), he raised his head of glory to the Lesser Bear. This sinner and evil-doer did not deserve that his offences should be forgiven or his faults covered up. But the grace and favour of the Emperor have conferred on him a new life and unimaginable honour. In every matter he will carry out the imperial orders in the manner that he has been directed. He will now take leave of Mirza Rajah and go home to make preparations for this expedition (against Bijapur), and join the Rajah with a party of followers (the strength of) which has been reported to your Majesty in the despatch of that chief of Rajahs,—close to the date chosen for the marching of the imperial army (against Bijapur.) He is confident that, through the grace of God and the lofty fortune of the Emperor, some (valuable) service may be rendered by this slave, as amends for his past failings,—whereby he may earn the pleasure of the Emperor, and discharge a small part of the heavy debt of gratitude which he owes for these favours. It was necessary for him to report this matter. (Prayers for the Emperor.)

Note.—Fast couriers took the happy news of Shivaji's submission to the Emperor in eleven days. He confirmed what his general had promised to Shivaji in anticipation of his sanction. The above *farman* conveys this fact to Shivaji.

VIII

SHIVAJI'S VISIT TO AURANGZIB AND AFTER

I. Discovery of primary Sources

The most important discovery of original sources of information about Shivaji, after that of Jai Singh's despatches described in the preceding section,—but even more valuable because covering a virgin field,—has been made in the Jaipur State archives in the year 1939. The body of letters written by the officers of Kumar Ram Singh, who was Jai Singh's representative at the Emperor's Court in Agra during Shivaji's visit there in 1666, has been traced. These are all written in the Dingal dialect or the Rajasthani variety of Hindi. In this chapter I shall supplement my summary of their contents by a few Persian *akhbarats* (news-letters) and historical letters from other sources.

These Dingal letters are unique in value as they faithfully report the conversations held in Ram Singh's house daily at night after his return from the Emperor's Court or during the visits of Shivaji to the Kachhwah prince who was his responsible care-taker during his stay at Agra. They also embody the news from various centres circulating in Agra which was the imperial capital for the time being, as well as the purport of the letters to Ram Singh received from his father the Mirza Rajah in far off Deccan. Sometimes these letters were written in the very night of the conversation and sent off next morning to the Jaipur capital (Amber) where they had been lying in undisturbed repose and ungarbled by later fabricators, till the year 1939, when we dragged them into light. In them we get the earliest and most authentic report of that interview in the Agra palace-fort which ultimately revolutionised the course of Indian history, and also priceless pen-pictures, by competent and critical Hindu eye-witnesses, of Shivaji's personal appearance, conversation, retinue, equipment &c.

The next piece of invaluable information we have now obtained is that contained in two Dingal letters informing us that Shivaji reached home (Rajgarh) only *twenty-five* days after escaping from his Agra prison, and that he lay severely ill for some weeks after, and had a relapse after an interval of convalescence from the first illness. This proves conclusively that he travelled very fast, utterly disregarding rest and comfortable meals, by the broken and obscure Deccan path through Gondwana, avoiding the better known but carefully watched royal highway through Dholpur, Narwar and Akbarpur or Handia (on the Narmada.) His object was to forestall at every mountain-pass and ferry the lazy Government couriers who were sent from Agra, immediately after the discovery of his escape, to all local officers with orders to stop and search all travellers going to the Deccan. And this he successfully achieved, but only at the cost of a ruinous strain on his health.

We must therefore now discard as pure fiction all the stories told by Khafi Khan and others about Shivaji's romantic adventures during his flight through Allahabad,

Benares and Gaya—and even Jagannath-Puri, according to a Maratha fabulist. The rigid time-limit of 25 days, by a rather bow-shaped route, bars out all these anecdotes as impossible.

These old Jaipur records also illustrate the marvellously efficient intelligence service of the English in India, in an age when they were poor traders in the Konkan, with no agency at Agra or Delhi. They corroborate the following contemporary Surat Factory report about Shivaji's chief grievance during his interview with Aurangzib:

"His spirit could not bear such humiliation as the other Umaras to wait at a distance with their hands before them, like mutes. The thought thereof put him into a fever, which the king hearing (it is said) sent to comfort him with promises of great preferment."

LETTERS

Emperor Aurangzib to Shivaji, 25th December, 1665.

Whereas I have learnt from the despatches of Mirza Rajah Jai Singh that you are, at the head of a good force, firmly engaged in my service and have exerted yourself greatly in the conquest of forts Phaltan and Thathvada belonging to the Adil-shahi kingdom, and in punishing the Bijapuri army which was in Tal-Konkan,—

Therefore I graciously praise you and send you a robe of honour and a jewelled dagger along with this *farman*....Written on 27th Jamadi-us-sani, regnal year 8.

Through the agency of Jafar Khan.

Emperor Aurangzib to Shivaji, 5th April, 1666.

The letter which you addressed to me reporting your having started, by the advice of Mirza Rajah, for the purpose of saluting the threshold of my Court, has been placed before me. It has become the cause of increasing my favour towards you.

Come here without delay, in full confidence in my grace and perfect composure of mind. After you have obtained audience of me, you will be glorified with my royal favours and given permission to return home. I am herewith sending you a resplendent *khilat* as a mark of honour.

Written on 10th Shawwal, 9th regnal year=5th April 1666.

Through Jafar Khan.

2. How Shivaji entered Agra

Agra, 23 April, 1666.

A letter has been sent by Maharaj-Kumar Ram Singh to Shivaji asking him to arrive at Agra by the 11th of May and to have his audience of the Emperor....The Emperor has ordered that the Kumar and Fidai Khan should advance one day's march from Agra and welcome Shivaji on the way and conduct him to the capital. Shivaji will be presented at Court on the 11th of May. Tej Singh, the son of Kanhaji, who has been deputed by the Maharajah [Mirza Rajah Jai Singh] to accompany Shivaji, is also coming.

Agra, 15 May.

On 11th May Shivaji reached Maluk Chand's serai and halted there. Then Kumar Ram Singh gave to Girdhar Lal Munshi a special robe (*sar-o-pa*, complete suit) and a *bargir* horse with silver trappings and said to him, "Do you go and convey my *Ram! Ram!* (salutation) to Shivaji." So, Girdhar Lal went there with 35 to 40 horsemen, gave Shivaji his master's salutations, and informed him of the arrangements for their meeting which had been communicated to him by Ram Singh. Shiva dismissed Girdhar Lal after bestowing on him one robe and Rs. 200 in cash.

On 12th May it was Ram Singh's turn to patrol [round the royal palace.] After posting his troops [for this purpose], he rode out to welcome Shivaji by advancing towards his camp. Earlier in the day he had sent Girdhar Lal Munshi to go, mount Shiva and conduct him to Agra. The Munshi went, mounted Shiva and brought him by the route of the Dahar-ara garden. The Kumar with Mukhlis Khan went forward by the path of eunuch Firoza's garden, where the Kumar's camp was situated. On the way he learnt that Shiva was coming by the Dahar-ara garden route; so he deputed Dungar-mal Chaudhuri and Ramdas Rajput to conduct Shiva to the road of Firoza's garden. These two went away and guided Shiva to the road leading to the Kumar's camp through the market-place. Further on was the Nurganj garden, where the two chiefs met each other.

Tej Singh (son of Kanha) told Shivaji, "That is Kumar Ram Singh!" and next coming up to the Kumar's side pointed out Shivaji to him. Shiva wished it in his heart that the Kumar should make the first move by advancing and receiving him, so he delayed coming up to the Kumar. Then the Kumar himself moved forward and embraced Shiva who was still seated on his horse's back. Next Mukhlis Khan met Shiva.

The Kumar had eight elephants (male and female) with him, on seeing which Shivaji told him, "Why are you taking these along with us? There will be crowding further on." Therefore, the elephants were sent away. The Kumar had set up tents for Shivaji close to his own camp; Shiva was conducted there and duly welcomed with music etc.

3. Shivaji's audience with Aurangzib within Agra Fort

Afterwards Kumar Ram Singh and Mukhlis Khan started for leading Shivaji to the Court. In the meantime the Emperor had left the *Diwan-i-am* and taken his seat in the Select Audience Hall (the *Diwan-i-khas.*) Shivaji was conducted to the latter place. The Emperor ordered Asad Khan Bakhshi to bring Shivaji forward and present him for audience. Asad Khan led him up to the Emperor. Shivaji presented one thousand *mohars* and two thousand Rupees as his *nazar* and Rs. 5,000 as *nisar* (propitiatary gifts.) Shambhaji, the son of Shivaji, was introduced to the Emperor and he offered 500 *mohars* and

Rs. 1,000 as *nazar* and Rs. 2,000 as *nisar*. Shivaji was made to stand in the place of Tahir Khan, in front of Rajah Rai Singh. The Emperor neither talked with nor addressed any word to him.

It was the Emperor's birth-day, and the betel-leaf (*pan-bira*) of the ceremony was distributed to the princes and nobles, and Shivaji too got one. Next the *khilats* for the occasion were presented to the princes, to Jafar Khan (the grand wazir) and to Rajah Jaswant Singh. At this Shiva became sad and fretful; he flew into a rage and his eyes became wet. The Emperor noticed it and told the Kumar, "Ask Shivaji what ails him." The Kumar came to Shiva's side and Shivaji told him, "You have seen, your father has seen, your Padishah has seen what a man I am, and yet you have deliberately made me stand up so long. I cast off your *mansab*. If you wanted me to stand, you should have done so according to the right order of precedence." After saying this, he then and there turned his back (to the throne) and roughly walked away. The Kumar caught hold of his hand, but Shiva wrenched it away, came to one side [room] and sat down there. The Kumar followed him to that place and tried to reason with him, but he would not listen, and cried out, "My death-day has arrived. Either you will slay me or I shall kill myself. Cut off my head if you like, but I am not going to the Emperor's presence (again.)"

As Shiva could not be persuaded, the Kumar came back to the Emperor and reported the matter to him. The-

Emperor ordered Multafat Khan, Aqil Khan and Mukhlis Khan to go, console Shiva, invest him with a *khilat* and lead him back to the Presence. These three nobles came over and asked Shiva to wear the *khilat*, but the latter replied, "I refuse to accept the *khilat*. The Emperor has deliberately made me stand below Jaswant Singh. I am such a man, and yet he has wilfully kept me standing. I decline the Emperor's *mansab*; I will not be his servant. Kill me, imprison me, if you like; but I won't wear the *khilat*." So they returned and reported all this to the Emperor, who told the Kumar to take Shiva away with himself to his own residence and persuade him. Ram Singh led Shiva away to his tents, seated him in his private chamber and reasoned with him; but Shiva would not listen. After keeping Shivaji for an hour, the Kumar dismissed him to his own camp.

In the presence of the Emperor, many nobles who hated Shivaji said, "Shiva committed such a [gross] breach of etiquette, and yet your Majesty overlooked it!" Sayyid Murtaza Khan remarked, "He is a wild animal. If he has not accepted the *khilat* today, he will wear it tomorrow."

That the Mirza Rajah might be satisfied, Kumar Ram Singh sent Gopiram Mahata after the third quarter of the day to Shiva's camp with a present of dry fruits. Gopiram offered a *nazar* of nine Rupees to Shivaji, who gave him in return a full robe (*sar-o-pa.*) At sunset the Kumar sent Ballu Sah and Girdhar Lal Munshi to Shiva's tent to persuade him....Shivaji listened to Ballu Sah's reasoning and replied, "Very well, I shall send my son with my brother (*i. e.*, Kumar Ram Singh) to serve as an imperial officer. I too shall go back to the *darbar* after a couple of days." After the two envoys had made this settlement, Siddi Fulad (the police prefect of the capital) and Partit Rai *harkara* (courier or spy) came to Ram Singh early in the night, to convey a message from the Emperor that the Kumar should conciliate Shiva. So, Ram Singh came out, called Shivaji from his tent to his own and reasoned with him. Then he went to the Emperor and reported, "I have returned after persuading Shiva."

Next day (13th May) when the Kumar went in the morning to pay his respects to the Emperor, the latter asked him, "Is Shiva coming?" The Kumar replied, "He had fever and therefore will not come today." Later, when the Kumar went to attend the sunset *darbar*, he took Shiva's son along with himself and kept him standing by his side. The Emperor gave the boy one full robe (*sar-o-pa*), a jewelled dagger and a pearl necklace as *inam*. Shiva has not since then up to today, 15th May, attended the Emperor's audience.

4. ANTI-JAI SINGH COURTIERS SET EMPEROR AGAINST SHIVAJI

Rajah Jaswant Singh, Jafar Khan, the Begum Sahib and other nobles of that party spoke to the Emperor, "Shiva displayed such rudeness and contumacy, and yet your Majesty overlooked it! The report of it will spread from kingdom to kingdom." Hence the Kumar did not take Shivaji with himself to the *darbar* any of these days. The Kumar is interceding and will secure assurance for him and arrange for the grant of a *mansab* to him.

The Begam Sahib, Jafar Khan, and Rajah Jaswant Singh had spoken to the Emperor against Shiva before, and today (16th May) too they have repeated with great insistence, saying, "Who is this Shiva that in your royal presence he behaved with such contumacy and insolence and yet your Majesty passed over his conduct? If this goes on, many Bhumias (petty land-holders) will come here and act rudely. How would the Government continue then? The news will travel to every country that a Hindu displayed such audacious rudeness [with impunity], and all would begin to be rude." Rajah Jaswant added, "He is a mere Bhumia, and he came and displayed such discourtesy and violence! It is your Majesty's concern if you overlook it. But he ought to be punished." The Begam Sahib, too, urged strongly, "He has plundered Surat, he has carried away Shaista Khan's daughter [not true], and acted with such rudeness in the royal presence. And you ignore it! How far is this policy advisable?"

Then it came into the Emperor's heart, or the policy was agreed upon [in the secret Council], either to kill Shiva or to confine him in a fortress, or to throw him into prison. He ordered Siddi Fulad to remove Shiva to

Rad-andaz* Khan's house. The news of it reached Kumar Ram Singh. He went to Muhammad Amin Khan's house and argued with him thus, "It has been decided by His Majesty to kill Shiva ; but he has come here under a guarantee of safety [from my father.] So, it is proper that the Emperor should first kill me and then only—after I am dead—he should put Shiva to death or do to him as he likes." Muhammad Amin Khan reported this speech to the Emperor, who replied, "Ask Kumar Ram Singh if he will stand security for Shiva, so that if Shiva escapes or does any mischief, the Kumar will take responsibility for the harm. The Kumar should sign a security bond."

Amin Khan called up the Kumar and communicated this proposal, at which the Kumar replied, "Very well, I shall sign the bond." Then he came to his own camp and in the night of 14th May acquainted Shiva with the facts. In the morning of 15th May, Shiva came over to the Kumar's tent and there worshipped Mahadev, and pouring water on the idol gave his solemn assurance [of good conduct.] Then the Kumar signed the security bond and, in the evening, handed it to Amin Khan in the

* Rad-andaz Khan, a man of humble origin but reckless bravery and pride, had become a favourite of Aurangzib and now held the high post of commandant of Agra fort. For his ruthless suppression of the Satnami sect he was further promoted and entitled *Shujaet Khan*. Rising still higher (5-hazari mansab), he was cut off by the Afghans in the Karapa Pass in 1674. (My *History of Aurangzib*, vol. iii. p. 235.)

Diwan-i-khas. The Khan reported the fact to the Emperor, who took the bond and remarked, "Tell the Kumar—Go to Kabul with Shiva; I post him under you to that province. Look out an auspicious day for starting." The Kumar replied, "This very moment is the most auspicious of times. His Majesty has ordered it well. Give me formal leave (*rukhsat*), so that I may start." But the Emperor said, "Select an auspicious hour, some six or seven days later, and start then. Get your equipment, baggage and materials ready. Send out *parwanas* (requisitions) for assembling the carts for your luggage, your horses, servants &c. Summon your Rajputs to muster for the march...."

When the plan of killing Shivaji was decided upon [at Court], Rad-andaz Khan said, "Kumar Sahib! I have been appointed to command your vanguard [during the march to Kabul.]"

5. SHIVAJI'S PERSONAL APPEARANCE AND RETINUE FULLY DESCRIBED

You have inquired, How many retainers has Shiva brought with himself? With what equipment has he come to the royal interview?

Well, he has come alone, with only one hundred retainers, and his escort numbers 200 to about 250 in all. Among the latter one hundred are mounted on their own horses (*i.e.*, are *khud-aspa* or *silehdars*) and the rest are *bargirs* of the *paga* (*i.e.*, mounted on horses supplied by their master.)

When Shiva rides out in a *palki*, many footmen. wearing Turkish caps, big like *Khandails,* go before him. His flag is orange and vermilion coloured, with golden decorations stamped on it. In his train the camels are few, and meant for carrying luggage, so that they are very heavily loaded. The Banjaras are a hundred [each with a] pair [of pack-oxen.] All his high officers have *palkis* to ride in, and therefore he carries many *palkis* with him.

At sight Shivaji's body looks lean and short. His appearance is wonderfully fair in complexion, and even without finding out who he is, one does feel instinctively that he is a ruler of men. His spirit and manliness are apparent. He is a very brave high-souled man and wears a beard. His son is nine [really seven] years old and very marvellously handsome in appearance and fair in complexion.

Shivaji has come with a rather small contingent, but with great splendour of equipment. A large elephant goes before him carrying his flag. An adavance-guard of troopers also precedes him; the horses have gold and. silver trappings. The Deccani infantry too marches before him. In this manner he has come to Agra, with the whole of his contingent moving with great care and pomp. He has two female elephants saddled with *haudas* which follow him. A *sukhpal* (*i.e.*, a sort of *palki* with a dome-shaped top) is also carried before Shiva; its poles are covered with silver plate, and all its tassels have large hanging knobs of silver. His *palki* is completely covered with silver plates and its poles with gold plates. With this splendour has he come.

The people had before been praising Shivaji's high spirit and courage. Now that after coming to the Emperor's presence he has shown such audacity and returned such harsh strong replies, the public extol him for his bravery all the more.

6. SHIVAJI'S CONVERSATIONS

One day when Ballu Sah, Tej Singh and Ran Singh were sitting together, Maha Singh Shekhawat said, "Shivaji is very clever, he speaks the right word, after which nobody need say anything more on the subject. He is a good genuine Rajput, and we have found him just what he was reported to be. He tells us such appropriate things marked by the characteristic qualities (or spirit) of a Rajput, that if they are borne in mind they will prove useful some day."

One day [in a general talk in Ram Singh's tent] Shivaji addressed Tej Singh thus, "It is sheer destiny that has brought me here. But when there were four good men of high rank like you round the Mirza Rajah, why did you not speak to him (against sending me into Aurangzib's claws)? You should have reasoned with and dissuaded the Maharajah." Tej Singh replied, "The Maharajah listens to only one man, his Secretary Udiraj. Who else would venture to counsel him? Even when big vassals (*thakurs*) speak to him, our master does not heed their advice. Sur Singhji and Bhojraj-ji once spoke to the

Maharajah, "You have gained a great victory over Shivaji. Do not now undertake the expedition against Bijapur." To this the Maharajah replied, "If you speak to me these ten or fifteen days, my oath be on you." Dilir Khan said gently, "Maharajah! Don't invade Bijapur. You have conquered Shiva, let him manage things in the Deccan and conduct our business there." But the Maharajah answered, "Bhai-ji, don't you speak," to which Dilir Khan retorted, "I will not say anything more now. This campaign will end by ruining both you and me, and then I shall speak."

7. Shivaji negotiates at Court for his release

I hear that Shivaji has paid some money to Jafar Khan (the grand wazir) to win his support, and on other courtiers too he has spent more or less....

On 20th May, Jafar Khan presented Shivaji's petition to the Emperor and got him to pardon Shiva's offences and spare his life. Previously to this the Emperor had been ordering Shiva to go to Kabul and the latter was refusing to do so. A petition on this point was also submitted and the Emperor has rescinded the order posting him to Kabul... Here everything is going on happily, and we have hopes of Shivaji being very soon taken to the feet of the Emperor [for his formal pardon]; after this audience his *mansab* will be restored.

29th May.—Shivaji has written a petition to the Emperor and submitted it through Muhammad Amin Khan as his mediator, in which he states, " If your Majesty restores to me all my forts taken by you, I shall pay you two *krores* of Rupees. Give me leave to depart; my son will remain here in your service and I shall take every oath that you may ask for. I have come here in firm trust in your Majesty. My loyalty is strong. Wherever you plan a campaign, summon me and I shall attend there. Your Majesty is now at war with Bijapur. Let me go there, fight and die and thereby render service to you." To this the Emperor replied, " He has gone off his head because of my mildness towards him. How can he be given leave to depart for his home? Tell him firmly that he must not visit anybody, not even go to the Kumar's house." Therefore strong patrols have been posted round Shiva's residence.

8. SHIVAJI PREPARES FOR HIS OWN DELIVERANCE

8th June.—Shivaji has petitioned the Emperor requesting him, " Issue orders for a residence for me to which I can remove, but do not keep me here in the custody of the Kumar." The Emperor has replied, "He (Ram Singh) is such a faithful servant that there is none like him. You remain in his charge."

The Kumar's men are keeping a watch over Shivaji [in addition to the Kotwal's troops.] He is saying, "The Emperor has put Shivaji under my control also. If he escapes or kills himself, I shall have to answer for it to His Majesty." Therefore, Tej Singh and his retainers keep watch over the bed of Shivaji, while Arjun-ji, Sukh Singh Nathawat and other Rajputs patrol around.

Shiva has sent word to the Kumar, "You have given the Emperor a bond of security for me. Take it back now, and let the Emperor do what he likes with me." The Kumar is trying to reason with Shiva and console him, but the latter would not listen to him. We are waiting for the Mirza Rajah's reply.

On Friday, 7th June, Shivaji sent all his servants away, telling them, "Go away; let none remain with me. I shall stay here all alone. Let me be killed if the Emperor desires it." His men struck their tents and loaded their transports for departure, informing Ram Singh that they were about to go away The Kumar reassured them and advised them, "Don't stay there, but remove thence to the garden behind my camp and live at that place."

Shiva has sent word to the Emperor directly through Fulad Khan, "I have given my men leave to depart. I beg that they may be granted pass-ports for the journey."

Note.—Shivaji's escort and officers on their return journey crossed the Narwar pass about 15 Aug., and must have left Agra about 25th July.

16th June.—Recently Shivaji had petitioned the Emperor asking permission to go to Benares, as he wanted to renounce the world and turn a religious mendicant. The Emperor replied, "Let him turn *faqir* and live *in*

Allahabad fort. Bahadur Khan, my subahdar of that place, will keep a good watch over him!" So, this question too remains unsettled. Round Shiva's residence a patrol of the Emperor's troops has been posted. The Kumar too is enforcing all strictness of caution [by posting his own watch at night *within* the enclosure of Shivaji's camp,—as we learn from another letter.] Ram Singh takes Shiva's son with himself to the *darbar*. The Emperor has written about Shiva to Maharajah Jai Singh, but no reply has yet arrived here.

It is rumoured that Shivaji is secretly soliciting the nobles for his release. He sent a note to Muhammad Amin Khan and Aqil Khan and [through them] petitioned the Emperor, "I am willing to cede all my forts* to His Majesty as my tribute. Let him permit me to go to my own country. My mere sending orders from here will not do, as my officers will not obey them. If I go there, I shall fight them and hand the forts over to the imperial agents." The Emperor declined, saying, "Why need he go there in order to hand the forts over to me? Will not his men yield them from his writing?"

*A characteristic speech of Shivaji in Ram Singh's inner council is reported in this connection:—When the Kumar asked Shivaji to surrender his remaining forts, the Maratha Rajah replied, "Your father gave the Emperor 23 of my forts and got Tonk pargana as his reward. You are now trying to get my other forts for the Emperor. Tell me what pargana you are thinking of gaining by doing so; will it be Toda?" On hearing this the Kumar remained silent.

[*Introduction.*—Shivaji had run out of funds during his unexpectedly prolonged stay at Agra, especially because he had to grease the palms of the Mughal ministers and influential courtiers heavily to induce them to plead his cause before the Emperor. He had besides made some purchases of precious things at the capital, as every rich visitor has to do, often against his cooler thoughts. By the middle of July, or two months after his arrival, he appealed to Kumar Ram Singh, who advanced him Rs. 66,000, to cover which Shivaji issued a *hundi* or cheque payable by his own officers to the Mirza Rajah in the Deccan. This amount was duly paid there.]

9. SHIVAJI'S ESCAPE FROM AGRA

Ballu Sah to Kalyandas, diwan of Amber,
Agra, 18th August, 1666.

This morning Shivaji was found to have fled away from Agra. Immediately on the receipt of this letter, please issue *parwanas* that watch should be kept at all the paths and *ghats* to prevent him from escaping through them. If any one in the garb of a *jogi* or *sannyasi* passes that way, he should be questioned and searched. Give very strict orders. Any one who can capture him will be duly rewarded....Open the *ghats* (to traffic) only when you receive orders to that effect.

Same to same, 20th August.

Later in the day of Shiva's flight, the Emperor told the Kumar to go and search for Shiva. So the Kumar has started towards Dholpur and has sent his men to all sides.

Ballu Sah to Mukund-das Sah, Agra, 2nd September, 1666.

You must have heard the news of the flight of Shiva. There was the patrol of Fulad Khan also [around his camp.] But the Kotwal Fulad Khan made an outburst of violence and had it reported to the Emperor that Shiva had escaped from the side of the Kumar's patrols. Hence, the Emperor got angry and has ordered the Kumar's rank (*mansab*) to be reduced, and all the *parganas* of Kot Putli &c. have been taken away from him and his *pargana* of Mandawar has been transferred to the jagir of Daud Khan.

Parkal-das to Meghraj, Agra, 3rd September, 1666.

When the day was four *gharis* old, the news came that Shiva had escaped....from within the thousand men of the watch around him. On that day nobody could ascertain by what device he had fled away, and during whose period of watch. Afterwards it became known that he had slipped out by crouching down in the baskets [of sweetmeats] which used to be sent out [of his camp.]

Parkal-das to diwan Kalyandas, Agra, c. 26th August, 1666.

Baliram Purohit, Jivo Joshi, Srikishan and Harikishan were on guard over Shiva [on that day.] They have been imprisoned in charge of Fulad Khan. The Khan has threatened them with lashes (*kora*) and the thrusting of salt into their nostrils, and pressed them to make a confession that Kumar Ram Singh had collusively let

Shiva escape. In fear of beating they admitted it in his presence, and added "We alone were not there, but five other men of the Kumar were also present. Ask them."

Tej Singh, Ran Singh, Girdhar Lal Vakil, Girdhar Lal Munshi and Ballu Sah were then taken to Fulad Khan, and sent by him to Fidai Khan, with the message, "These too have confessed that the Kumar had let Shiva escape."

These men, after inducing Fidai Khan to dismiss Fulad Khan's servants, told the Nawab that they had made the confession in fear of torture, but were now solemnly asserting that the Kumar had no hand in the flight, and added, "We are Brahmans, we shall have to answer before God. Had the Kumar sent Shiva away, we should have said so; but the Kumar has done nothing like that." Fidai Khan remarked, "So, by force he has made you say so! Tell Fulad's men to take them away and inform him that I have myself interrogated these people, and now he should not beat them."

10. SHIVAJI'S LEFT PROPERTY

From a Persian *akhbarat*.—When Shivaji was under confinement (at Agra) he entrusted his pearls, *huns*, and gold mohars to the couriers of Mulchand sahukar for being conveyed to his home. But when Shiva escaped, the couriers turned back from the way and returned to the sahukar. He placed these articles through Fidai

Khan before the Emperor, who ordered them to be handed over to Iftikhar Khan.

From a Dingal letter, dated 11 Oct. 1666.—On 9th October the Emperor marched out of Agra for Delhi. On being asked for orders about Shivaji's [confiscated left] property, he replied, "Hand it over to the Qazi. It belongs to the *bait-ul-mal*; it is *haram* (unlawful) property. Sell it and distribute the sale proceeds among the *faqirs*." The jewels, elephants, horses and camels fit for the Emperor's service will be purchased by the imperial Government; the remainder will be sold in the bazar. As for the miscellaneous articles tied up in cloth bundles, the Qazi is saying, "What can I do with these here? Have I porters enough to transport them to Delhi? Hand them over to me at Delhi only."

11. SHIVAJI'S HOME-COMING

From a Persian akhbarat, dated Delhi 15th November, 1666.

The Emperor has learnt from the news-letter of Aurangabad that a son has been born in the house of the wretch Shiva and that he himself is ailing.

From the Dingal letter of Ballu Sah to diwan Kalyandas, from Delhi, 19th November.

For many days past there had been public rumours of Shivaji having reached his fort. And now news-letters from the Deccan have come to the Emperor to the effect that it has been learnt from the reports of spies that Shiva, after slipping out of that place (*i.e.*, Agra) at midnight, reached his fort in 25 days; that his son who accompanied him had died on the way, but one other son had been born to him there (at Rajgarh.) For many days Shivaji lay ill, and afterwards became well again; but is now suffering from some other malady. Thus has the *waqia-navis* written.

[*Note.*—This would give 12th September as the date of the fugitive Shivaji's return to Rajgarh. He lay low for some weeks, prostrated by the fatigue of the long journey and the hardships of the jungle route. The spies probably got the above news about him in the middle of October next.]

12. PARAMANAND, SHIVAJI'S POET LAUREATE

Parkaldas to diwan Kalyandas, Agra, c. 15th July, 1666.

Shivaji has a poet entitled *Kavindra Kavishwar*, to whom he gave a male elephant, a female elephant, one thousand Rupees in cash, a horse and a full suit (*sar-o-pa.*) He has promised to give one more elephant to the poet, and he is going to give it. Shivaji is saying, "The Emperor does not grant me a pass-port, or I might have gone out of Agra, as I had entered it, on horse back. I will now give away my horses and elephants and will sit down here as a mere *faqir.*"

Bimaldas to diwan Kalyandas, written from Amber, 23rd August, 1666.

On the receipt of Ballu Sah's letter from Agra urging us to close the *ghats* in the kingdom, we sent out orders to that effect to all the *parganas*. That very day Purohit Manohardas and Nathuram reported from Dausa that Paramanand the Kavishwar of Shivaji had arrived there with one male and one female elephants, two camels, one horse, forty infantrymen (? or foot runners?) and two pack-oxen. Paramanand is falsely claiming the female elephant as a gift from Shivaji to himself; (it has a *hauda* on its back.) He says that the packs on his bullocks contain clothes, but is refusing to open them for our inspection.

I have replied to Manohar-das to detain the poet and search the bullock-packs thoroughly.

Gharibdas to Kalyandas, 28th December, 1666.

Manohardas and Nathuram have written to say, "Kavindra Kavishwar Paramanand, of Shiva's service, had been detained here [since 23rd August.] Later an order came from the Mirza Rajah to release him. So, we set him free. Then followed a fresh order to keep him under guard wherever he might be. We made enquiries and learnt that he had gone on to Udai, intending to proceed to Benares....

So on hearing this news, I sent off four horsemen and fifteen footmen that very day. They overtook him in Chandangaon, in the Hindaun pargana, and brought him back on Wednesday, 26th December. He is now saying, "I want to go to Delhi"....Order me what I should do with him. Please expedite your reply as he is babbling a good deal. He carries much baggage with him, including two horses, two camels, one *sukhpal* with twenty porters (*kahar*) and footmen.

13. Mughal Government conciliates Shivaji.

After the death of Mirza Rajah Jai Singh (on 28 Aug. 1667), no Mughal subahdar was willing to face the prospect of a war with Shivaji,—least of all the next viceroy of the Deccan, the ease-loving prince Muhammad Muazzam (Shah Alam I) and his favourite lieutenant Rajah Jaswant Singh, "whose back Shivaji's soldiers had seen so often." So, they arranged for a peace with him to which the Emperor agreed as his hands were now full of the Yusufzai revolt.

6th May 1667.—[From a Persian *akhbarat*]

The Emperor ordered the prime minister to summon the *wakil* of Shiva, reassure him and send him to his master, on condition of returning in two months, in order to inform Shiva that his offences had been pardoned by His Majesty, that his son had been enrolled as an imperial officer (*mansabdar*), and that he was at liberty to seize as much of Bijapur territory as he could, or else he should remain firm in his own place and obey the Emperor's son [Prince Muazzam.] A letter "By Order" (*hasb-ul-hukm*) to this purport was handed to the *wakil*.

The family of Muhammad Quli (*alias* Netaji) has been brought, by order of the Emperor, from the Deccan to Delhi. One of his wives is staying in the Deccan, and two others came to Delhi. They were asked, by order, to turn Muslims, but refused. The Emperor then ordered Netaji to go to them and persuade them, and if they still refused to accept conversion he should marry a Muslim wife. Neta spoke to them and they then agreed to embrace Islam, after which His Majesty ordered them to be remarried to him according to Islamic rites and gave them ornaments worth Rs. 5,000.

21st August, 1667.—[From a Persian *akhbarat*]

Shivaji has written to Shafi Khan [Diwan of the Deccan] thus, "The Emperor has conferred the *deshmukhi* rights on me, but the imperial collectors obstruct me in realising these dues, and most of the ryots living in the neighbourhood of the forts surrendered by me [to the Emperor] do not pay the due rent to me. If I am permitted, I can punish them and establish my own revenue administration fully. I have been created a 5-*hazari* (both *zat* and *sawar* rank) and expect that a jagir corresponding to this rank would be granted to me."

The Emperor ordered the following reply to be sent to him:—"I give subsistence allowance (*jagir tankha*) only to men who render service either in my presence or in a subah. You are present neither with me nor with the subahdar (of the Deccan). How can you be given *jagir tankha* for your *mansab*? As for your *deshmukhi* rights, let not my officers obstruct your collection. I have granted them to you around the forts ceded."

3rd October, 1667.—[From a Persian *akhbarat*] :—

The Emperor received a letter from Prince Muhammad Muazzam (the new viceroy of the Deccan) to this effect :—Shivaji has written a letter to me saying "I am a hereditary slave of the imperial Court and my son Shambhaji has been created a Commander of Five thousand (with 5,000 troopers rank), but has received no jagir as *tankha* (or subsistence allowance.) I now beg that His Majesty would pardon the offences of this servant, restore the *mansab* of my son and assign a *jagir* to him. I am ready to render service in person wherever I am ordered." As Shivaji is at present manifesting great misery of heart, I beg Your Majesty to forgive his past misdeeds and to restore the *mansab* formerly [*i.e.*, in 1665] granted to Shambhaji.

His Majesty after reading the despatch, handed it back to the prime minister and remarked, "I order the restoration of the *mansab* of Shambhaji. Do you assign him *jagirs* in the territory of the forts surrendered to me [by Shiva.] He should come [with a contingent of troops] and render service under the Prince [Muazzam.]"

Dilir Khan to Rajah Shivaji.

After expressing my great friendship for you, it is the aim of my loving heart (to tell you) that,—praised be the Lord of the Universe for it !—at the prayer of this the humblest of the servants of the Emperor, your firm fidelity and honesty have been and will be covered with the Emperor's favour, as far as the heart desired, nay, even more than that. Your son, too, has been honoured with a *mansab* of six [really five] thousand in rank and six thousand troopers (of whom 5,000 are with two and three horses,) a bounty of two lakhs of Rupees, and the right to use the kettledrum and standard. It is necessary that immediately on the receipt of (this) letter you should quickly summon Shambhuji to you, that he may be glorified by imperial favours in return for good service. The favours which the Emperor, out of his regard for the lowly and his wish to cherish his household slaves, has ordered in (your) case, will become known to you from the letter of Muhammad Said,* the best of nobles, the head assistant [*peshdast* to the wazir.] It is a matter of congratulation to you and us alike. God willing, all that friendship and brotherhood demand will, as we have mutually agreed, be made evident to the world. What more need I write?

Prince Muhammad Muazzam to Shivaji, 9th March, 1668.

Rajah Shivaji! Out of the kindness which I feel for you, I have written to His Majesty about your loyalty and firm devotion. His Gracious Majesty has elevated your head by granting you the title of *Rajah*, which was the extreme point of your desires. You ought, in due recognition of this imperial favour, be even more devoted in loyalty and service than before and thereby hope for further favours.

---

* A Khushnavis of the Court of Aurangzib.

As requested by you, I have reported your desires to His Majesty, and I shall carry out whatever orders he may be pleased to issue on them. Be composed in mind in all matters and rest assured of my princely grace to you.

Written on 5th Shawwal, regnal year 11 = 9th March 1668.

14. Later Persian letters relating to Shivaji

Letter of Pratap Rao Gujar, Senapati of Shivaji, c. 1672-3.

Know all ye officers, *qanungoes*, *desais*, merchants, *mahajans*, brokers, captains of the English, French and Dutch, and the general public of the port of Surat, living between fear and hope,—

That at this time the Maharajah (Shivaji) has ordered a true estimate to be made of the annual custom duties on goods and merchandise in Surat, and one-fourth (*chauth*) of this revenue to be levied as tribute to the lion-like swordsmen (of his army). For the performance of this work he has appointed me, the humblest of his slaves. Therefore, in accordance with his royal order I write to you that if you, under the guidance of good fortune, deem obedience and submission to this order as politic and tending to your own good, obey the agent (*gumashta*) sent by me, and correctly show the records of collection, it will be the cause of your good and the prosperity of the kingdom. Otherwise, soon expect the heroes of my army to come to this country for a tour and hunt, and to raze all the houses of the place to the ground, so that no vestige of habitation will be visible; all the inhabitants of the place will be seized in the grasp of our wrath and fury, and not a man of them all will find the path of escape from the claws of the lion-hunting soldiers. If you fondly hope for help from your Emperor, you will be utterly ruined, as we have already trampled on this realm twice, and what remedy has he done? Should the smoke of (your) artillery and muskets perchance befog you brains, and make you consider your city-wall as an impregnable fortress, then, God willing, very soon will our splendid army arrive (here), scatter to the winds every stone of your fortress as cotton is scattered by the cotton-dresser, and with those very guns and muskets will they demolish the houses of your city.

Although the forts of Salher and Mahuli rival Alexander's rampart (in strength) and none (else) has grasped their battlements even with the noose of his imagination, we captured them, through our King's luck, in as short a time as it takes to speak a word. Your fort of Surat is no better than a wall. How long can it bar the path of our hill-climbing heroes? You may have heard in what misery and disgrace your Emperor's generals, Bahadur Khan and Dilir Khan bit the back of their hands, struck the ground with their arms (in despair), and were glad to flee from Salher to Poona.

It is simply out of graciousness to the humble that I have shown you pity and refrained from despatching our army before the arrival of your answer. If Providence befriends you and you pull the plug of negligence out of your ear of discretion, and listen to the words of advice and good plan,—then it will in every way result in your profit and your heart's content. Otherwise, there will be no other consequence than your humiliation.

Reply of the Surat Officers to Pratap Rao.

After giving sacred praise to the Creator of the world and of men,—who hurls into the dust oppressors like Shaddad and Nimrod, by entangling them in the meshes of fate and striking them with the stone of negligence,

Verses

O God, you created the high and the low,
You created the oppressor and the oppressed, too,—

Be it known to the quick mind (*rai*) of Pratap Rai (Rao) and the Maratha Brahmans, Naikwars, and *bargirs* (ordinary troopers) of the army of the fugitive Rai, that the letter of this unlucky-faced man has just now come to the knowledge of the officers and clerks (of Surat.)

Don't slay your prisoner, when you have vanquished your enemy,
You yourself will be captured by misfortune if you slay your captive.

O you wicked scoundrel (*paji*) and cruel oppressor! the Mirza Rajah (Jai Singh) was a mere servant of our Emperor and yet he with very slight and slack effort succeeded in putting the rope of humility round the neck of your Shiva and in forcing him to gain the honour of kissing the Emperor's feet. And (the Kings of) Bijapur and Haidarabad,—of whom Shahji was a mere servant,—consider it an honour to show welcome to and kiss the ground before those (imperial officers) who have rubbed their foreheads (on the carpet) in front of our Emperor; and year after year they pay fixed tributes and thereby secure their own repose and honour.

What power have you and your servants that you can know His Majesty, with all your indecent language—which will lead to your tongue being cut off and yourself being stoned to death?

The cat plays the tiger in seizing a mouse,
But turns into a mouse when facing leopards.

O, you cruel fool, you faithless man! Surat has now got another aspect (*surat*). (The path of) these mouse-like hole-seekers having been stopped*, it has now become the roaming-place of lions and elephant-conquerors (*i.e.*, the Mughal troops).

You should give up your impossible project, and quickly seek refuge in some other quarter. Don't spare to do whatever your wicked and foolish self can do in the next two or three days, because the victorious Prince† is coming to this region with 70,000 troopers clad in armour. God willing, he will make you the food of the kites of his army. Or, if you desire your own good, reflect within yourself: restore to Nawab Bahadur Khan and Dilir Khan, whatever

* By building a brick wall round the city, after its first plunder by Shivaji in 1664.

† The text reads *Sultan Mahmud*, but Aurangzib had no son or grandson of that name. Evidently Sultan Muhammad Muazzam (Shah Alam), his second son and viceroy of the Deccan, is meant.

in cash and kind you have collected from the imperial *parganas*, villages, and highways of Surat and other provinces, make them your intercessors, and go to wait on the Prince,—which will in every way be the means of your life being spared.

Verses

It is better that he should be gentle to me,
Should weep and make excuses (for his past conduct).

Note—Kartoji Gujar was made by Shivaji his *Senapati* or Commander-in-Chief with the titles of Pratap Rao and *sar naubat* of horse. In 1672 when the Mughals were besieging Salher, a relieving army under Pratap Rao routed the Mughals under Ikhlas Khan "with prodigious slaughter" and forced them to raise the siege, Ikhlas himself being captured with 31 of his principal officers. (*Shivaji*, p. 190.) To this exploit a vaunting reference is made in Pratap Rao's letter. Bahadur Khan, afterwards surnamed Khan Jahan Bahadur, was appointed viceroy of the Deccan after 1672. Pratap Rao's meteoric career was cut short in a rash charge on the Bijapuri army under Abdul Karim near Nesari, on 24th February 1674. (My *Shivaji*, 3rd ed., p. 203.)

Surat was first plundered by Shivaji, with 4,000 cavalry, in January 1664. Its mud walls were soon afterwards replaced by a brick rampart, by order of Aurangzib. But in October 1670, Shivaji sacked the town again. These are the two raids referred to in Pratap Rao's letter, which must have been written at the close of 1672 or in 1673.

15. Summary of Persian Documents relating to Shahji Bhonsla

[This excludes the references to his doings in the Eastern Karnatak to be found in Aurangzib's letters during his second viceroyalty of the Deccan as given in *Adab-i-Alamgiri*.]

30 January 1642. Farman of Muhammad Adil Shah to Shahji :—Rustam-i-zaman Randaula Khan has been appointed commander of the army in Karnatak, with four deputies,—Rahmat Kh., Khudabanda Kh., Ghazi Kh. and Afzal Kh. You must obey them.

29 January 1643. Farman of Muhammad Adil Shah to Shahji Bhonsla :—You have reported the loyalty of Tirumal Nayak [of Madura, reign 1623-1659] to me. So, I am sending to you a *farman* for him.

8 April 1643. Farman of Muhammad Adil Shah to Maharaja Shahji Bhonsla :—You have written professing your loyalty to me.

21 July 1643. Farman of Muhammad Adil Shah to Maharaja Shahji Bhonsla :—I learn from the speech of Narsingh Rao that you have been displeased on reading my *farman*.

22 Dec. 1646. Muhammad Adil Shah to Asad Kh. :—Baji Ghorpare has been ordered to go with Ambar Khan [Bijapuri] to Karnatak. Therefore you should give *congee* to the contingent of Baji Ghorpare now under you.

22 March 1647. Muhammad Adil Shah to Shahji Bhonsla :—I had previously issued orders that money for buying presents and elephants should be sent to me. But the roads are unsafe. You should supply an escort to Azam Kh. up to the limits of Bangalore district, and your son Shambhaji Bhonsla will conduct them from Bangalore to my Court.

9 April 1647. Md. Adil Shah to Bachan-appa Raghu Nayak :—Ten lakhs of *hun* and 25 elephants have been seized by Qutb Shah. You ought to wrest them from him. Shahji and Ambar Khan have been ordered [to assist you.]

4 May 1647. Md. Adil Shah to Maharaja Shahji Bhonsla :—Seventeen pairs of spies are being sent ; pay them at the rate of 3¼ *huns* per month.

23 Aug. 1651. Same to same :—The tax on tobacco is to be spent in buying elephants &c.

6 Feb. 1653. Same to same :—The lesser Balapur has been assigned for your residence. But Khan Muhammad, my wazir, raised objections. I now order him to leave it to you.

19 March 1657. Ali Adil Shah II to [addressee's name missing] :—From Shahji's letter I learn that you are loyal. I send a *qaul* and *karar* (= safe assurance and agreement) for you. Obey Shahji and render me service.

9 June 1657. Ali Adil Shah II to Maharaja Shahji Bhonsla :—Narhar Timaji the envoy (*hajib*, chamberlain) in attendance on me, had been previously ordered to write to me the news of your subah. He is now summoned to Court.

9 February 1658. Same to same :—Informs him of the appointment of Afzal Khan Muhammad Shahi as subahdar of [Western] Karnatak.

8 April 1659. Same to same;—I learn from Ibrahim Khan's letter that you are truly loyal to me. I do not pay any heed to the misrepresentations made against you.

23 January 1661. Ali Adil Shah II to Chokkalinga Nayak of Madura:—Reporting the submission of Shahji Bhonsla. [Is the date a copyist's error for 1663?]

10 March 1663. Farman of Ali Adil Shah II to the Desais and Naikwars:—For some time past the jagirs of Shahji lay under confiscation. They are now restored to him. Details about the *parganas.*

Note.—An English Factory letter, P. Gyfford to Surat, written on 20 July 1663, informs us "A spy of Adil Shah who met a man from Kolhapur swears that before he came out of Bankapur [where Ali Adil Shah was then in residence, for suppressing the rebellion of Shivappa Nayak], he saw irons put on Bahlol Kh. and Shahji, Shivaji's father, but taken off the latter in two days, who is now with the King without any command."

29 Jan. 1664. Ali Adil Shah to Yekoji Bhonsla.

10 April 1664. Same to same.

10 June 1664. Four farmans. Same to same:—About giving in farm the revenue collection of Muhammadabad *alias* Kulahal, of Turgal, of Trinomali *alias* Qadirabad and the grant of the *deshmukhi* and *desh-kulkarni* rights. Grant of Islampur *alias* Bangalore to Yekoji.

31 January 1670. Same to same.

10 Oct. 1671. Same to same:—About *parganas* Kaveripatan and Tiru-pattur and fort Jagdevgarh.

IX

THE LEGACY OF SHIVAJI

Source

There is a short list of Shivaji's possessions at the time of his death (1680) given in the earliest Marathi life of that king, which was written by Krishnaji Anant Sabhasad in 1694. Another life is contained in a somewhat later work which is known as the *Ekanavvi qalami Bakhar* (the English translation of which, made by Lt. Frissell, is printed in Forrest's *Selections*: *Maratha series*, as the *Raigarh Life*.) I prefer to call it the *Dattaji-Malkare Bakhar*. An expanded Persian version of it is given in India Office (London) ms. No. 1957 (Ethe's *Cat.* No. 485) and also in a British Museum ms. (Rieu's *Cat.* i. p. 327.) This I.O.L. ms. was acquired by Warren Hastings, probably about 1772, and I translated the whole of it in the *Modern Review* in 1907. Leaves 42—44 of this work give a very interesting inventory of the various kinds of property left behind by the great Shivaji. A curious light is here thrown on the life's acquisition of an Indian king two and a half centuries ago, and the character of the articles stored by him illustrates the state of society in that age. The author writes :—

Translation

" Shambhaji after his accession to the throne ordered all the clerks of the royal stores to submit lists of the property, in cash and kind, accumulated by the late Maharajah Shivaji. Instead of delegating the work to others, he personally inspected them. Below is given the detailed list of the property :—

TREASURE :

Gold ornaments	..	four *nalo* (cylinders) nine *candy* (khandi).*
Hun	..	five lakhs.
Copper	..	13 *nalo* 3 *candy*
Ironware	..	20 candy
Lead vessels	..	450 *nalo* 450 *candy*
Mixed metal (zinc and lead) vessels	..	400 *nalo* 400 candy
Muradi (tankas?)	..	6 lakhs
Silver	..	4 *nalo* $5\frac{3}{4}$ candy
Bronze	..	275 *nalo* 275 candy
Steel ingots	..	40 in number
Advanced as loan to the provincial governors	..	3 lakhs of *hun*

In the different forts 54 pitchers containing 30 lakhs of *hun*.

WARDROBE :

Mungipatan or gold-embroidered cloth, 1 lakh (pieces)
Do-patta, gold-embroidered and plain, 1 lakh (pieces)
Silk cloth .. 4 lakhs (of pieces)

**Khandi*, is a measure of weight varying at different places. At Poona it consisted of 20 Poona maunds of 25 lbs. each.

·*Hun*, a South Indian gold coin, then worth Rs. 5.

Shawl and other woollen fabrics ..	1 lakh pieces
Waist-band	50 *than*
Kinkhab (brocade)	1 lakh *than*
Kinkhab, plain	1 lakh *than*
Scarlet (broad cloth)	1 lakh pieces
White paper	32,000 quires
Zar-afshani (paper sprinkled with gold dust)	11,000 quires
Ba'apuri paper	20,000 quires
Daulatabadi paper	2,000 quires

SPICES :

Cloves ..	20 *nalo* 20 candy
Jawlri	3 candy
Falfal (pepper)	30 „
Saffron	4 „
Ambergris	10 „
Arkaja	2 „
Sandal ..	50 *nalo* 50 „
Krishnaguru chandan (black sandal wood)	1 „
Camphor	4 „
Aloe wood	2 „
Gulal	20 „
Rakta chandan (red sandal wood) ..	20 „
Dried grapes	1 „
Walnut	3 *nalo* 3 „
Almond	2 „
Date (khurma)	30 „
Indian date (khejur)	40 „

Cocoanut kernels	50 candy
Cardamon	3 „
Scented oil of *Mugra* (*i.e.*, Bela) ..	4 „
„ „ *Sugandh-rai*	4 „
„ „ of Chameli	1 „
„ „ of aloes	30 „
„ „ of Champa-bel ..	2 „
Betel-nut	70 „
Incense (gugal)	1 „
Turmeric	500 „
Haritaki (myrabalan)	100 „
Zangi haritaki	1,000 „
Snuff	8,000 „
Red pepper	50,000 „
Poppy seed	100 „
Mercury	2 „

JEWELS :

Diamond
Manik
Panna (ruby)
Pokhraj
Pearl
Coral
Lahsunia (a white precious stone, bulb-like)
Sapphire
Topaz
Rings
Jewelled sashes (for hanging swords from)
Padak or *dhukdhuki* (pendant or locket)

Pearl bunch (torah)
Aigrette (sarpech) jewelled
Chandra-rekha
Sis-phul
Nag-bini (a flower worn on the nose)
Fan
Bracelet
Ear-ring
Tunkal (?)
Kaṇkan
Palliạ (a broad wristlet)
Dheṇṛi (jewelled shield for the ear)

GRAIN:

Shali paddy	.. ..	17,000 candy
Kodru (Paspalum frumentaceum)	..	2,00,000 ,,
Vetch (gram)	.. ..	50,000 ,,
Peas (*mash*)	.. ..	12,000 ,,
Mung(? unbroken)	.. ..	25,000 ,,
Arhar	.. ..	1,000 ,,
Masur	.. ..	500 ,,
Ghee	.. ..	25,000 ,,
Mustard oil	.. ..	70,000 ,,
Hing (asafœtida)	.. ..	30,000 ,,
Sandhav salt	.. ..	270 ,,
Zira	.. ..	200 ,,
Gum	.. ..	300 ,,
Gopi-chandan	.. .	200 ,,
White *til* seed	..	1,000 ,,

Orpiment arsenic (*hartal*)	..	..	1,000 candy
Mica (*abrakh*)	..	..	1,000 ..
Indigo	..	..	1,000 ..
Sulphur	..	..	200 ..
Vermilion	..	..	30 ,,
Kaiphal	..	..	50 ..
Verdigris	..	..	2 ..
Long pepper	..	..	2 ..
Pippal	..	..	2 ..
Opium	..	..	100 ..
Ajwan	..	..	100 ..
Honey	..	..	100 ..
Musadar	..	..	100 ..
Iron filings	..	..	900 ..
Black *til* seed	..	..	200 ,,
Raibhog rice	..	..	100 ,,
Lala ,,	..	..	200 ..
Taliasar ..	..	..	100 ,,
Malwar ,,	..	..	100 ,,
Firisal ,,	..	..	400 ..
Arhar dal	..	..	20,000 ,,
Mung dal	..	..	200 ,,
Masur dal	..	..	100 ..
Sugar	..	..	1,500 ..
Sugar candy	..	..	300 ..
Molasses	..	..	1,600 ,,
Salt	..	..	1,500 ,,
Garlic	..	..	5,000 ..
Onion	..	..	300 ,,

ARMOURY:

Swords	300	pieces
Khanda	200	,,
Aiti	600	,,
Spears	4,000	,,
Jamdhar (dagger)	1,000	,,
Pattah (narrow-bladed straight rapier with a gauntlet hilt)	1,000	,,
Shield	1,300	,,
Chhara	1,100	,,
Arrows	4,000	quiverful
Cuirass	4,000	pieces
Coats of mail (*chhata*)	1,100	,,
Baneti (rod ending in spikes)	5,000	,,
Helmet	4,000	,,
Axes	3,000	,,
Pickaxes	1,100	,,
Thapiya	3,000	,,
Krot (? *garasi*, knife for cutting bushes)	5,000	,,
Gunpowder	2,00,000	candy
Palkis for riding	3,000	numbers
Umbrellas	12,000	,,
Buckets for drawing water	1,500	,,
Cotton	7,000	candy
Wax	1,300	,,
Resin (*ral*)	1,000	,,
Iron balls	1,00,000	numbers
Drums	600	,,
Kettledrums	1,200	,,
Bugles	8,000	,,

STABLE:

Arab horses	..	..	6,000
Turkish ,,	..	..	8,000
Deccan ,,	..	..	1,000
Mares	..	..	9,000
Other kinds of horses	..	..	7,000
Ponies (pack horses)	..	..	1,000
Camels	..	..	3,000
Elephants	..	..	500
Cows	..	..	1,000
Oxen	..	..	5,000
Cow-buffaloes	..	..	5,000
Sheep	..	..	1,000

Entrusted to the cavalry *Bargirs* 5,000 horses (of which 3,000 were male and 2,000 mares) and 125 elephants.

SLAVES:

Males	..	..	1,000
Females	..	..	600.

Our Indian historian has recorded material things only, and left it to an European writer to point out Shivaji's most precious legacy to his people:

"The territory and treasures, however, which Sivajee acquired, were not so formidable to the Mahomedans as the exmaple he had set, the system and habits he introduced, and the *spirit* he had infused into a large proportion *of the Mahratta people*'" (Grant Duff's *History of the Mahrattas*, i, 300.)

X

SHIVAJI AS SEEN BY EUROPEANS

1. Anthony Smith in 1664

During Shivaji's first sack of Surat (January, 1664), a merchant of the English factory there named Anthony Smith, when returning from the Swally harbour was seized by the Marathas and kept in Shivaji's camp for three days, after which he was ransomed for Rs. 300. There is no reason for doubting the veracity of Smith, because though the President of the Surat Factory wrote against him to the Directors in England, as a faithless servant.. the charge was not proved and Smith continued in the English E. I. Company's service for some years afterwards. Escaliot, the English chaplain at Surat, in a letter to a friend at Home gives the full narrative of what Smith saw during his captivity and adds the following description of Shivaji :—

" His person is described by them who have seen him to be of mean (*i.e.*, medium) stature, lower somewhat than I am (when) erect, and of an excellent proportion. Actual (*i. e.*, active) in exercise, he seems to smile, a quick and piercing eye, and whiter than any of his people."

The French traveller Thevenot reports (*c.* 1666) on

hearsay, "The rajah is small in size any tawny (in complexion), with quick eyes which indicate abundance of spirit."

2. Niccolao Manucci, 1665

Manucci, a young Italian adventurer in India, then about 24 years of age, was employed by Mirza Rajah Jai Singh as a diplomatic envoy to the petty princes of Western India. In his master's siege-camp before Purandar, he met Shivaji in June 1665 and gives the following account of him :—

A few days after my arrival Shivaji gave himself up and came into our camp. Since I went at night to converse and play cards with the rajah (Jai Singh) whenever he so desired, it happened one night during this period that we were having a game,—the rajah, his Brahman and I,—when in came Shivaji. We all rose up, and Shivaji, seeing me, a youth well favoured of body, whom he had not beheld on other occasions, asked Rajah Jai Singh of what country I was the rajah. Jai Singh replied that I was a Farangi rajah. He wondered at such an answer, and said that he also had in his service many Farangis, but they were not of this style....This was the opening which afforded me occasion many times to converse with Shivaji [in the Hindustan language.] I gave him information about the greatness of European kings, he being of opinion that there was not in Europe any other king than the king of Portugal. I also talked to him about our religion. (From Irvine's translation, in *Storia do Mogor*, ii. 136.)

3. Henry Oxinden at Shivaji's Coronation June 1674

"The 6th June.—About 7 or 8 of the clock went to Court and found the Rajah seated in a magnificent throne and all the nobles waiting on him in very rich attire, his son Shambhaji Rajah, Peshwa Moro Pandit, and a Brahman of great eminence (*i.e.*, Gaga Bhatt) seated on an ascent under the throne, the rest, as well officers of the army as others, standing with great respect. I made my obeisance at a distance and Narayan Shenvi held up the diamond ring which was to be presented to him. He presently took notice of us and ordered our coming nearer even to the foot of the throne, where being vested, we were desired to retire, which we did, but not so soon but that I took notice on each side of the throne were hung, according to the Moors' manner, on heads of gilded lances many emblems of Government and dominion, as on the right hand were two great fishes' heads of gold with very large teeth (=*mahi wa maratib*), on the left hand several horses' tails, a pair of gold scales on a very rich lance poised equally,—an emblem of justice,—and as we returned, at the palace gate there were standing two small elephants on each side and two fair horses with gold bridles and rich furniture."

4. ENGLISH MERCHANTS OF RAJAPUR, 1675

"The Rajah (*i.e.*, Shivaji) came on the 22nd March about midday, accompanied with abundance of horse and foot and about 150 *palankins*. So soon as we heard of his near approach, we went out of our tent and very near met him. He ordered his *palankin* to stand still, called us very near him, seemed very glad to see us and much pleased that we came to meet him, and said the sun being hot he would not keep us now, but in the evening he would send for us....

"The Rajah came. He stopped his *palankin* and called us to him. When we were pretty near him we made a stop, but he beckoned with his hand till I was up close with him. He diverted himself a little by taking in his hand the locks of my periwig and asked us several questions; at length asked us how we liked Rajapur.... He would (he said) order things for the future to our full satisfaction." (*F.R.*)

5. FRENCH ENVOYS FROM PONDICHERRY, 1677

Introduction.—In 1923 I secured transcripts of the passages relating to Shivaji in the manuscript diary of Francois Martin, the founder of Pondicherry, preserved in the Government archives of Paris, and published a condensed translation of them in the *Modern Review.* Since then these *Memoires* have been printed under the editorship of M. Alfred Martineau (vol. II in 1932), and I here give extracts from my translation as filled out from the printed volume.

Translation

Messrs. Germain and Cattel and the Brahman (the three envoys from Martin to Shivaji) returned to Pondicherry on 9th August 1677 (*New style.*) They had reached the camp of Shivaji on the bank of the Coleroon river, where he lay with his army. They were introduced to the audience of that lord by the minister (Janardan Pandit) who had attended our Brahman in the camp (of Shivaji) before Vellore. Our presents were offered; Shivaji made light of them, but he had been informed that we were not very rich, and that we were making no trade (at this time)....They remained only three days in the camp. Shivaji delivered to them a farman in due form for our security in Pondicherry.

I have already remarked that Shivaji had some claims against Ekoji, his step-brother, on account of the succession to their defunct father. Ekoji had entered into possession of that one-third of the territory of Jinji which their common father Shahji Maharajah had as his share. It is held also that he had appropriated (their father's) movable property of value. Shivaji demanded his share of these goods. He had written many times to Ekoji to come and see him in order that they might make a settlement between themselves; but the latter had put it off. At last, after taking all the sureties from his brother that he wished for,—in the form of oaths used among them, but which are not inviolable among men who value their interest more than their religion,—Ekoji crossed the Coleroon and came to see Shivaji. The first meetings merely gave evidence of amity and love. Then they proceeded to negotiation, in the course of which Ekoji noticed that his brother would not release him unless his claims were satisfied. So, he too used cunning, and while he gave good words (in reply) he searched for ways of retreating from such an evil pass. He succeeded in it one night; his men kept for him a catamaran (raft) ready on the bank of the Coleroon. Under the pretext of certain personal necessities (*i. e.*, purifying bath),—because he was watched (by Shivaji's agents),—he approached the bank of the river, threw himself on the catamaran, and passed over to the other bank which was his own territory and where he had troops assembled. On the fact being reported to Shivaji, he arrested the officers of Ekoji who were living in his camp, and among the number was Jagannath Pandit, a Brahman who commanded Ekoji's troops, a man of spirit and enterprise.

The camp of Shivaji is without pomp, without women and without baggage. It has only two tents,—but of simple coarse stuff and very small,—one of them for himself and the other for his prime minister.

Shivaji's horsemen ordinarily get two pagodas as their pay per month; all the horses belong to the Rajah.... There are ordinarily three horses to every two men, which contributes to the speed that he usually makes. He thus frequently surprises his enemies who believe him to be far distant when he falls upon them....He also pays his spies handsomely, which greatly helps his conquests by the regular information which they give him.

XI

PRINCE AKBAR IN MAHARASHTRA

Introduction

Prince Muhammad Akbar, the fourth son of the Emperor Aurangzib Alamgir, had been employed by his father in commanding one divisional army in the invasion of Rajputana after the death of Maharajah Jaswant Singh and the annexation of Marwar by the Mughal Government. He failed miserably in his campaigns against Maharana Raj Singh of Udaipur and was again and again sharply censured by his father. At last he lent a ready ear to the appeals of Durgadas Rathor and the envoys of the Maharana to seize his father's throne with Rathor and Sisodia help and thus save the Mughal empire from disruption as the consequence of Aurangzib's bigoted persecution of the Hindus. The conspiracy failed and Akbar was forced to save himself by fleeing to the Deccan, where he took refuge in the territory of Shambhuji, arriving at Pali (renamed *Padishahpur*) on 1 June 1681. He spent several years in Shambhuji's territory, latterly in Banda (Savant-Vadi) and Bicholim, being a constant threat and source of anxiety to Aurangzib, but could achieve nothing, and finally left India in February 1687 for Persia where he died in exile. His full career is given in my *History of Aurangzib* vols. iii ch. 37 and iv ch. 44 and 47, and *Studies in Aurangzib's Reign*, ch. 6.

1. MUHAMMAD AKBAR TO SHAMBHAJI

Shambhaji, the chief of great Rajahs, &c. hope for my boundless favours and know that,—

From the beginning of his reign it was the intention of Alamgir to utterly ruin all the Hindus alike. On the death of Maharajah Jaswant Singh this intention became revealed to all. His war with the Rana (Raj Singh, of Udaipur) was also the outcome of this design.

As all men are the creation of God, and He is the protector of them all, it is not proper for us as Emperors of India to try to uproot the race of landowners, for whom is India. Emperor Alamgir had carried matters beyond their limits, and I became convinced that if these men were overthrown then Hindustan would not continue to be in the hands of our family. Therefore, with a view to saving my heritage and also taking pity on this race (Rajput Rajahs) who have been loyal to us from olden times,—I decided, at the request of Rana Raj Singh and Durgadas Rathor, to ride to Ajmir and fight a battle for the throne, so that the intention of God might become known. In this state of things, as the Rana happened to die, the business was delayed. One month afterwards, Rana Jai Singh submitted the same prayer of his father (to me,) through Padishah Quli Khan,—who had gone to Jilwara in order to plunder his dominions,—saying, "If you wish that the honour of Hindustan should remain (inviolate), then we all, laying our hands on the skirt of your robe, hope for our deliverance and benefit from your Majesty."

At the request of these two great clans, I set about to take possession of my heritage. I arrived within two miles of the encampment of Alamgir. It was three hours after sunset,—the battle having been fixed for the next morning,—when Death dragged the coward Padishah Quli Khan bound (with ropes, as it were,) to the Court of Alamgir, who slew him immediately on his arrival. Although the going away of any one was not really subversive of my undertaking, yet, as Padishah Quli Khan had been the intermediary in bringing over to my side the Sisodias and Rathors, both these clans were seized with a groundless suspicion that the whole affair was a stratagem (of Alamgir.) So they decamped towards their homes, without informing me. At their departure my soldiers lost heart and fled away, so that the battle was not fought [16th January, 1681].

At this I took a small portion of my family retainers with me and went towards Marwar. The night of the next day Durgadas Rathor saw me with all his troops, and decided to accompany me. I made two or three tours and circuits in the kingdom of Marwar. As Muazzam,—who had been appointed to pursue me,—could not overtake (me) in these rambles, he divided his troops and stationed them in different parts of the kingdom of Marwar as outposts. Therefore, I passed (into the dominion of) Rana Jai Singh, and he, after offering to me horses and other presents, begged me to remain in his kingdom. But as his country was close to the seat of the Emperor, I did not consider it prudent to stay there. Therefore, bearing in mind your bravery and high spirit, I decided to march (to your country.) So. helped by the favour of the gracious Accomplisher of Tasks, on the 1st Jamadi-ul-awwal, year 1092 A.H. (9th May, 1681), I safely forded the river Narmada at Bhaiswarah. Durgadas Rathor is with me. Keep your mind composed about me and cherish the hope that, God willing, when I have gained the throne, the name will be mine and the State will be yours. Fully realising Alamgir's enmity to yourself and to me, set your heart on this that we should act so as to promote our business. (*Verses*)

As the world does not stay in the same condition,
It is better to have a good name, which will endure as a memorial.

This is what we expect from a man and a hero. What more need I say than that 'A hint is enough for the wise?' Written on 3rd Jamadi-ul-awwal, year 1092. (11th May, 1681).

Notes.—Maharana *Jai Singh* was the son and successor of Raj Singh. *Jhilwara* is a village at the eastern mouth of the Deosuri pass leading into Mewar from the Marwar side. Akbar forded the Narmada "at one of the crossing places appertaining to the ferry of Akbarpur, at a distance of 16 miles, close to the frontier of Rajah Mohan Singh," according to Khafi Khan (ii. 276). Akbarpur is south of Mandu. The word written as *Bhaiswarah* in the ms is a copyist's error for Maheshwar.

a noted ferry 8 miles east of Akbarpur. The year is wrongly given in the ms as 1098.

2. Muhammad Akbar to Shambhaji

This chief of the Rajahs of Hind ought to act in accordance with this letter, that it may be the source of his good name in this world and the next. I wrote another letter before this; but most probably it has not reached you, or else you would have sent me a reply. It is proper that you should not now fail in sending letters till my arrival, as my heart has been for a long time seeking for news about this devoted chief. What more except the desire of meeting you? (Written *c.* 20 May 1681.)

3. The Diwan of Muhammad Akbar to Shambhaji

The Prince has at this time learnt from the news-letter of Tal-Konkan that your servant named Naro Kanar (Konher ?), has taken up his abode in the village of Dapuli, after coming from the *pett* of Apta appertaining to the *pargana* of Chaul, and seizes on the way the peasants of Danda Rajpuri who having fled from that place come to the city of Chaul, and sends them to you with their property. Your men have forcibly seized the boat, rice and buffaloes of Vittoji, a resident of Chaul. This matter has distracted the hearts of the peasants (of Chaul); so, a copy of the news-letter is sent with this letter, and you will be able to learn the facts from it.

I have been ordered by the Prince to write to you about the matter, asking you to withdraw your men from the village of Dapuli, to send the money and goods taken from the peasants back to their respective owners, care of Karim Beg, the *diwan* of Konkan, and to take steps that no *ryot* may be put to loss (in future). After acting according to this order, write an explanation which I may place before the Prince. What more shall I write? Written on 26th Zihijja, in the 2nd year of the reign; (27 December 1681.)

Note.—This *Dapoli* was a small village *north* of Danda and the city of Dapoli, 40 m. *south* of Danda. The Siddis sacked *Apta* on 7 Dec. 1681. 1092 A.H. was the 2nd year of the nominal sovereignty of Akbar.

4. PRINCE AKBAR TO RAJAH RAM SINGH OF AMBER (JAIPUR), 22ND MAY, 1682

Aurangzib's treatment of the Hindus has become manifest and is known to you. As for instance, in the affair of Kumar Kishan Singh (the son and heir of Ram Singh, who was murdered by an Afghan near Parenda fort on 10th April 1682),—though it happened owing to his youthfulness, yet it too was a sign of the bigotry of Alamgir which he displays to that community in every way. Therefore, out of my regard for the hereditary servants of our house, who have generation after generation been treated with kindness by our august dynasty, I exalt and cherist you by conferring on you the title of Mirza Rajah and the mansab and cash reward of your father, and on your son Bishun Singh that *mansab* which you held when you were a Kumar.

Hope for the daily increasing favours of my imperial Majesty, and remain ready with your ears alert for the news [of my coming.] When I march with my victorious army towards Hindustan. you should join my victorious followers and exert yourself greatly in my imperial service, which will be the cause of your being favoured at Court and honoured. The usual jewels and robe of honour are not being sent to you, on account of the insecurity of the roads.

5. Shambhuji Rajah to Rajah Ram Singh of Amber

Written c. November 1682.

[After five long sentences of traditional eulogy]

Shri Shambhu Raja craves your friendship and after enquiring about your welfare communicates to your highness his own words in this letter.

We have received your communication and understand your object to mean that no opposition should be offered to the Emperor of Delhi, but that his suzerainty should be accepted.

Thereafter you came to know how your son Krishna Singh met his ruin for having intrigued with Sultan Akbar; and after full consideration of the political situation you again wrote to us in laudable terms that we acted rightly in offering shelter in our dominion to Sultan Akbar, that you approved the course we followed and that as we are Hindus, you signified your readiness to execute whatever was considered expedient in the circumstances.

If such indeed is your real intention, then you yourself ought to take the lead in this affair. The present wicked Emperor believes that we Hindus have all become effeminate and that we have lost all regard for our religion. Such an attitude on the part of the Emperor we cannot any longer endure. We can not put up with any thing derogatory to our character as soldiers (Kshatriyas). The Vedas and the codes enjoin certain injunctions of religion and caste, which we cannot allow to be trampled under foot, nor can we neglect own duty as kings to our subjects. We are prepared to sacrifice every thing, our treasure, our land, our forts, in waging war against this satanic Emperor. With this firm resolution we have for these two years extended our hospitality to Akbar and Durgadas. We have killed many a brave captain of the Emperor, imprisoned several, released some after exacting ransom, and some out of compassion; several effected their escape by offering bribes. In this way the imperial commanders have proved themselves utterly incompetent. The moment has now arrived when the Emperor himself can be captured and made prisoner with the result that we can rebuild our temples and restore our religious practices. We strongly assure you that we have resolved to execute all this in the near future.

But we are in comparison with you young and inexperienced. We have seen and heard so much about your valour and your zeal for religion. You at present fully possess the seven arms of kingship, so that if you muster courage and co-operate with us in the task of annihilating the power of this Emperor, what may not be accomplished! When we ponder on this situation, we feel extremely surprised to find that you keep yourself so quiet and so unmindful of your religion.

There is another point. You and we have well observed what sort of a man Durjan Singh Hada is and what wealth he possessed. But he sacrificed his wealth and relying on his own personal valour created such a havoc at our instigation, as you being so near must have fully learned about. We from our side are doing our best. We are planning to despatch Akbar and Durgadas into Gujarat, so that you on your side must courageously execute whatever is possible. Shah Abbas of Persia has signified his willingness to support the cause of Akbar; but it does not in our opinion behove us to accept Muslim help in this cause and enable Abbas to gain the credit. Was it not your own revered father Jay Singh who gained the honour of helping Aurangzib to capture the throne of Delhi? You can now follow the same example and obtain the same credit by helping Akbar (to the throne). If he becomes the Emperor of Delhi with the help of the Muslims of Persia, they will gain predominance. It is necessary to prevent such a contingency. If you and we join our forces and place Akbar on the throne, we shall get the opportunity of protecting our religion and on your part you will shed lustre on the house of Jay Singh.

My ministers Kavi-kalash and Janardan Pandit are writing to you separately at length. You will also learn all the details personally from (our deputed agent) Pratap Singh and from the trusted spies who will meet you. Please write constantly about your own welfare. What more is there for us to write, when we are sure you comprehend all matters so intelligently?

Note.—This letter was written in Sanskrit and the English translation is the work of G. S. Sardesai. For *Durjan Sal Hada*, a noble of Bundi, see my *History of Aurangzib*, Vol. V. Ch. 58 § 5. All the other letters have been translated from Persian mss.

6. Muhammad Akbar to Kavi-kalash

I visited Jetapur on 14th Rabi-ul-awwal (20 Feb. 1684). Immediately on the receipt of this order, set out for seeing me, so that you may quickly arrive near. God forbid that through delay, the affair should take another turn. Most probably Kirat Singh has been given permission to depart. Know the matter to be urgent. Consider what has been written as ordered from my mouth.

Note.—The text has a word *jijab* which I have emended as *ujlatan*. This Kirat Singh was not the younger son of Mirza Rajah Jai Singh, but an envoy sent by Shambhaji to Goa on 9 Dec. 1683.

7. Muhammad Akbar to Kavi-kalash

Received your letter and learnt its contents. You (have written) about your arrival at Pachwar and interview with him (Shambha). As for the envoy of Muhammad Azam who has arrived there, it is not known to me why he has come and what agreement you have made with him. If you consider it to be expedient for yourself, make peace; otherwise I am not myself much inclined towards peace. There is no harm in your writing in reply, but your coming (here) is necessary and very convenient,—as many *rajkarans* will be accomplished. Know that the season for *rajkarans* is the monsoons. Don't remain careless in reliance on the peace (negotiations), because there is (really) no peace. After the rainy season that very trouble of Bhimgarh will come before you. You know best what is for your future benefit. Dated 24th Shaban (27 July 1684).

Note.—Rajkaran, a Marathi word meaning, 'a state counsel, a deep and political project.' The date is wrongly given as 1090 in the ms. *Bhimgarh*, is a jungle 27 miles east of Goa; here Rajah Shambhaji retreated from his invasion of Goa territory (Dec. 1683), on learning that Prince Shah Alam was descending upon his rear by the Ramghat pass. Shambhaji soon afterwards went back to Raigarh. *Pachwar* is the village at the foot of the Raigarh or Rairi hill fort, the official capital of the Maratha kings. After Shambhaji had thus fled away, Akbar and Kavi-kalash remained at Bhimgarh (and later at Phonda) negotiating with the Portuguese for a peace, (Jan. 1684.)

8. Muhammad Akbar to Kavi-kalash

I had heard before this that you were ill. Probably you have by this time gained some relief. The question of peace is entirely at the discretion of the Rajah and yourself. But it is far (from wise) to remain careless in reliance on the conversations for peace—which is in reality a mere word and sound,—as the season of rains is over. Probably you have forgotten the business of Bhimgarh. As for the peace with the Feringis, in which you have dragged me in as intermediary, it is not known to me how their affair has been concluded. What has the envoy of Muhammad Azam stated? What agreement has been made with him? What is the state of the Bijapur business? Written on 19th Ramzan, 1095 A.H. (20 Aug. 1684).

9. Muhammad Akbar to Kavi-kalash

Received your two letters addressed to me and learnt their contents. My standards had set out from the *Rajbari* [Bicholim] for this purpose that you might enjoy the favour of an audience at this very place. But it was not feasible. You have now fixed the 3rd of the month of Muharram (corresponding to 30 Nov. 1684), as the date of your interview with us. From the first to the tenth of that month are the ten *ashura* (' ten holy days'). According to our laws and faith, to begin any good work during the ten *ashura* days is contrary to the practices and rules of piety. You should inform me after fixing the eleventh or the twelfth of the month for your interview, and on that very day my standards will march out of Sakharpen and arrive at Malkapur. Write to me very quickly; the matter is urgent.

Note.—As the road from Kolhapur to Ratnagiri, after crossing the Ambaghat (that marvellous feat of British engineering) ten miles north-west of Malkapur, descends into Konkan, *Sakharpen* is the first important town on it. Here one road runs westwards to Ratnagiri and another runs north-west to Devrukh (7 miles away.) *Malkapur* is 25 miles north-west of Kolhapur in a straight line, and 13 miles east of Khelna (also called Vishalgarh) fort.

10. Muhammad Akbar to Kavi-kalash

Received your letter. You have written that as it is necessary for you to go to Kolhapur on the occasion of the bathing at the eclipse on 13th Muharram (10 Dec. 1684), you would come to Malkapur on the 16th of the present month and have audience with me on the the 17th of that month. I delayed only on account of the ten *ashura* days. When they are over, I shall march out of Sakharpen on the eleventh (of Muharram), and get down at Malkapur. You ought to come to Malkapur on that date and see me. Thereafter you may go to Kolhapur, so that there will be no delay. The matter lies in your hands.

11. MUHAMMAD AKBAR TO SHAMBHAJI

After (conveying my) boundless desire (for meeting you), be it not concealed from this brother (*bhai*) that you have come and your coming is very good. I, too, have come to Malkapur. It is proper that the interview and business should be soon accomplished. What more, except longing to see you? (*c.* Dec. 1684.)

12. MUHAMMAD AKBAR TO SHAMBHAJI

Chief of august princes, cream of grand Rajahs, devoted follower, *Chhatrapati* Rajah Shambhaji! receive my imperial favours and know that,—the facts about the descent of the Mughals and the exertions and firm stand made by Kavi-kalash, have reached my knowledge from the letters of Muhammad Jan and Khidmatparast Khan. Kavi-kalash is a very good and faithful servant of yours. Heaven avert that he should be ruined by any (other courtier) through jealousy! You ought to do everything to protect him. It is certain that by this time the Mughals have gone away, (or, otherwise) you have marched with your army, as you had written to me, towards Khelna. If you write, I too shall go and join you in the campaign. Written on 22nd Safar, 1096 A. H. (18 Jan. 1685).

Note.—The year is wrongly given in the ms. as 1092. On 14th January 1685, Kavi-kalash repulsed Shihabuddin (Ghaziuddin), who had descended the Bhor ghat, at Gagoli. [Jedhe.]

XII

REIGN OF SHAMBHUJI

1. Best Sources

For the reign of Shambhuji (May 1680 - February 1689) the historical material in the Marathi language is even more meagre, longer subsequent to the occurrences and more unsatisfactory than for the reign of his father the great Shivaji. The Chitnis Bakhar, which is now the only resource for Marathi readers, was written in 1810 and has been proved untrustworthy almost throughout. But with the help of the English, French and Portuguese records it is now possible to reconstruct this prince's history without any gaps, on the sure basis of *contemporary* written documents and with amplitude of correct details in respect of several incidents. The Persian *Akhbarats* (*i.e.*, news-letters), still in manuscript, give absolutely accurate dates and here and there information of primary importance. The "eye-witness" Bhimsen Burhanpuri in his Persian memoirs (named *Nuskha-i-Dilkasha*) has rather neglected this reign and gives only occasional references to it. The Persian sources on Aurangzib, especially Khafi Khan and the *Akhbarats*, fully detail only the abortive siege of Ramsej, but pass over the rest of the reign ; evidently the information received by their writers was scanty. For Prince Akbar's exile in Maharashtra, the Portuguese records are our mainstay and these have been made available by Chevalier Panduranga S. Pissurlencar; the *Akhbarats* giving occasional glimpses of the Mughal side. The fully detailed Portuguese narrative of the Maratha Rajah's invasion of Goa in 1683 was first published in India by me in 1920 from the ms. English version preserved in the India Office, London. The *Jedhe Shakavali* (in Marathi) is useful for dates and accurate information (however brief) about the home affairs of the Marathas.

In this chapter the English and French records are given, but the siege of Ramsej, the fights with the Siddis of Janjira, the negotiations with the Bombay merchants, and the long war with the Portuguese have been omitted, in order to save space. These can, however, be read in fair detail in my *History of Aurangzib*, vol. IV, which also deals fully with Aurangzib's measures against the Maratha king. Some of the documents excluded from the present chapter were printed by me in South Indian journals many years ago.

2. Accession of Shambhuji

28 April 1680.—We have certain news that Shivaji Rajah is dead, it is now 23 days since he deceased, it is said, of a bloody flux, being sick 12 days. How affairs goes (*sic*) in this country we sball advise as comes to our knowledge. At present all is quiet, and Shambhaji Raja is at Panhala. [F. R. Surat, vol. 108, Bombay Council to Surat.]

27 April 1680.—Shambhaji has taken upon him to govern and title of king. He has sent for all persons that were in command as *subahdars, havildars* etc., some he imprisoned and some he discharges of their employs. We have lately come here a new *subahdar* sent by him. [Rajapur factors to Bombay.]

3 May 1680.—Shambhaji is proclaimed and put in his father's place. Moro Pandit and Annaji Pandit &c. are gone to Panhala to receive his order. Ramraja is at Rairi.... All the *subahdars havildars* &c. are continued in their several employments; no alteration made. [Bombay Council to Surat.]

30 June 1680.—Shambhaji is now at Panhala, where he has made ready 5,000 men, given them two months' wages beforehand. He has settled subahdars and all officers of his. Annaji Pandit's head is cut off. Moro Pandit is in favour, but no trust as yet. The country begins to be a little settled. [*Ibid.*]

12 July 1680.—Shambhaji Rajah is now at Rairi: his young brother [Rajaram] he used with all kindness, and continues as yet to do.....Annaji Pandit is alive,.... but in great trouble and laden with chains. The country begins to be well settled, and Shambhaji publicly declared Rajah. He hath an army of 20,000 men now together; what he designs them is not known; report speaks him very diligent and careful. [*Ibid.*]

20 August 1680.—Report goes that Shambhaji Rajah intends, after the rains, to give Bahadur Khan [subahdar of Mughal Deccan] battle in open field, and has sent him word as much. [Chopra factors to Surat.]

10 Nov. 1680.—We are hotly alarmed of Shivaji's forces being abroad. It is reported here that there is a party of horse and foot designed to march towards Surat, another against Burhanpur, a third to keep Bahadur Khan in play, who is removed from these borders further towards Deccan. [*Ibid.*]

27 Nov. 1680.—Augee Pandit, a person of great esteem and quality in Shivaji's time [who] commanded the army next under Moro Pandit, came to the island [of Bombay] on the 20th instant with a letter from Shambhaji complaining of our harbouring the Siddi. [Bombay Council to Surat.]

3. Shambhuji and the Eastern Karnatak

(From the French *Memoires* of F. Martin, the founder of Pondicherry.)

Mons. Clement, chief of our Company's factory at Rajapur, in his letter of 29th April [New style, corresponding to 19th of the unreformed calendar] gave me the news of the death of Shivaji Rajah, twelve days earlier. The deceased may well hold a high rank among the great men of India, although all the conquests which he made during his life were done more by skilfulness and cleverness than by open force. There were difficulties among his leading officers after the death of the Rajah, in finding out a successor to him. His eldest son,

Shambhaji Rajah had all the right to the succession; but as he was the declared enemy of the Brahmans, most of his officers who belonged to that caste were unwilling to recognise him. He had the cleverness, however, to gain the chief ones over and the others followed. He was established [on the throne] by them.

The news of his death created a great confusion among the chief officers in these parts [*i.e.*, the province of Jinji or Eastern Karnatak.] Some of them seemed to desire to stay in their governments and render themselves independent. However, after a general meeting which they held among themselves, they resolved to be bound by what would be decided by the chief officers of the late Rajah who were on the other (*i.e.*, western) coast.

Oct.-Nov. 1680.—Although the officers of this province had recognised Shambhaji Rajah as their sovereign, they nevertheless were in fear on receiving the news that the new king had caused to be arrested and put in fetters many Brahmans among the principal officers of the late Shivaji,—among others Janardan Pandit, the brother of the Governor-General of this province [Raghunath Narayan Hanumante.] No good is predicted of the Government of Shambhaji Rajah from his having arrested officers of such importance and experience, who had followed his father in all his conquests and whom they had served with success.

Things changed in this province at the beginning of the year 1681. The Governor-General had written to me asking for a surgeon to treat a malady in his ear which had troubled him for many years, and which the English Dutch and Indian surgeons had failed to cure....I sent Mons. Petitbois on 9th January 1681, but I was surprised to see him returning on the 12th. He told me that he had arrived outside Jinji on the 10th, but found the gates of that city closed and that he was informed that there was great disorder in that place.

The governor (*i.e.*, *qiladar*) of Jinji and other chief officers had received orders from Shambhaji Rajah to arrest the Governor-General of the province. That officer, having entered Jinji with only a few followers, for celebrating there the *pongal**, a famous festival of the Hindus,—did not suspect anybody. The garrison of the place had surrounded his palace and the governor sent to tell him (*i.e.*, Hanumante) that he had received orders to arrest him. But the affair had not yet been pushed further forward, as they were waiting for [more] troops at Jinji.

We learnt some days later that the Governor-General had been arrested in consequence of Shambhaji Rajah having been informed that this officer had come to a secret understanding with the king of Golkonda and with certain Hindu princes in order to make himself sovereign of this country. The common belief, however, is that his enemies had falsely accused him out of envy and the

*The beginning of the Tamil year, when the Sun enters the sign of the Capricorn (*Makar*), about the 12th of January.

desire to rob him of the wealth which he had amassed during his governorship. The subahdar of the province was suspected of having written most strongly [against Hanumante.] People are asserting that the Governor-General has amassed more than eight lakhs of *ecus** in less than three years of rule. He has not been put in prison, only confined to his palace, pending the receipt of Shambhaji Rajah's orders,—his family living with him and his soldiers around. People could visit him on business... The French surgeon paid a second visit to Jinji and cured him. Shambhaji's generals are keeping watch on his frontier, as they have heard that Ekoji wished to profit by the occasion. [*Memoires*, ii. 192, 201, 211-212.]

4. Prince Md. Akbar seeks refuge with Shambhuji

21 June 1681.—Sultan Akbar is at a place called Pali, near Nagothan....He is a white man of middle stature, of about 25 years of age: he is lodged in a large house covered with straw, at the foot of Pali-garh: it has *tallah* walls; but since his being there, are pulled down; it is lined within with white calico, and spread with ordinary carpets: he sits open: with him of any note is but one man, called Durgadas, a Rajput.....in great esteem with his master, about five hundred horse, and but fifty camels; a small parcel of foot:....they are most

*An old French coin worth 3 francs; here probably used as an approximate equivalent to a Rupee (which was then worth about 2½ francs.)

Rajputs, very few Moors. Without them is quite round placed about three hundred foot, Shambhuji Rajah's man, who keep guard....About four days ago came from Shambhuji Rajah to him, one Hiraji Farzand, a person of great quality and esteem. He brought with him a letter from his master, and a present that was laid down at the Sultan's feet, 1,000 pagodas, a large string of great pearls, hanging to it a rich jewel set with a very large diamond and a large jewel of diamonds for the head, with many pieces of rich India and Persia stuffs. [Bombay Council to Surat.]

16 July 1681.—Akbar's force increases daily. He hath now about 1,500 horse and at Trimbak [there] awaits him 5 or 6 thousand horse more. Shambhuji is daily expected to wait on him, and it is said will with 2,000 horse conduct him to Burhanpur, where all the Hindu Rajahs will meet him and some *umaras* that are his friends. From thence they intend to march for Delhi. [Bombay Council to Surat.]

5. Shambhuji crushes Conspiracy against his Life

30 Aug. 1681.—Shambhuji hath been in great danger of his life. He had like to have been dispatched by poison put into a dish of fish. But a boy privy to it prevented his eating of it; he gave some of it to one of his servants and a dog; both died in a few hours. Those that conspired against him was (*sic*) Annaji Pandit, Kesho Pandit, Prahlad Pandit etc., all in hold laden with iron. [Bombay Council to Surat.]

8 Sep. 1681.—The conspirators against Shambhuji was (*sic*) Annaji Pandit, Ramrajah's mother, and Hiraji Farzand, who would have brought Sultan Akbar in, but he would not, but immediately gave Shambhaji notice of it by a messenger,—which hath so much gained on the Rajah that he hath promised the Sultan 30,000 horse that are making ready to accompany him to Burhanpur. [*Ibid.*]

12 Oct. 1681.—Shambhuji is now at Rairi. For plotting against his life he hath put to death Annaji Pandit, Hiraji Farzand, Bowgec Pandit [=Balaji Prabhu], and five more, bound and put under elephants' feet. Twenty more are to suffer death. The Rajah will march for Burhanpur with Akbar in a few days. [*Ibid.*]

27 Oct. 1681.—Shambhuji Rajah is making ready great forces, both horse and foot, to assist Sultan Akbar. It is said, in a month more they may march out of these parts and that they intend to march Surat-way for Burhanpur: God help you and the Hon'ble Company's concerns from them. Ramrajah's mother [Soyra Bai] is dead by report, poisoned by Shambhuji Rajah's contrivance. [*Ibid.*]

21 April 1680.—Anaji Surnis enthrones Rajaram, [variant 6 May.]

18 June 1680.—Shambhuji enters Raigarh.

20 July 1680.—Sh. enthroned.

Dec. 1680.—Sh. arrests Raghunath N. in Karnatak.

Aug. 1681.—Sh. puts to death Anaji Datto Sachiv, Anaji Pant [Surnis], Bala Prabhu, Somaji Datto, and Hiraji Farzand,—arrests Shamji Nayak in Karnatak.

13 Nov.—Shambhuji meets Akbar. [*Jedhe Shakavali.*]

Dec. 1681, Fr. Martin's diary.—Shambhuji Rajah continues his executions of the Brahmans. It is pertinent to note....the hatred of this prince against the men of that caste, joined to the condition into which he frequently falls by his excess in drinking. It is particularly during that time (*viz.*, that of intoxication) that he orders the execution of those who come to his mind. It is known that he has killed 14 of them on the information that he had received, or what served as a pretext to him, that they had formed a party for seizing him, taking his brother Ramraja out of prison and putting him in his place. [ii. 280-281.]

24 April 1682.—We have no reason to think Shambhaji Rajah our friend because of the Siddi's being continually supplied by our Island [of Bombay], and yet he continues fair with us,—not out of any respect to us but of kindness to himself, [he] reaping a great benefit from our trading to the *Kurlas*, which brings into him a great deal of money yearly. We hope he will not concern himself so much as to quarrel with us for Avji Pandit's coming on the Island, [he] being a person he (*i.e.*, Shambhuji) hath no esteem for, but turned him out of his favour and pay, and coming from Ghor-bandar we account him so wholly disregarded, as let him be where he will, the Rajah matters not; otherwise he would have prevented his leaving his dominions or been concerned at the Portuguese entertaining him. [Surat Council to Bombay.]

1 June 1682.—The King's [*i.e.*, Aurangzib's] *chela* [*i.e.*, slave, named Mahmud Razzaq] and Avji Pandit are arrived here [from Bombay.] They intend to set forward towards the King in a few days. [*Ibid.*]

28 Nov. 1682.—The chiefest minister of State [at Raigarh] is Prahlad Pant and (*sic*) Kavi-kalash. [Bombay Council to Surat.]

6. THE DOWNFALL OF SHAMBHUJI

(Translated from the *Memoires* of F. Martin)

Nov. 1683.—Shambhuji Rajah continues to exercise his cruelty with regard to the other officers of his father, particularly against the Brahmans. It can be [easily] foreseen that this prince will ruin himself by his wicked conduct; the Brahmans never forgive, and besides their character is to govern among the Hindu princes. [ii. 338.]

May 1685.—The bad conduct of Shambhuji Rajah,—his excesses, his cruelties,—drove many of his chief officers to form a conspiracy against him. It was discovered and many were executed. Two *desais* fled to Goa. The prince demanded their surrender; on the refusal of the Viceroy to do so, we believe war will soon recommence between the two nations. [ii. 390.]

Shambhuji Rajah had rendered himself odious to his subjects by his violence, his cruelty, and his debauchery.

This made some of his leading Brahmans conceive the design of destroying him. To these men a secret understanding with the officers of the Mughal Emperor appeared less criminal than the carrying out of the murder themselves. They previously informed certain [imperial] officers to place troops in ambush at a place which was convenient for their purpose; they next engaged Shambhuji Rajah in the diversion of hunting and caused the prince to be led into the ambuscade, where he was enveloped [by the Mughals.] His head was by order of the Mughal Emperor, carried to various provinces and publicly exposed in many cities. [ii. 454.]

7. WAR, PEOPLE'S SUFFERING AND ECONOMIC RUIN

4 Feb. 1682.—Nawab Hasan Ali Khan is come to Kalian Bhivandi, with it is said 20,000 horse and 15,000 foot, burning all places in Shambha's country as he comes along, and 8 or 9 Portuguese villages by mistake... Shambha has raised his siege from Danda Rajpuri and with Akbar is fled up into their strong *garhs*. [Bombay Council to Surat.]

3 January 1682.—Sundarji Baji [=Balaji] has arrived in Bombay as ambassadar from the Maratha King.... Since the burning of Apta, the Siddis have been at Upper Chaul and done much mischief both by fire and sword, taking several prisoners and much plunder. This has so enraged Shambhuji that he is gone with a full resolution utterly to destroy Danda Rajpuri. [*Ibid.*]

28 Aug. 1682.—The Siddi hath robbed the *Kurlas*....

He hath brought away the *havladar* of Ganuan* [as prisoner] and cut off the noses of several inhabitants there besides a great many [that he] hath taken from Nagothan. [*Ibid.*]

26 Nov. 1683.—About two months past the Sultan [Akbar] gave the Duch a visit. Shambhuji has employed Durgadas as an ambassador to sue for peace with the Portuguese. [Karwar factors to Surat.]

4 Sep. 1683.—The Portuguese have done such action already in burning men alive and destroying pagodas that Shambhuji will not easily put up [with them.] Europe commodities are afraid to come into Shambhuji's country by reason of his ministers' exactions, who not only take custom of us (*i.e.*, the European importers) but from the [native] merchants too, with a *peshkash* exacted according to the quality (=rank) of the person, which is really our loss. [Karwar factors to Bombay.]

28 January, 1684.—At the change of the Government [*i. e.*, usurpation of Bombay by the rebel Richard Keigwin] an ambassador of Shambhuji was prisoner to one of the Mughal's generals and was intended to have cut off his head. But hearing Bombay was proclaimed your Majesty's, he suspended the execution and sent the prisoner to me, who[m] I safely sent to Shambhuji. [Keigwin to King Charles II.]

6 Nov. 1684.—This Government is eager and hungry after present interest, which suits ill with the rules of

*Is it *Gavan*, at the southern point of Trombay Island ?

saving so much recommended to us [by the Home authorities]....With the Rajah down to the plowman the infection of *peshkash-ing* is so prevalent that nothing can be well done without it, or withstand it. [Karwar factors to Surat Council.]

2 April 1685.—The weavers that came from Thana and Chaul was (*sic*) about a twelve month, since when the latter was besieged by Shambhuji Rajah, and since there is come none. There was in number about 600 families; 400 for want of encouragement did forsake this place in Keigwin's time, 150 of the remainder are dead; so that there are now about 50. [Bombay Council to Surat.]

12 April 1685.—In former years there was a quantity of pepper, about 1,500 candy; it grew in and near about Rajapur; but now grows not the tenth part, since that place hath been in Shivaji's hands,—not only the pepper is lost, but [it is now so] decayed in trade that it is a miserable poor town. [Surat Council to England.]

22 May 1685.—The Karwar factors are asked to supply slaves for export, some 20 or 40 at Rs 15 per head. But you may obtain them cheaper, [there] being such troubles, we know at such times they may be had at a pagoda a head. Three pairs of dwarfs (male and female) are to be sent Home to His Majesty. [Surat Council to Karwar.]

18 July 1685.—The ways are being molested by Delvi Desai, one of Shambhuji's Governors who has lately revolted from him (in Kanara.) [*Ibid.*]

8. Capture and Execution of Shambhuji
(Translated from the *Masir-i-Alamgiri* or the official History of Aurangzib's reign.)

While the Emperor was staying at Akluj, the ears of the world were gladdened by a happy news from the Invisible Power; the merry music of a victory, for the report of the occurrence of which Islamic ears had been longing, resounded through the sky. Peace and safety were restored through the grace of the Emperor's justice and virtue; disturbance sank down; Satan was chained. To speak more plainly, the infernal infidel Shambha was captured by the army through the power of the Emperor's fortune.

Shaikh Nizam Haidarabadi, surnamed Muqarrab Khan, a brave general, in recognition of his military capacity had been given along with his sons and relatives, a total mansab of 25 thousand *zat* (21,000 troopers.) Before this he had been detached by the Emperor from Bijapur to capture the fort of Panhala from Maratha possession. Like a prudent and watchful man he had sent out spies to bring news of the infidel. Suddenly they conveyed to him a true report that Shambha, on account of his feud with the Shirke family who were connected with him by kinship [*i.e.*, his step-mother's clan], had gone from Raigarh to Khelna, and after making a settlement with that family and satisfactorily provisioning Khelna fort, had proceeded to Sangameshwar, where his minister Kavi-kalash had constructed lofty mansions and gardens, and was there sunk in merrymaking and pleasure.

The Khan, out of devotion to the Emperor, in utter disregard of his life started from Kolhapur, from which Sangameshwar was 45 *kos* distant, and the path full of crags and passes so difficult and dangerous that travellers have not seen the like of them on earth,—with a band of honour-seeking devoted followers, and proceeded by forced marches. Although the spies of Shambha informed him that the Mughal troops were coming, that foolish pride-intoxicated man, by making the signal of a frown had them beheaded, crying out, "You careless fellows, are you mad? Can a Mughal force possibly reach here?"

The Khan, after patiently enduring much fatigue and hardship, came upon him with the speed of lightning and wind. That accursed wretch charged him with the support of four or five thousand Deccani spearmen. But Kavi-kalash was accidentally wounded with an arrow and after a little fighting they took to flight. Shambha concealed himself in a hole in Kavi-kalash's mansion hoping that none would detect him. Spies gave the Khan correct information about his hiding place, and he, without going out in pursuit of the fugitive (troops), surrounded the mansion. His son Ikhlas Khan with a party of brave men entered it by the steps aud dragged that low fellow and Kavi-kalash out by the hair of their heads and took them to the elephant on which Muqarrab Khan was seated.....Twenty-five of Shambha's chief followers with their wives and daughters were made prisoners.

The news of this event reached the Emperor at Akluj which was henceforth named *Asad-nagar* (Most Auspicious City.) He ordered Hamid-ud-din Khan, the provost-marshal of his camp, to hasten to Muqarrab Khan and bring the captives chained hand and foot. The victorious Khan returned from that country (in safety) by prudent management. Through the good luck of Alamgir, none of the infidel chiefs made any attempt (to rescue Shambha.)

On 15th February 1689, when the imperial army, after marching from Asad-nagar, had encamped at Bahadurgarh, Shambha was brought to the Court. The Emperor, out of his devotion to Islam, ordered that from four miles before the camp, Shambha should be made an object of ridicule and his comrades should be clad in the dress of buffoons, punished in various ways, mounted on camels, and led into the camp and the imperial darbar with drums beating and trumpets pealing,—so that the Muslims might be encouraged and the infidels disheartened by the sight. The night in the morning after which he was brought to the Court was, without exaggeration, the *Shab-i-barat*, because nobody slept till the morning in the joyous expectation of seeing the spectacle; and the day was like the day of *Id* because all men, old and young, went out to see such a scene of joy and happiness.

In short, that man, deserving of a degrading public parade and execution, was taken through the whole camp and then brought to the Emperor, who was seated in the Hall of Public Audience. He ordered him to be removed to the prison of retribution. That moment the Emperor descended from the throne and kneeling down on the carpet of prayer bowed his head to the ground in thanksgiving and raised his hands in prayer to the Judge of Actions and the Promoter of Hopes. The cloud of the display of the handiwork of Providence was shaken and drops of marvel (at God's power) fell from his far-seeing eyes. (Verses)

The peak of his cap reaches high heaven, [but]
His head is ever bowed down to the earth in reverence.

As Shambha had previously ignored the value of the Emperor's mercy and fled away,—first from the Emperor's Court in his father's company (in 1666) and the second time from the late Dilir Khan (in 1669),—therefore, that very night his eyes were deprived of the power of seeing, and the next day the tongue of the deceitful speaker Kavi-kalash was cut out. The victorious [Muqarrab] Khan was rewarded for this splendid service with the title of Khan-i-Zaman Fath Jang and....promotion to the rank of 7,000 (*zat* and *sawar*); his son Ikhlas Khan gained the title of Khan-i-Alam, &c.

As the destruction of this wicked infidel, in consideration of the harshness and disgrace that he had inflicted by slaying and imprisoning Muslims and plundering the cities of Islam, preponderated over the reasons for keeping him alive, and the decision of the doctors of the Holy Law and the counsel of the dignitaries of the Church and the State were in favour of despatching this hellish robber,—therefore, after the arrival of the Emperor at Koregaon (henceforth) named Fatihabad, he was executed along with Kavi-kalash by the sword on 11 March 1689.

(From the Persian history, *Fatuhat-i-Alamgiri*, written by Ishwar-das, a Nagar Brahman of Patan in Gujrat.)

After two days the Emperor ordered Ruhullah Kh. to ask Shambha where he had kept his treasure, jewels and other property [of value] and which of the imperial *umara* used to correspond with him in secret. In these circumstances, as it is well-known that if a man has washed his hands of [all hope of] life he speaks whatever he pleases, that haughty man opened his mouth in shameful and vain words about His Majesty. But the Khan did not report to the Emperor fully what had fallen from the wicked tongue of the accursed rebel, but merely gave a hint as to its nature. So, the Emperor ordered him to be blinded by driving nails into his two eyes. It was done as ordered. But that proud man, from his high spirit, gave up taking any food from that day onwards. His guards urged him in vain, and he fasted for some days. At last the case was reported to the Emperor. By his order Shambha was taken to the place of execution, and his limbs were hacked off one after another. His severed head was publicly exposed from Aurangabad to Burhanpur, and taken to Delhi and hung on the gate of that city. [Br. Mus. ms. f. 156 *a* & *b*.]

(Translated from the Persian history of Khafi Khan, ii. 384-389.)

With the object of travelling and bathing in the river Man-Ganga, which flows close to the boundary of the Sangameshwar pargana, one day's march from the ocean,—Shambhuji went from Khelna fort to Sangameshwar, where his diwan Kavi-kalash had built a lofty mansion full of pictures and laid out a garden of fruit trees and flower-beds...Relying on the inaccessible nature of the hills and forests around and the difficulty of the paths, he stayed there off his guard, with 2,000 or 3,000 horsemen. Unlike his father he indulged in drinking wine and making merry with beautiful women, and now remained sunk in pleasure. The fast spies of Muqarrab Khan brought to him intelligence of Shambhuji's residence and condition. The Khan, taking no thought of his life, started from Kolhapur, his base, with 2,000 brave horsemen and one thousand select foot musketeers,.... crossed the difficult Amba-*ghat* and other lofty defiles,.... always dismounting (himself first and his followers after him) in order to thread every narrow pass or thick jungle on foot, and thus by forced marches arrived near the doomed man.

It is said that when some spies of that worthless dog reported to him the approach of the Mughal troops, the fellow, intoxicated with the wine of negligence and futility, believing in the impenetrability of the place, and with his pride doubling the effect of wine, ordered the tongues of the spies to be cut out for giving him false intelligence.

He did not engage in equipping for battle or fortifying the place.

Suddenly Muqarrab Khan, who had arrived with only his son, nephews and 10 or 12 of his brave relatives and 200 to 300 swift-moving horsemen, delivered an attack upon that bewildered victim. Shambha,....when it was too late, turned to girding his and waist and taking up arms with the few soldiers who still remained with him,—most part of his escort having fled away. Kavi-kalash, his wazir, who was known as his brave and devoted confidant, placing Shambha behind himself, advanced to confront the Mughals at the head of a party of noted Marathas.

At the very beginning of the fight, an arrow* hit Kavi-kalash's right arm and rendered that limb incapable of action. Falling down from his horse he cried out, "I shall stay behind." Shambha, who was planning to flee away, also leapt down from his horse and shouted, "Panditji, [text reads *P-a-n-j-i*] I too shall remain here." As soon as four or five other Marathas dismounted, the rest of Shambha's troops took to flight and Kavi-kalash was captured. Shambha betook himself to the shelter of a temple [*butkhana*, a possible variant is *taikhana*, cellar] and remained concealed and invested there. After much search his hiding place was discovered, he made a fruitless attempt

* *Tir* may also mean a bullet,—which is more likely here. Shivaji's defeat near Jalna in 1679 was mainly due to the abundance of Mughal fire-arms.

to fight, but at last after giving up some of his followers to death, he too was made prisoner with his family—26 men and women, besides two other women, the wives of his high-placed relatives and comrades, were included among the captives. They were all dragged by the hair, with their hands tied together, to the feet of Muqarrab Khan's elephant. Although in this short time Shambha had shaved off his beard and rubbed ashes on his face and put on another dress [like a *sannyasi*], he was recognised by the pearl necklace peeping out of his dress and the gold ring found on the fetlock of his horse. The Khan placed Shambha on his own elephant in the back seat; the other captives were chained and conveyed on elephants and horses, with every precaution and watchfulness, back to his camp.

XIII

A HERO OF OLD MAHARASHTRA

Shantaji Ghorpare

In the long history of Aurangzib's struggle with the Marathas, after the sun of Maratha royalty had set in the red cloud of Shambhuji's blood and the people's war had begun, two stars of dazzling brilliancy filled the Deccan firmament for nearly a decade and paralysed the alien invader till at last they clashed together with fatal results. They were Dhanaji Jadav and Shantaji Ghorpare, and the history of Southern India from 1689 to 1698 is very greatly the biography of these two men.

Dhanaji Jadav was the great-grandson of Shivaji's mother's brother and was born about 1650. He first saw service under Pratap Rao Gujar, the Commander-in-Chief of the Great Shivaji and continued to fight under the Maratha banner ever afterwards. His first great achievement was the defeat that he inflicted upon a Mughal detachment in the plains of Phaltan, shortly after Rajaram's accession (1689), for which he was given the title of Jai Singh. He accompanied this king in his flight to Jinji, in the Madras Karnatak, in the autumn of that year.

Like him Shantaji Ghorpare was a Maratha of Shivaji's caste and descended from that branch of the Ghorpare family which lived at Kapshi in the Kolhapur

State. Entering Shivaji's service with his father and two brothers, he won an extensive *jagir* for his family in the Kopal district north of the Tungabhadra.

Shantaji had an inborn genius for handling large bodies of troops spread over a wide area, changing his tactics so as to take prompt advantage of every change in the enemy's plans and condition, and organising combined movements. The success of his tactics depended on the rapid movement of his troops and on his subordinates carrying out his orders punctually to the minute. He, therefore, insisted on implicit obedience from his officers and enforced the strictest discipline and promptness in his army by draconic punishments for disobedience or slackness. As Khafi Khan writes (ii. 446), "Shanta used to inflict severe punishments on his followers. For the slightest fault he would cause the offender to be trampled to death by an elephant."

The man who insists on efficiency and discipline in a tropical country makes himself universally unpopular, and, therefore, we are not surprised when we learn from Khafi Khan that "most of the Maratha nobles became Shanta's enemies and made a secret agreement with his rival Dhana to destroy him"

The first recorded exploit of Shanta was done during Rajaram's flight to Jinji. After that king had been surprised by the Mughals on an island of the Tungabhadra and escaped with his bare life, he hid himself in the territory of the Rani of Bednur (now the Nagar division in the N. W. of Mysore) for some time. Aurangzib sent a large force under Jan-nisar Khan, Matlab Khan, and Sharza Khan to invade this country; but as the Emperor's official history admits, "Shanta triumphantly opposed them, till at last the matter was settled by the Rani paying a small fine under the name of tribute." (*M.A.* 329.) Shanta's younger brothers Bahirji (surnamed Hindu Rao) and Maloji were included among the companions of Rajaram who were captured on the island and lodged in Bijapur fort, whence they contrived to escape by bribery. [*Ibid.*]

Rajaram, when going to Jinji, had left Shanta in Maharashtra, charging him to act under the orders of Ramchandra, the *Amatya*, who had been practically invested with a regent's full powers for Maratha affairs in Western Deccan. (Sane, letter 433.) For some time he did so, and we find him co-operating with the Amatya and other generals in defeating the famous Bijapuri general Sharza Khan (now in the Mughal service with the title of Rustam Khan) near Satara on 11th May 1690. Sharza offered a long resistance, but was worsted and made prisoner with his wife and children; the entire baggage of his army was seized together with 4,000 horses and eight elephants; and he had to ransom himself by paying one lakh of Rupees. (*M.A.* 336, K.K. 416, *Jedhe.*)

Late in 1692 Shanta and Dhana were sent by Ramchandra to the Madras Karnatak, each at the head of 15,000 cavalry to reinforce Rajaram, who was threatened in fort Jinji by a new imperial force despatched by Aurangzib under Prince Kam Bakhsh and the Wazir Asad Khan, a year earlier. Shanta arrived first and burst into the Conjeveram district. The terror inspired by his raiding bands caused a wild flight of the inhabitants far and near into Madras for refuge (11th to 13th December 1692). When the Maratha force arrived near Kaveripak, Ali Mardan Khan, the Mughal faujdar of Conjeveram, went out to encounter it, being deceived by the screen of cavalry as to his enemy's vast numbers. He could not avoid a battle when he learnt the truth. In the course of the fight, his corps of Bahelia musketeers deserted to the enemy, and Ali Mardan in vainly trying to retreat to Conjeveram was hemmed round and captured with 1,500 horses and six elephants. His entire army was plundered by Shanta (13th Dec.) (Fort St. George *Diary*, *Dilkasha* 108*b*, *Jedhe*.) The defeated Khan was taken to Jinji and held to ransom for one lakh of *hun*. Dhana Jadav similarly defeated, captured and pillaged another great Mughal general Ismail Khan Maka, at the same time. [Martin's *Memoires*, iii. 266-269.]

Zulfiqar and Asad Khan, in utter despair of opposing the victorious Marathas or even of saving themselves and the Emperor's son Prince Kam Bakhsh under their care in the siege-camp before Jinji, paid a large sum to Rajaram and his minister and were thus permitted to withdraw with their entire army to Wandiwash without serious opposition. This lame conclusion of their wonderful victories caused a rupture between the Maratha generals and Rajaram, which is thus graphically described by the governor of Pondicherry:—The commanders of the reinforcements which had come to Jinji (from Maharashtra in December 1692) were extremely irritated that without their participation, Ramraja, by the advice of his minister alone, had made a treaty with the Mughals. They bore a particular grudge against the latter (*i.e.*, the minister) whom they accused of having received a large sum for leaving to the Mughals a path open for their retiring in safety to their own territory. It was quite evident that the Marathas could have held them all at their discretion—namely, Sultan Kam Bakhsh, the wazir Asad Khan and his son and a large number of persons of rank who were in that army. They (the Maratha generals) represented that they could have extracted large sums as their ransom, besides being able to secure an advantageous treaty with the Mughal Emperor by restoring to him men of such importance. Shantaji Ghorpare.. incensed by this act (of Rajaram) withdrew with his troops to some leagues from Jinji. We believe that Rajaram had acted from gratitude, as he know well that it would have been easy for Zulfiqar to take Jinji.

All this mutual accommodation between the two parties (*viz.*, Zulfiqar and Rajaram) was the result of a secret understanding which they had formed between themselves. In view of the expected death of the aged Emperor and the inevitable war of succession among his sons, Asad Khan and Zulfiqar planned to, establish themselves as independent sovereigns in that country, with Maratha help. They had in view the union of the kingdom of Golkonda and the Karnatak [under their own sceptre], while Ramraja was to get, as his share, the kingdom of Bijapur....That prince, in order to recall to his side his army commanders (who had left him in disgust) apparently disclosed to them his reasons for having acted in that manner (towards the hard-pressed Mughal generals); presents were joined to it; he visited Shantaji Ghorpare. Thus the complaints and murmurs ceased in part, but their spirits still remained ulcerated. [*Memoires*, iii. 286.]

After the Mughal siege-army had purchased its retreat to Wandiwash and Jinji had been freed from danger (January 1693), Shantaji laid siege to Trichinopoly, the ruler of which was at chronic war with Rajaram's first cousin and firm ally, Shahji II., the Rajah of Tanjore. Rajaram himself arrived on the scene soon afterwards and the Trichinopoly Nayak had to make peace in April.

Early in May Shanta quarrelled with his king and went back to Maharashtra. Rajaram, in anger, took away Shanta's title of *Senapati* (Commander-in-Chief) and gave it to Dhana Jadav.* (*Jedhe.*)

Malhar Ramrao Chitnis, who is usually wrong in his dates and names, reports an earlier quarrel (in 1690) and describes it thus:—"When Rajaram went to Jinji, he commanded Shantaji Ghorpare and his two brothers to obey the orders of the Amatya (Ramchandra.) But

* This is how I interpret the phrase *Dhanajis namzad kele*, according to the Persian idiom.

Shanta did not co-operate at the siege of Panhala and did not act according to his instructions. Remaining in the Sandur district, he waged war up to the Tungabhadra, captured the fort of Guti, seized some frontier *thanas* and stayed there. The Amatya reported these things to the king at Jinji, who was displeased and took away the post of Commander-in-Chief and conferred it on Mahadji Pansabal in 1690.

"He wrote about it to Ramchandra, and sending two men to Shanta took away his *Sikke-katar* and placed them in charge of Ramchandra......Then Shanta tried in vain for a fortnight or a month to interview Ramchandra, who declined to see him. So, he went to the king at Jinji and staying there gave an undertaking to serve like all other officers to the satisfaction of the king, while his two brothers would remain under the orders of Ramchandra. Making this agreement he went to Jinji to oppose the army sent by the Emperor......" (ii. 34.)

"For his great services....Rajaram greatly liked Dhana and....now gave him honour equal to that of the Senapati with the right of playing the *naubat*...." (ii. 36). Mahadji fell in battle at Jinji and Shanta was made Senapati in his place. (ii. 40.)

Chitnis reports a later quarrel which I am inclined to place in May 1693 :—"For some reason or other Shantaji Ghorpare quarrelled with the courtiers of Rajaram and insulted them. Thereafter, the king sent Mane to attack

Shanta, but the other sardars after much reasoning dissuaded him....So, Shanta was merely censured and his post of Commander-in-Chief was given to Dhanaji. Things went on in this way for two or three years." (ii. 42.) Much of Chitnis's account is unsupported by contemporary sources, and I am inclined to regard it as confused and partly inaccurate.

Returning home about the middle of 1693, Shantaji acted as his own master and devoted his time and resources to carving out a principality for himself in the Bellary district. He refused to obey the orders of the king's *locum tenens* and did not lend his aid to the national party when they raised Prince Muizz-ud-din's siege of Panhala in November next.

His brother Bahirji, too, had left Rajaram in a huff (March 1693). The reason for the rupture I infer to be the usurpation of the real control of the Government by the Brahman ministers at Jinji in consequence of Rajaram's sinking into debauchery and imbecility, so that the men of the sword rebelled against their own loss of influence at Court and the appropriation of the wealth of the State by the men of the pen. Bahirji joined another malcontent, Yachapa Nayak (who had made himself master of Satgarh fort) and probably tried to imitate his example of winning an estate for himself. The Maratha royal forces attacked the two deserters near Vellore in May. But the quarrel was made up and Bahirji returned to his master's side in February 1694.

While thus "fighting for his own hand" and pursuing an independent career of depredation in imperial territory, Shanta was defeated after a long chase and a three days' running fight by Himmat Khan at the village of Vikramhalli (early Nov., 1693). Three hundred of Shanta's own soldiers and 200 of his Barad allies were slain, and 300 mares, some flags, kettledrums &c., were captured by the Mughals, who suffered a heavy loss in killed and wounded. But the pursuit failed through a quarrel between Himmat Khan and his coadjutors Hamid-ud-din and Khwaja Khan, so that Shanta, without any fear, sent 4,000 men under Amrit Rao towards Berar, while he himself led 6,000 cavalry towards Malkhed—Karnul hills—Haidarabad &c. In March 1694 we find him in the Mahadev hills. (*Akhbarat*, year, 37).

Another cause of Shanta's attitude of aloofness from the Government was his being drawn into the cross-currents of ministerial rivalry at the western capital of Maharashtra. He sided with Parashuram, the rival of the Amatya, while Dhana belonged to the faction of the latter (*Dil.*, 122*a.*)

But in October 1694, Shankarji Malhar (the *Sachiv*) formed a plan of joint action and sharing of profits with Shantaji and persuaded him to march to the Madras Karnatak, saying, "Go with your troops and do our master's work. Hasten to the Raja with light equipment (literally, alone). Remain there showing due respect. Raise the siege. Don't violate your faith." He took an oath from Shanta to act in this spirit, and added to his forces the contingents of Hanumant Rao Nimbalkar and other generals, making a total of 25,000 horse, which marched in a compact body, firing its artillery on the way. Shankarji made an agreement with Shanta to conduct the revenue (collection) in concert and to remain faithful (to each other's interests), and sent his brother (?) Yesaji Malhar as his representative with this expeditionary force.

Meantime Zulfiqar Khan had concluded a successful campaign against the Raja of Tanjore and exacted from him a bond to abandon the cause of Rajaram which he had hitherto helped most usefully with money and provisions, and to pay a tribute of thirty lakhs of Rupees every year. (May 1694.) Then he came back to Jinji and renewed his pretended siege of it, occupying the country around. (*Jedhe;* Fort St. George *Diary.*)

Shanta seems to have effected nothing for his master this time, and soon returned to the north-western corner of Mysore. In November 1695, Dhana was sent to prop up the Maratha cause on the Madras side, which he succeeded in doing, by driving away Zulfiqar from the siege of Vellore.

But in this very month, Shanta performed the most glorious achievement of his life,—one which still further raised his reputation for invincibility and made him the dread of even the greatest Mughal generals.

Shanta was reported to be going back to his own estate in the Chittaldurg district, heavily loaded with booty from the imperial dominions. Aurangzib, then encamped at Brahmapuri (on the Bhima), ordered Qasim Khan, the able and active governor of the Sera country (western Mysore), to intercept the raiders. To reinforce Qasim Khan, he sent a detachment from his own camp under some of his highest younger officers,—Khanazad Khan (afterwards Ruhullah Khan II and Lord High Steward), Saf Shikan Khan, Sayyid Asalat Khan and Muhammad Murad (the Paymaster of Prince Kam Bakhsh's army),—with a command of 25,000 men on paper but five to six thousand troopers in actual muster. It was, however, a very choice corps, being composed of men from the imperial guards and personal retinue and the contingents of the nobles who had to patrol round his tent on different days in the week (*haft chauki*), with artillerymen. They joined Qasim Khan about 12 miles from the Marathas' expected track, early in November. Shanta, who had been roving at a distance, heard of his enemy's position and movements, came up with them by swift marches, and matured his plan for their destruction with consummate skill which the luxury and thoughtlessness of the Mughal generals crowned with the most complete success imaginable.

Khanazad Khan was a Persian of the highest descent, being the son of the late Paymaster-General Ruhullah Khan I, and great-grandson of the Empress Mumtaz Mahal's sister. With him had come some officers of the greatest influence and favour in the Emperor's personal circle. Qasim Khan rose to the height of hospitality required by such guests. Discarding the simple and light kit of a general who wishes to wage war with the Marathas wisely, he brought out of his stores in Adoni fort, his 'show' articles, such as unused Karnataki tents; gold, silver and China vessels of all kinds, etc., and sent them six miles ahead of his halting place to be kept ready for himself and his guests when they would arrive there at the end of the next day's march. (*M. A.* 375.)

But on that day doom overtook him in the person of Shanta Ghorpare, who showed the highest tactical power in making his dispositions and moving his three distinct and scattered divisions so as to ensure the perfect timing of their movements and exact co-operation among them. He divided his army into three bodies, of which one was sent to plunder the Mughal camp, another to oppose the soldiers, and the third was held in hand ready for action wherever required. The zamindar of the Chittaldurg district sided with the Marathas in the hope of a share of the spoils and thus the Mughals were ringed round by enemies and cut off from all information (*M. A.* 375.) (*Dil.* 117*b.*)

An hour and a half after sunrise, the first Maratha division fell upon Qasim Khan's advanced tents (six miles to the front), slew and wounded the guards and servants, carried off everything they could, and set fire to the heavy tents. On the news of it reaching Qasim Khan, he hurried towards the point of attack, without rousing Khanazad Khan from his sleep or maturing any plan of concerted action. Before he had gone two miles, the second body of the enemy appeared in sight and the battle began. This awoke Khanazad Khan, who left his camp, baggage and everything else on the spot and quickly advanced to the aid of his friend. But the enemy's numbers were overwhelming and they had a very large body of *Kala-piada* musketeers,—the best marksmen and bravest infantry of the Deccan,—in addition to their numberless mobile light cavalry. "A great battle was fought and many were slain on both sides. In spite of the steadiness of the imperialists and the destruction done by them, the enemy did not yield one foot of ground or show the least wavering. Then the reserve division of Shanta fell upon the camp and baggage left behind and looted everything. This news reached Qasim and Khanazad in the heat of the battle and shook their firmness. They took counsel together and decided to go to the small fort of Dodderi* close to which the advanced-tents had been sent and where there was a tank. Fighting for two miles they reached the tank in the evening and halted; the enemy retired from the attack but encamped close by."

The fort of Dodderi was small and the food-store in it limited. So "its imperial garrison shut its gates upon their

---

* Dodderi, 14°20' N., 75°46' E., in the Chittaldurg division of Mysore, 22 miles east of Chittaldurg, and 96 miles in a straight line south of Adoni. South of it stands a large reservoir.

"The imperialists, giving up all plan of fighting, took the road to Dodderi in confusion, reached the place with extreme difficulty, and were invested." (*Dil*, 118*a*.)

newly arrived comrades. The two Khans shared with the other officers the food they had brought with themselves, and the common soldiers found nothing to eat except the water of the tank; grass and gram for the elephants and horses were nowhere. As the night closed, the enemy completely encircled them. The imperialists stood to arms ready to meet any attack. But for three days the Marathas only appeared in sight without fighting, till some thousands of infantry sent by the zamindar of Chittaldurg—who had been reduced to humility by Qasim Khan—seized the opportunity and made an attack. On the fourth day, before sunrise, ten times the former number of *Kala-piadas* darkened the plain and began to fight. The imperial artillery munitions had been plundered in their camp and what little was carried with the soldiers was now exhausted; so after vain exertions for some hours, they sat down in despair. The enemy's hail of bullets destroyed many men in this situation."* Fully one-third of the Mughal army had been slain at the two camps, during the retreat, and on the banks of the tank of Dodderi. Then the chiefs decided to save their own lives by sneaking into the fort, and a disgraceful scene ensued which is thus described by Khafi Khan (ii. 331):—

* This is the contemporary record compiled from State papers like despatches and newsletters, (*M.A.* 375-377). But more than 30 years later, Khafi Khan (ii. 429), gave the following different and seemingly inaccurate account:—

"A party of the enemy fell upon Qasim Khan's tents......and

"In this extremity of distress, Qasim, Khanazad and Saf Shikan, who had dismounted close to one another, secretly planned to enter into the *garhi* without informing Muhammad Murad and other comrades who were at a distance. They began to send within such stores as were left after the enemy's plunder, pretending to lighten themselves for fighting. The first night Qasim Khan, on the pretext of patrolling, left his post and entered the fort by scaling the wall with ropes, as it was not advisable to enter by the gate owing to the crowd assembled there (outside). Then Khanazad and Saf Shikan entered by the gate by charging the crowd of common soldiers round it. Lastly Muhammad Murad and other officers, learning of it, came in with the greatest difficulty. Saf Shikan,

10 to 12 thousand horsemen attacked the baggage of Khanazad...... 7 or 8 thousand more appeared between the two Khans, so that neither could reinforce the other. The battle raged till sunset.... All night the chiefs remained on their elephants and the soldiers holding the bridles of their horses, to repel night-attacks. At dawn the Marathas renewed their attack......in this way the imperialists were attacked for 3 days, at last (on the *fourth* day) they marched fighting all the way and took refuge under the *garhi* of Dodderi. For these three days they had no food. In the same way 3 or 4 *more* days were passed, the imperialists entrenching and repelling charges under shelter of the walls of the *garhi* day and night, while their camels, horses and oxen were carried off by the Marathas. As the gates of the *garhi*......had been closed upon them, the grocers of the *garhi* threw down to them grain from the top of the wall, charging one or two rupees per *seer*. On the 4th or 5th day (*i.e.*, the 7th or 8th day after the first battle) the two Khans decided to enter the *garhi*."

turning to Muhammad Murad, cried out—'How gallantly we have brought ourselves here!' Murad's nephew retorted—'Shame on the type of valour you have shown in coming here, of which you are bragging!'"

The Marathas besieged the fort* on all sides, being confident that hunger would destroy its defenders. On the day of entering the fort, the soldiers, high and low, were all given bread of millet (*jawari* and *bajra*) from the local stores, while the transport cattle fed on the old and new straw-thatching pulled down from the roofs of the houses. On the second day no food was left for either man or beast. Many of the cattle of the army had been carried away by the Marathas, many others had perished from hunger,—"They chewed one another's tails, mistaking them for straw," as the graphic exaggeration of a Persian writer well describes it;—and the remaining oxen 'lean like the ass's tail,' were now eaten up by the Muslim soldiery. Then they faced utter starvation. Qasim Khan was a great eater of opium, his life depended on the drug, and the lack of it caused his death on the third day. (*M. A.*, 378; but many suspected that he had committed suicide to escape disgrace by the enemy and the censure of the Emperor.) Of the common soldiers, many in the agony of hunger leaped down from the fort walls and sought refuge in the enemy's camp, who took away the money they had concealed in their belts. The traders of Shanta's camp-bazar used to come below the wall of

* They overthrew one tower of it and attacked all sides. (*M.A.* 378.)

the fort and sell fruits and sweets at fancy prices to the starving Mughals on the top, who threw down money tied in rags and drew the food up by means of ropes. (*K.K.*)

When the food supply was absolutely exhausted and the water in the fort became scanty and unwholesome, Khanazad Khan, in despair of relief, sent his diwan and a Deccani captain of the imperial service to Shanta to beg for terms of capitulation.

Shanta at first demanded a lakh of *hun* besides the elephants, horses and property of the imperial army. But the treacherous Deccani captain whispered to him, "What is this that you are asking for? Raise your terms. This amount will be paid by Khanazad Khan alone as his ransom." At last the ransom was fixed at 20 lakhs of Rupees; and all the cash, articles, jewels, horses, and elephants of the doomed army were to be given up, each general being allowed to go away on a single horse with the clothes he wore on his person. The generals individually signed bonds for their respective ransoms and each left a kinsman or chief servant as security for its payment. The terms were faithfully kept on the Maratha side, thanks to Shanta's iron discipline. (*K.K.* corrected by *M.A.*)

Shantaji sent word that the men might come out of the fort without any fear and stay for two nights in front of its gate; those who had any money need fear no extortion but might buy their necessaries from the Maratha camp. The lean woe-begone and bedraggled remnant of the imperial army filed out of the fort after the 13th day. The enemy gave them bread from one side and water from the other. Thus they were nursed back to life and strength in two days. On the third day Khanazad started for the Court with a Maratha escort. He had lost everything, but the other imperial officers on the way supplied him and his men with horses, tents, dress, food and money to relieve their urgent distress. (*M. A.* 378, *K.K.* 433.)

Meantime, the Emperor who was then at Brahmapuri, 280 miles north of the scene of the disaster, on hearing of the danger to Qasim Khan, had sent Hamid-ud-din Khan from his side and Rustam-dil Khan from Haidarabad to support him. They had united near Adoni, but in time only to receive and help Khanazad on his return. Here Khanazad's army was reclothed and newly furnished with the gifts and forced contributions from the officers and residents of Adoni. (*M. A.* 379, but *Akhbarat*, year 39. sh. 72 differs.)

In less than a month from this, Shanta achieved another equally famous victory. Himmat Khan Bahadur, who had been deputed to co-operate with Qasim Khan, had taken refuge in Basavapatan (40 miles west of Dodderi) on account of the smallness of his force, not more than one thousand cavalry, though he had received the impossible order to go out and punish Shanta. (*M. A.* 379.)

After the fall of Dodderi, Shanta had established his

own garrison there and told off two forces to watch and oppose Hamid-ud-din (in the north) and Himmat Khan (in the west). On 20th January he appeared before Himmat Khan's position at the head of ten thousand cavalry and nearly the same number of infantry. His Karnataki foot-musketeers—the best marksmen in the Deccan, took post on a hill. Himmat Khan, with a very small force, advanced to the attack and dislodged them from it, slaying 500 of them. Then he drove his elephant towards the place where Shanta was standing, when suddenly he was shot by a bullet in the forehead and fell down unconscious into the *hauda*. His driver wanted to turn the elephant back, but the Captain of his contingent (*jamadar*), Ali Baqi, told the driver—'The Khan is alive. Urge the elephant onward. I shall drive the enemy back.' But he, too, was wounded, thrown down to the ground and carried off by the enemy. Then his son fell fighting. Shanta received two arrow-wounds. The leaderless imperialists fell back to their trenches. At midnight Himmat Khan breathed his last. Three hundred of his men were dispersed and fled to various places. The rest held their fortified enclosure successfully for some days, after which the Marathas withdrew from its siege and went away with the captured baggage of the Khan.*

* This narrative is based upon the despatch received by the Emperor on 2nd February and included in the *Akhbarat* of the next day, with some additions from *M. A.* The rest of *M. A.* and the whole of Khafi Khan (gossipy fabrication) have been rejected by me. Khafi Khan writes (ii. 433-434): Shanta, on hearing of the near approach of Himmat Khan, formed his army in two divisions

Flushed with these far-resounding victories, Shantaji went to Jinji to wait on Rajaram (March 1696). He seems to have claimed the office of Senapati, contrasting his own brilliant performances with Dhanaji's poor record of victories. Hitherto Prahlad Niraji (the Pratinidhi or regent) had, with great tact and diplomacy, kept peace between the two rival generals and taken great pains to show in all the acts of Government that the king treated the two as absolutely equal. But he was now dead, and his successor in the king's council was less clever and could not keep the balance even. (Sardesai, i. 661.) Shanta's vanity, imperious temper and spirit of insubordination, roused to an inordinate height by his recent triumphs, gave great offence to the Court at Jinji and the result was an open rupture near Conjeveram (May 1696). Rajaram sided with Dhanaji and placing Amrit Rao Nimbalkar in the van of his army, attacked his offending general. But Shanta's military genius again triumphed; Dhana was defeated and driven precipitately to his home in Western India; Amrit Rao fell on the field. (*Jedhe*. But *K. K.* and *Dil.* wrongly give the victory to Dhana.)

---

and hastened by two routes to meet Himmat Khan. At a distance of 32 miles Himmat Khan encountered the first of these divisions (led by Shanta). Severe battle; many slain on both sides, Marathas fleeing drew Himmat Khan's army near their second division. Shanta had posted crack marksmen in dense jungles at various places across the path of Himmat Khan. The latter was shot through the forehead by a *Kalia* musketeer from a tree top. All his baggage, elephants and stores were looted.

This victory is thus graphically described in *Masir-i-Alamgiri*, which wrongly places it in October 1689:—"On the way to Jinji, this wretch had a fight with Dhana Jadav, who was escorting Rajaram there, on account of an old quarrel. Shanta triumphed, and caused Amrit Rao, the brother (-in-law) of Nagoji, the comrade and assistant of Dhana, to be crushed to death by an elephant. He also captured Rajaram, but Dhana escaped. The next day Shanta appeared before Rajaram with his wrists bound together, saying—' I am the same loyal servant (as before). My rudeness was due to this that you wanted to make Dhana my equal and to reach Jinji with his help. I shall now do whatever you bid me.' Then he released and conducted Rajaram to Jinji." (401.)*

Of Shanta's doings in the Eastern Karnatak this year we have full information from the English factory-records of Madras and the Persian memoirs of Bhimsen. On his arrival at the head of 15,000 horse, Maratha bands spread into several parts of the country, the Mughal army with its reduced numbers was powerless to defend its many outposts, and Zulfiqar Khan was forced to hold himself in the defensive in the fort of Arcot, after repelling one attack of Shanta near Arni. Indeed, he made a secret understanding with the Marathas for mutal forbearance.

* Rajwade, XV. 45, is a letter styling Shanta *Senapati* in June 1695; but I cannot accept this date in defiance of the *Jedhe Chronicle*, which says (as I interpret it) that Dhan was given that title in May 1693. Shanta's outbreak in May 1696 ended in his victory and Rajaram could not have ventured to disgrace him *then*.

In November it was reported that treasure for the Mughal army sent from the Court had reached Kadapa. Shantaji immediately marched to that side to intercept it. Zulfiqar set out after him to defend the convoy; but hearing that Shanta had changed his plans, the Mughal general fell back on Arcot after making three marches only. Shantaji entered the uplands of Central Mysore and returned home, Zulfiqar marching to Penukonda (75 miles north of Bangalore) to join Prince Bidar Bakht.

In the Maratha homeland an internecine war now raged between Dhana and Shanta, all other captains being ranged on the two sides. They fought together in the Satara district in March 1697. But fortune at last deserted Shantaji; his severity and insolence had disgusted his officers and most of them were secretly corrupted by the agents of Dhana. Hanumant Rao Nimbalkar, in concert with Dhana's troops, fell on Shanta's baggage train, and most of the latter's officers deserted to Dhanaji, while the rest were killed or wounded. Shantaji, despoiled of all and deserted by his army, fled from the field with only a few followers to Mhaswad, the home of Nagoji Mane whose wife's brother Amrit Rao he had killed. With Nagoji, however, the sacred rights of hospitality to a refugee rose higher than the claims of blood-feud; he gave Shanta shelter and food for some days, and then dismissed him in safety. But his wife Radha Bai followed her brother's murderer with a woman's unquenchable vindictiveness. She had urged her husband to slay their guest, but in vain. And now when she saw him escaping unscathed, she sent her surviving brother after him. One of the many diverse accounts* of his death (given by Khafi Khan) is that the pursuer (wrongly called Nagoji Mane by both Khafi Khan and *Jedhe*) came upon Shantaji when, exhausted by fast travel, he was bathing in a *nala* near the Shambhu Mahadev hill, in the Satara district. The party from Mhaswad surprised him in this helpless situation and cut off his head. "Mane (*i.e.*, Nimbalkar) threw it into the saddlebag fastened behind his horse....On the way the bag got loose and fell down. Firuz Jang's spies, who had spread in that hilly region, in pursuit of Shanta, picked it up, recognised it as that general's head, and sent it to Firuz Jang, who sent it to the Emperor. The severed head was paraded through the imperial encampment and some cities of the Deccan." (*M.A.* 401-402, *K. K.* 447-448, *Dilkasha* 122*a*.) The date of his death is given in the *Jedhe Chronicle* as *Asharh* 1619 *Shaka*, or June, 1697. Bhimsen places it (without date) *before* the fall of Jinji in January, 1698. But the *Masir-i-Alamgiri* records it (without stating the day or even month) at the conclusion of the events of the 42nd year of Aurangzib's reign (3rd March 1698—20th February 1699), but I have

* Admittedly diverse and conflicting, according to *M.A.* 402, which omits all of them. The Mane family "old paper" printed in Parasnis's *Itihas Sangraha*, *Junya Aitihasik Goshti*, ii. 45, is so palpably incorrect as to suggest an opium-eater's tale. Khafi Khan after giving the account followed above, adds, "There is another story current (about his end). God alone knows the truth," (ii. 448).

not found all the dates of this work unimpeachable. Khafi Khan places it in the 39th year (5th April 1695—24th March 1696); but his chronology is palpably confused.

Thus died Shantaji Ghorpare most ignominiously at the end of a most dazzling military career, like Charles X of Sweden. But his greatest monument is the abject fear he inspired in all ranks of the Mughal army *, which is faithfully reflected in the curses and abuses invariably used as epithets to his name in the Persian histories.

The two life-long rivals, Shanta and Dhana were both army leaders and organisers of the highest ability, courage and activity, but with contrasted characters. Dhana Jadav made war like a gentleman; he knew that the fickle goddess of Fortune might desert him in the field any day; therefore, he never went to an extreme. He was moderate in victory, generous to the vanquished, polite in his address, practised in self-control, and capable of taking long views and making statesmanly settlements. His inborn courtesy to the Mughal generals who had the misfortune to encounter him, is noticed with praise by the Muslim historians. Moreover, he served his country's Government unselfishly for many years.

---

* "When the news arrived that Shanta had come within 16 or 18 miles of him, Firuz Jang (Aurangzib's highest general) lost colour in terror, and making a false announcement that he would ride out to oppose him, appointed officers to clear the path, sent his advanced tents onward, but then fled towards Bijapur by a roundabout path"! (K. K. ii. 446).

Shantaji Ghorpare, on the other hand, was in comparison with Dhana, a barbarian devoid of culture or generosity, unable to restrain his passions or to take thought of the distant future. He loved to hustle all whom he met with, not excepting his king. The hour of his victory was the hour of the gratification of his vindictiveness. He showed no mercy and expected none. Therefore, he excited among the Mughal generals, as well as his Maratha adversaries, a feeling of mingled terror and repulsion. By his temperament, Shanta was incapable of co-operating with others and he had not the patriotism to subordinate his own will to the needs of his nation. He lived and died merely as a most successful raid-leader and selfish adventurer, and exercised no influence on the political history of the Marathas, or even on the general effect of Aurangzib's campaigns. He flashed through the Deccan sky like a lonely meteor without ever having a companion or ally, or even sharing the counsels of his nation's leaders, among whom he might have naturally claimed a place.

AURANGZIB'S REMAINING LETTERS.

AURANGZIB TO PARSHURAM TRIMBAK

31 October, 1699.

Trimbak, commandant of the fort of Panhala, be hopeful and know that my army is now marching to conquer the forts in the possession of the miserable (Raja-) Ram, and to extirpate him. In a few days the imperial camp will be pitched at Murtazabad (Miraj) and, through God's power all the forts and places belonging to that wretch will be conquered and annexed to the imperial dominions. The luckless Rajaram, like his brother now in hell (*i.e.*, the deceased Shambhuji) will be captured by the holy warriors of Islam and quickly put to death.

As the men of some (Maratha) forts are inclined to the imperial side, if you, according to my former letter, be led by good fortune to yield the fort to my servants, you will, God willing, be exalted with the gift of a high rank and other kingly favours. Otherwise, through the power of the All-powerful, the fort will be quickly conquered, and you will see what you will see: you will be imprisoned and executed along with all your women and children and all members of your family, old and young. Written on the 17th Jamadi-ul-awwal, in the 43rd year of my reign (31 October, 1699 A.D.)

AURANGZIB TO RAMCHANDRA PANT BAURIKAR

31 October, 1699.

Ramchandra, hope and know that the letter, which at this auspicious time you have been guided by foresight and good fortune to write to my general Tarbiyat Khan, has been placed before me, and all your demands have been accepted. I, (therefore,) now issue the order that you should be firm and constant in the straight path of good faith and fidelity, quickly perform what you have written, and abandon that wretched vagabond (Rajaram, the second son of Shivaji). If a few moments of the evanescent life of that doomed man be yet left over, and that slaughter-worthy man should desire to flee anywhere (else) in fear of the imperial troops, it is fitting that you should present all his forts to the imperial Court as your tribute. After you have, under the guidance of your good star, done either of these two acts, you will (God willing) be honoured with excellent favours and many splendid gifts, and be exalted high above your peers, and raise your head in trust and glory. If (however) through ill-luck you do not distinguish between benefit and harm, and your letter be (a mere collection of) words void of truth, then the vanquished infidel (Rajaram),—who knows that he has given (me) great offence and done improper acts,—will (God willing) be soon captured in the claws of the holy warriors of Islam and executed like his brother in hell (*i.e.*, the deceased Shambhuji). And, through God's power, you, too will see (what you will see); losing your house and life, you will be imprisoned and slain with your women and children and all members of your family, great and small. Dated the 17th Jamadi-ul-awwal, 43rd year of my reign (31 October, 1699 A.D.)

Notes

In the Persian ms. both letters are dated in the 46th year, which would amount to the 28th of September, 1702. This is clearly wrong, because in September 1702 Aurangzib was painfully toiling through the muddy roads and flooded rivers to effect his retreat to Bahadurgarh, and not, as these letters represent him, setting out on a victorious campaign. (*Masir-i-Alamgiri*, 467.) I have, therefore, emended the figure into the 43rd year.

After a four years' stay at Barhampuri (Islampuri), the Emperor Aurangzib set out in person, 19th October, 1699, to ravage the Maratha country and capture the Maratha forts. After 20 days' march he reached Miraj (*Masir-i-Alamgiri*, 408). At this time the above two letters were written by him inviting the two Maratha commanders to submit.

Ramchandra Pant Baurikar, was appointed commander of the Maratha forts with the title of *Hakumat-panah*, 1690, (*Duff*. i. 367). Parshuram Trimbak, a Brahman, rose from the humble rank of hereditary *Kulkarni* of Kinneye, acted very ably as the assistant to Ramchandra, surprised Panhala from the Mughals in 1692, was appointed *Pratinidhi* about 1704, and died in 1720 (*Duff*. i. 367, 396, 471). Rajaram, the second son of

Shivaji, succeeded Shambhuji on the throne, and died in March, 1700, (*Masir-i-Alamgiri*, p. 419 states that the news of his death reached Aurangzib in Maharashtra on the 5th March, 1700). Tarbiyat Khan was the *Mir Atish* or Head of the Artillery in Aurangzib's army. Grant Duff (i. 392) says that during the siege of Satara (8 December, 1699-21 April, 1700) Aurangzib wrote a letter to Ramchandra which fell into the hands of P. Trimbak. Was it the above letter?

AURANGZIB TO PARSHURAM TRIMBAK
27 May, 1702.

Parshuram, submissive to Islam, hope and know that, although your great offences do not deserve pardon, yet, ...inasmuch as the beloved Prince Muhammad Bidar Bakht Bahadur has reported to the Emperor that you have repented of your past sins and offered with all humility and submission to surrender the fort of Khelna (Vishalgarh) to the imperialists on condition that (1) the imperial army does not march to the conquest of your forts, but returns to the former (Mughal) territory, (2) you are assured of the pardon of your faults and the sparing of your own and your companions' lives, by the issue of an imperial *farman* (order), and (3) you are honoured by the acceptance of your requests stated in writing to the Prince,......

Therefore, at the request of the Prince, the gracious Emperor issues this order that when you wait (on the Prince) and surrender the fort of Khelna, your offences will be pardoned, you and your comrades will be spared your lives, and the imperial army will not march towards you to conquer your forts and country, but will (God willing) march back to the old imperial dominion after taking possession of Khelna. You should soon deliver Khelna to the imperial officers and leave the fort with your comrades in peace of mind, remain firm and true to your promises, and regard it as very necessary to avoid doing the contrary. Written on the 11th Muharram, 46th year of the reign, (27th May, 1702 A.D.).

Note.—On 7th November, 1701, Aurangzib started from Wardhan-garh to besiege Khelna (Vishalgarh), which he reached on 6th December. After a long siege, the fort was surrendered by Parshuram Trimbak, whose terms were acceped by the Emperor at the intercession of Prince Bidar Bakht, the eldest son of Azam (the 3rd son of the Emperor), on 7th June, 1702. (*Masir-i-Alamgiri*, 448-457).

XIV

THE HISTORIAN RAJWADE

HIS PLACE AMONG MARATHA HISTORIANS

Though he had been dead to history for the last eight years and had made Vedic philology and Aryan prehistory the sole pursuits of the evening of his life,—the news of the actual passing away of Vishwanath Kashinath Rajwade on the 31st of December, 1926, came as a painful shock to all who really knew and cared for Indian historical studies. The greatest discoverer, the lifelong searcher, the exclusive devotee without a second love, the most fruitful collector of the raw materials of Maratha history,—and at the same time their most painstaking (if occasionally inexact or perverse) editor, and their most speedy and prolific publisher,—has been lost to us for ever. Time may bring forth others to carry on his work; but they will be merely a tamer race of the after-born, scanty gleaners after his copious harvest; not one of them will devote,—as Rajwade devoted—all thoughts, all passions, all interests of a long mateless professionless life to the ceaseless exploration of all possible and impossible "find-spots" of historical records, amidst hopelessly defective means of transport, discomfort, privation and lack of helpers, in the teeth of ignorant suspicion and hostility, neglect and inertia from a local public whom he had to humour, coax, educate, and when necessary delude. But his life's mission was achieved: he alone revolutionised historical methodology in the Deccan and—by that example—in other parts of India as well.

Rajwade was a penniless collector,—slighted by the rich whose scorn he flung back in double measure in the spirit of a Diogenes,—suspected and (as he fancied) hampered by the instruments of law and order against whom he railed without bound, without season, like a man possessed. But his actual performance, in spite of the severe handicaps of his poverty, temper and environment, was wonderful. He was our pioneer *par excellence.* He not only blazed the trail for us, but he was also the most daring, the most indefatigable, the most extensive and continuous digger in our historical "reams of gold."

True, K. N. Sane had got possession of a bundle of Marathi historical letters and V. V. Kharo had set himself to examine the old Patwardhan sardars' archives earlier and had actually begun the publication of their records some years before Rajwade sent his first volume of State papers to the press. But the former two had found their materials ready to hand and could do their copying and editing comfortably at home. Rajwade, unlike these, was the adventurous explorer. He was the true "wandering scholar," the typical Brahman mendicant-pilgrim (vowed, however, solely to Saraswati) roaming all over the land year after year in quest of every obscure shrine and sanctuary of his adored Goddess of History. Every scrap of old paper he found was a sacred relic to him in his careful handling and meticulous annotation of it.

In his passion to save and publish the raw materials of his country's history he disregarded the laws of ownership —the unnatural ownership of the ignorant and the unworthy. He often carried on his own shoulders the bundles of historical papers that he could beg borrow or steal, (or more correctly wheedle out of ignorant villagers),—and deposited them in secret refuges selected by him. These places were never made known to the public, and they cannot be learnt from his friends,—because that eager, uncompromising, solitary spirit had no friend, at least not for long. He had, after a time, parted company with every body who had befriended him; his collaboration with other Marathi historical workers had been broken off by his acrid criticism of them in public. But no such devoted explorer, collector and editor of mss. has been known since the days of the Renaissance in Europe. His finds were, no doubt, more modern, their world-value far less; but the difficulties he had to surmount were incomparably greater.

Education and Early Aims

Vishwanath, the son of Kashinath Rajwade, was born at Vadgaon (some 20 miles north-west of Poona) on 12th July 1864. He has given a graphic account of his school-life, with a rather lurid picture of the condition of private schools in Poona in those days, in an autobiographical paper of his *Sankirna Lekh Sangraha*. At the age of twelve (1876) he began to learn English, but left school after only four years, and finally returned to his village home, whence he passed the Matriculation examination (January 1882) as a private candidate. His college career was equally interrupted and unduly prolonged, not for any intellectual deficiency but for his financial difficulties and his wayward and reckless temperament. The story of his school and college education as given by himself in an autobiographical sketch, well illustrates the inconstancy, lack of discipline and wayward manner in which many modern Indians are brought up in the formative stage of their lives. Rajwade's inborn genius alone saved him from the pernicious effects of such a course, and enabled him to rise to greatness though it left some flaws in his temper and character.

He entered a vernacular Marathi school at the age of eight at a petty village and then removed to Poona. After 18 months' attendance, the boy spent the next 18 months at home playing, fighting and enjoying sights. No wonder he wrote later, "What I learnt in these three years I could have mastered in six months had I been placed under the care of a good teacher, and 2½ years of my life could have been saved." In 1876 his family put him in an English school—that of Baba Gokhle at Poona. But he soon afterwards went over to a rival school newly started by Kashinath Natu (a lawyer!), who lured away many boys from Gokhle's school. After three months here he was induced to transfer himself to a third and still newer school, started by Vaman Rao Bhave and Lakshman Rao Indapurkar, and here he was given rapid promotion in the middle of terms in reward of his desertion! In 1880, after three years at Bhave's, he left it to join Rev. Mr. Beaumont's mission school, but for two months only. Then he returned to his village home and in January 1882 passed the Matriculation examination as a private or non-academic candidate.

His college life was equally desultory and nomadic. He kept the first term at the Elphinstone College, Bombay (1882), but did not keep the second for financial and other reasons. He joined the Deccan College in Poona in June 1884, completed the second term and next year passed the Preliminary Intermediate examination (in the second division.) Then followed one year of voluntary rusticity at home. In 1886-87 he joined college again, but kept away from the normal examination at the end of the term, and at the close of the year 1887 left college, however, passing the First (or Preliminary) B.A. next year as a non-collegiate. After spending one year (1889) at Bhave's school in learning Botany, he went to the Deccan College again in 1890, and from here in January 1891 he took his Final B. A. degree, thus spending nine years in finishing a course that normally requires three years only. But the time had not been misspent. He read extensively and attentively in the Deccan College (Poona) library, and in addition studied Botany at Bhave's school for a year and a variety of additional subjects which were not strictly required for securing the B. A. degree.

At College he scorned delights and lived laborious days. He used to row five to seven miles on the river every evening, and by plain living and gymnastics acquired excellent health and staying power. As he tells us, "In the seven years from 1884 to 1890, I was not ill for a single day."

In his student days, though he neglected to prepare for his examinations, his favourite studies embraced practically every branch of knowledge on which books were available there,—European history, economics, ethics, politics, theology, logic, mental philosophy, all old and new, original and translated works. In addition he acquired an elementary knowledge of Persian and French.

Rajwade had been married young, but he lost his wife when he was only 25, and never married again, though a year or two before his death he vainly searched for a new helpmate to smooth the last days of his life.*

At first he took to teachership as a profession, but it was for three years only. Next with a friend he started a monthly magazine named *Bhashantar* ('Translation') in 1895, in which he began to publish his Marathi

*This statement was questioned by some admirers of Rajwade when my sketch of his life was published in 1927, but I have had it confirmed by the "Swamy" or *Yogi* whose advice he had sought on the question of marrying a widow in old age. Such a marriage would at least have given him an obedient cleanly cook. A Marathi novel then published about a lonely old scholar falling in love with a rustic beauty of the Gondwana forests, though it was popularly believed to refer to Rajwade, is pure fiction.

renderings of Plato's *Republic* and Montesquieu's *Esprit de Lois.* The venture perished in a short time in a fire which destroyed the press and all its materials. Freed from worldly ties by his wife's death, freed from business concerns by the fire in the press, Rajwade now devoted himself, in the spirit of a true *sannyasi*, to his life's work, the reconstruction of his race's history on an enduring basis. As early as 1888 he had first conceived the idea of correcting the "thousands of errors" in Captain Grant Duff's *History of the Mahrattas* (published in 1826) by research among original materials. To this task he was inspired by reading the original historical letters printed in the series called *Kavy-etihas-Sangraha*, and to this task he consecrated his remaining days.

In his college days, like most other Indian students he wrote his letters to friends in English and conversed in the usual mixture of English and Marathi; but in later life he decided to eschew the foreign language and use Marathi exclusively in speech and writing.

This change was due to the influence of Vishnu Krishna Chiplunkar's vernacular essays. He adds in his autobiographical fragment, "The historical letters in *Kavy-etihas-Sangraha* informed me that there is such a thing as my fatherland (*swadesh*) and the poems printed by Parashuram Tatya Godbole increased my admiration for Marathi litera ture."

When I first met Rajwade, in 1908, he urged me to write in my mother-tongue (Bengali) and not in English.

A mutual friend, himself a Deccani Brahman, asked Rajwade "If Sarkar had written in Bengali could you have read his histories, or even known his name ?" There was no answer.

He revolutionised the Historical Method in Marathi

The older generation of Maratha scholars like Dr. Bhalchandra and Justice Ranade had put their faith in unauthentic chronicles, formal histories, and later narratives. Rajwade, with an impatience and contempt which he cared not to conceal —pointed out that original contemporary documents, or State papers proper, were the only reliable materials of history. Even before the close of the 19th century he had been seized with the passion for *documents inedites* which began to rage in France and England a decade later. His third volume of historical letters (published in 1901) bore as the motto on its title-page the Sanskrit warning 'Write nothing without authority' and elsewhere he quoted the saying of Lamartine "No document, no history." It should be remembered that even Lord Acton in his lectures on the French Revolution speaks rather disparagingly of unprinted sources, among which a later scholar, Dr. Holland Rose, has worked with such striking success.

His college life, ill-spent from the point of view of the ordinary degree-seeking student, had admirably equipped him for this task both in body and mind. He constantly travelled throughout India from Rawalpindi to Cape Comorin and from Karachi to Benares. In Maharashtra he visited almost every village, walking on foot,—partly from poverty and partly from an obstinate desire* not to enrich the British by patronising their railways! He was not troubled by the need of carrying any baggage or money. At college he used to enjoy a sound sleep on two tables placed together with only a horse blanket thrown over them; and during his village tours he received free meals as a poor Brahman pilgrim. Indeed, with a grim humour, he once entered his profession in the Census return as "mendicancy"!

His quest yielded immediate and striking results. His first volume of historical letters, published in 1898, with its long, careful and learned introduction, at once established his fame as the foremost historical worker in Maharashtra. This volume started the series of *Original Materials for the History of the Marathas* (*Marathanchi Itihasanche Sadhanen*) of which there were to come forth twenty-one more before his death. It contained 304 historical letters, ranging in date from 1750 to November 1761, or eight months after Panipat, and is an invaluable source for the history of that fatal battle and the events leading up to it, as seen from the Maratha camps and Courts.

*This was, I believe, an invention of his witty friends. We can know the country and the people only by walking on foot and not by whisking through a province in an express train or a motor car. Even cheap public buses (unknown in his days) are more democratic, as I have found in my many tours in Maharashtra.

His Corpus of Original Historical Documents

On historical records, Rajwade's firm conviction was that it is the duty of their present owners to publish them, or if they are unable to do it themselves, to give every help in their power to some scholar to perform that task. This view he often expressed with a brusqueness and ferocity that startled the sleeping mediæval society around him. For instance, he inveighed thus against the Patwardhan *sardars* of Miraj and Kurundwad: "These Patwardhans have given no [financial] help to V. V. Khare who is editing and publishing their great ancestors' records. They are now enjoying those ancestors' *jagirs*. Khare is the true heir to those ancestors and has a greater moral right to their estates than the present *sardars* of the family." Again, when about to leave a village in disappointment, he turned fiercely upon the rustic owner of a bundle of historical letters who had refused to let him copy them, and cried out, "These papers are of no use to you, but important for my purpose. Give them to me.... You refuse! Well, I shall get them from your widow when she offers them for sale to some dry grocer as waste paper!" It would be pleasing to imagine that the churl was at last frightened by an irate Brahman's curse into delivering the papers to him.

Rajwade had rescued a bundle of waste paper from a dry grocer's shop at Paithan; it yielded 23 of these precious letters (in the original), 24 more were supplied by Vasudev Vaman Khare, a poor schoolmaster of Miraj,

75 by Govind Rao Bhanu of Wai, and 183 by Mr. Yerande, whose ancestor had served in Bundelkhand and the Doab in the Panipat period. These last, along with 517 other papers, had been kept in a cane basketbox in the lumber room of their family mansion at Wai in peace and neglect for over a century till April 1897, when Rajwade opened them.

The introduction to the volume covers 127 printed pages, and is full of varied information, restrained in tone, and free from verbosity. It strikes me as the best introduction he ever wrote, as it avoids the irrelevant prolixity which became a besetting sin with him in later years, when his introductions exceeded his texts in length and rambled over every conceivable subject under the moon.

But neither this volume nor any of its successors was a financial success. On the first volume he incurred a loss of Rs. 1,400 (a part of which was due to a fire). Friends of learning, like the Chiefs of Miraj and Inchal-Karanji, gave some help. Prof. Bijapurkar printed five of the subsequent volumes at his own expense at a cost of Rs. 2,100, and gave the author 50 copies of each, on the sale of which Rajwade lived! Thus, he got only Rs. 600 out of these books, as he tells us in the preface to his sixth volume. During his travels in search of historical papers up to 1905 Rajwade piled up a debt of Rs. 600, though he lived like a hermit. But the work went on. It is the most heartening example in our own days of the triumph of the human spirit and true devotion over every obstacle on earth. The *sannyasi's* austerities did win for him the attainment of his soul's quest, in spite of the world the devil and the flesh!

Rajwade's literary output forms 22 volumes of materials (*sadhanen*), six volumes of other historical works, and six volumes of miscellaneous papers. There was hardly an issue of the annual *Comple Rendu* and *Conference Report* of the Poona Itihas Mandal that was not enriched with his learned and informing papers.

Later in life, Rajwade left the Poona Itihas Mandal which he had helped to found in 1909,—he could not long agree with anybody—and joined the Ramdasi sect at Dhulia. His later writings and discoveries mostly appeared in the two monthlies *Itihas ani Aitihasik* and *Ramdasi*. His latest undertaking, left incomplete at his death, was a gigantic dictionary of the verb-roots in the Marathi language of which he collected about 20,000 examples. We may pass over his philological studies and excursions into the history of ancient Aryan culture, colonisation and ethnology as fanciful or hypercritical, like Tilak's ventures into the same field.

Apart from the peculiarities of his temper, "Rajwade was a very difficult person to satisfy with regard to food. He insisted on strict cleanliness,—(by which Dr. Ketkar probably means ritual purity and untouchability.) He had such fastidiousness regarding cleanliness that few families could achieve the standard. To the great annoyance of his hosts, he several times left their houses on the ground of uncleanliness." (Ketkar in the *Indian Herald*, Jan. 1927.) Thus, in his latter days, he had often to cook his meals with his own hands. After boiling the pots of rice and *dal* (lentil) he would pour them down on *two* banana leaves placed side by side (for he was a huge though simple vegetarian eater) and larding them with a copious supply of melted butter, consume the whole lot. His unwise dieting, in spite of his ceremonial cleanliness about cooking, at last deranged his bowels and sapped his splendid vitality. Two years before his death he began to feel that all was not well with him, and so he left Poona, where (he complained) he could not get proper food, and finally settled at Dhulia. Among the resolutions that he wrote down in youth was this one: "I will exact a hundred years of life from the god of Death." But alas! the gods willed it otherwise.

Nerves of a Literary Man

In search of a quiet rural retreat for his declining days, Rajwade left Poona and paid an unannounced visit to Kamshet, a small village on the Indrayani river, 29 miles north of Poona, early in June 1924. He had brought Rs. 500 in cash with himself and asked his host to build a tin shed for him *within three days*! In the afternoon a storm arose, followed by furious showers of rain and hail, the wind lashing the rain drops into the hut where the party was living. It was the first burst of the tropical monsoon. The wind threatened every moment to blow away the tin roof overhead. The storm abated towards the evening; but scorpions, crabs, and even snakes began to crawl in for shelter. Rajwade grew terribly afraid, huddled himself in a blanket in a corner on the floor and refused to eat his evening meal, appealing to his host to help him to escape in any possible way. Early next morning his host awoke at 5 o'clock, only to find that Rajwade had stolen away earlier, without informing him.

He then went away to Dhulia, in West Khandesh, where he was befriended by Shankar Shrikrishna Dev (a Ramdasi), Bhaskar Vaman Bhat and Govind Kashinath Chandorkar,—three lawyers, who built an outhouse for him, in which his books and papers were stored,

HIS POLITICAL OPINIONS AND INTERPRETATION OF NATIONAL HISTORY

In politics, Rajwade was typical of a certain section of the Chitpavan or Poona Brahmans. As his friend and admirer, Dr. S. V. Ketkar, writes :—

"Mr. Rajwade believed in the racial superiority of the Chitpavans (his own caste) and thus indulged in many controversies....He once told me that....he had taken the count of the first-rate men in India during the 19th century and mentioned among them the names of Nana Saheb [of Bithur] and Tatya Tope of the famous Indian Mutiny of 1857....He disbelieved that it is ever possible for Englishmen to do justice to India. The political duty of India is no other than to kick the British out of the land."

But there was a slight difficulty in carrying out this agreeable patriotic operation. The English are not only not kickable, but they are also very scientific. Rajwade had after all realised that "until the Indians became a *highly* scientific people they will *ever* remain slaves and subjects. ....The whole phenomenon of the disappearance of the Maratha Empire was simply the result of inferior science. European nations with their superior science were bound to capture India" (as he told Ketkar.)

This view is sound so far as it goes. But the ignoring of the moral factor in history that follows in the next sentence of his speech is pathetic in its simplicity when we remember Rajwade's age and education. He continues: " During the times of the last two Peshwas British India was regarded as more safe and therefore all the Maratha gold had already gone and settled in British territory prior to the Fourth Maratha War (1817); and the gold had gone there because the Englishmen had a gun with longer range and a more systematic judicial system....The Maratha Government....failed also in giving to its subjects the sufficient sense of protection by a systematic judicial system, the lack of which shows inferior *science* ".

Rajwade, with an insane hatred of modern Europe, could not realise, in spite of his omnivorous reading, that behind a modern European army there are years of self-control, hard training, exact co-ordination of individual effort, and the brain power of the General Staff,—that discipline is a moral product and not a matter of long-range guns,—that an honest law court implies something different from a knowledge of physical science or even of jurisprudence. To the gross venality of the Peshwas' officers, the debasing vices of the Peshwas' family, the selfish dissensions of their highest nobles and their lack of public spirit (not merely in the days of the last two Peshwas but even in Shivaji's time), the peculiar mentality of Rajwade made him blind.

He thus airily covers up the moral canker in the higher society of Maharashtra in the days of independence, —but I believe his view was based upon honest self-delusion: "Those who say that the Marathas destroyed themselves by dissensions forget that a people in whom a sense of inferiority has appeared and who are conscious of another and superior Power in their neighbourhood will always have dissensions. The neighbouring superior Power has always opportunities of creating dissensions." *Perfide Albion* once more and everywhere; yes, *we* are not to blame for our national downfall, but the hated English! An accomplished French philosopher and administrator, the Comte de Modave, who visited India in 1774-77 and died in the Deccan, has written,—"It is difficult to form an exact idea of the Government of the Marathas....By the ancient constitution the Government is monarchical, arbitrary and despotic,....but great changes have come upon it which have altered its outward form. The despotism is no longer in the hands of the king [the Chhatrapati]; it is in those of the hereditary Diwans [the Peshwas] who seized the authority in later times. Afterwards, the last revolutions having admitted the principal [military] chiefs to a share of that authority, it has followed that their power has been weakened at home [*i.e.*, Poona], without the General Estate of the Nation having gained thereby. Each great chief governs arbitrarily that portion of the affairs which he is in possession of, without rendering account to anybody. When these chiefs assemble at Poona for deliberating on the public affairs, bloody battles are waged among them,....so much so that one can say that the *Government of the Marathas is actually anarchical* when we consider it with reference to those who have seized it, and despotic in respect of all other subjects. They do not give themselves a Captain General by a majority of voices, as M. de Voltaire says. [But rather] the most powerful subdues or destroys the others, and his son succeeds him, if he has as much courage or cleverness as the former: otherwise a new civil war makes a new Captain General."

A perfectly true picture of the Peshwai after Panipat. But Rajwade could never see it.

The introductory essay of his very first volume illustrates his narrow caste prejudices. It is a sustained, but utterly unhistorical attempt, to find a scape-goat for the Chitpavan disaster at Panipat in the person of Govind Pant Bundele,—a Brahman of that Karhade section which the Chitpavan Brahmans hated and persecuted (sometimes even at Benares.) These caste squabbles, joined to his Maratha chauvinism, (*e. g.*, his claim that the annihilation of the Maratha army at Panipat proved a "great illusion" to the victorious Muslims), often vitiated his historical judgment and nullified his marvellous industry.

HIS LAST DAYS

Rajwade's Brahmanic pride, coupled with the vanity of authorship, at last drove him across the thin line which separates genius from madness. He hated the lower castes of Hindu society as unclean and ignorant beasts. On a public platform an attempt was made to hustle him for making some contemptuous remarks about the labouring classes. Once he was travelling in an evening train, when a party of workmen boarded the same third class compartment and he was disturbed by their loud talk and the overcrowding. Then he began to hold forth against the proletariat, crying out, "The English people complain of the white man's burden. But they have given democratic equality to this country, and it is *we* who have to bear the burden of the populace under British rule." Alas! the State-railways have made no provision for entire carriages being reserved for pure Chitpavan Brahmans (no admission for Karhades and Saraswats) by paying only single third class fares.

The intractable old man, soured by disappointment, was at last sheltered by three gentlemen at Dhulia (a town in West Khandesh) and tenderly cared for, like the opium-eater Samuel Taylor Coleridge in his old age. In his last illness he used to say, "If I had been born in Germany, I should have been lodged in the State hospital and the Education Minister would have visited me daily to inquire after my health. But here in India——." Just before his end, he sat up in his bed, cried out in English, "Gone! gone!" and then sank down into eternal peace. Thus, his last words were uttered in the language of the race that he hated with the insane fury of those Chitpavans who have misread their national history.

The wide synthetic power, the passionless superiority to time and place, the Olympic calm, the supreme common sense and the select and well-digested reading—I shall not say of a Gibbon—but even of many a second-rate European historian, were denied to Rajwade. And hence he lived and died a collector and could not compose a single history worthy of the name. His racial prepossessions, his fiery temperament, his lack of balanced judgment, and his indiscriminate uncritical reading unconsciously robbed him of intellectual honesty, and he was denied the historian's supreme gift of visualising the *truth* about past times, though he gained the applause of a certain class of narrow provincial (or rather caste) chauvinists, with whom past history is only the bondmaid of current politics of the stump orator brand. But, rest, perturbed spirit! rest. Others will reap where you could but sow.

Corrections.—The birth-place of Rajwade is Varsai, in the Kolaba district, not far from the Karjat railway station. The school where he learnt his alphabet was at Vadgaon; it was not the historical Vadgaon, 20 miles north-west of Poona, but one of the numberless petty hamlets bearing that name in this region. (*See* p. 247 above.) The first volume of his *Marathyanchya Itihasanchi Sadhanen* has some letters coming down to 1763 or two years after the battle of Panipat, (P. 253.) The Bharat Itihas Samsodhak Mandal was actually opened on 7th July 1910 (P. 256.) Rajwade did not himself enter the Ramdasi sect, but joined the body of workers at Dhulia who had undertaken research into the history and doctrines of that sect.

XV

KASHINATH NARAYAN SANE

It is said that when the old Emperor Wilhelm I and Prince Bismarck were standing bare-headed as mourners beside the unfilled grave of Von Moltke, one thought passed through the minds of both,—"Which of us will be the next?" Similarly, when the news of Rajwade's death on the last day of 1926 followed that of Parasnis in the preceding March, the thoughts of all who cared for Maratha history turned instinctively and silently to the venerable scholar whose tall taciturn and lonely figure until recently used to be seen walking the streets of Kalian every morning, though in his 76th year. The present writer made frequent inquiries about Sane's health from mutual friends in Bombay and was quite unprepared for the news that he had passed away on the 17th March 1927.

Kashinath Narayan Sane was born in a Chitpavan Brahman family in a village near Bassein in the Thana district of the Bombay Presidency, in 1851. After receiving his early education in that locality, he entered the Deccan College, Poona, from which he graduated in 1873. Soon afterwards he entered the Government education service, where his strenuous habits of work and love of strict discipline found favour with his superiors and led, in a few years, to his appointment as Principal of the Poona Training College, which he organised and developed with great energy and success. Then, for several years, he was Headmaster of the Government High Schools at Poona and Belgaum in succession. While he was at Belgaum the post of Educational Inspector, Southern Division, fell vacant and was given to Raoji Balaji Karandikar. Sane felt that his claims to this high office had been unjustly superseded; but his appeal was rejected by the authorities *, and Sane showed his sense of the injustice done to him by retiring on pension before his time.

Thereafter, he devoted himself entirely to the promotion of Marathi literature, especially history. A knowledge of the Marathi language was not demanded by the Bombay University in those days, and Hari Narayan Apte (the novelist) started a scheme for encouraging the study of their mother tongue among College students by granting some scholarships as the result of an examination in Marathi prose and poetry. Sane helped Apte in this good work by acting as honorary examiner for some years. He was on the executive committee of the Historical Society (*Mandal*) of Poona from its foundation (1910) and latterly its President. Government conferred on him the title of Rao Bahadur.

---

* A writer in the *Kesari* unjustly suggested that Government had got an inkling of Sane's strength of character and silent but blazing patriotism, and shelved him in that atmosphere of official excitement and suspicion against "Puna Brahmans."

Sane was at college with N. J. Kirtane (who was afterwards to print the *Chitnis Bakhar* of Shivaji) and Vishnu Krishna Chiplunkar, and imbibed a strong love of history which continued throughout his life. After leaving college he found that the only materials for Maratha history till then published were four or five instalments of the *Chitnis Bakhar* which had appeared in a general literary magazine named *Vividha-jnana-vistar*. He then began to think of bringing out a monthly paper to be specially devoted to the publication of old historical letters. Chiplunkar heard of the idea and urged that in the projected magazine, in addition to historical letters, old unpublished Sanskrit and Marathi poems ought to be included. After some discussion, the idea materialised; a monthly magazine named *Kavyetihas-Sangraha* came out in January 1878, the editors being Sane, Chiplunkar and Janardan Balaji Modak, who took charge respectively of the three sections, Marathi historical letters, Sanskrit poems and Marathi poems. The size was super-royal octavo, 48 pages a month,—sixteen pages being devoted to each section concurrently from month to month.

The magazine continued for eleven years. Chiplunkar retired at the end of the fourth year, but Modak carried it on to the end.

At the close of the first year the editors wrote: "Our undertaking has been greatly liked by those who read Marathi from Goa to Karachi and from Hubli-Dharwar to Gwalior and the Nizam's Dominions. We have received unexpected support from men of all classes,—from school masters on Rs. 10 a month to Rao Sahibs and Rao Bahadurs and rich merchants. True, the support has not been sufficiently liberal to enable us to conduct this work regularly and without anxiety. But it has filled us with the hope that it would increase."

Among the important helpers were 26 gentlemen at different centres, who secured old materials or carried on local investigations, sent old manuscripts or copied and annotated them for publication in the *Kavyetihas-Sangraha.* But delay in the payment of subscriptions led to delay in publication, till the number for December 1888 came out exactly twelve months later. Then the paper ceased to appear.

But the *Kavyetihas-Sangraha* could be proud of its achievement. In eleven years it had given to the world 6,300 pages, consisting of 22 historical works (great and small), 501 historical letters, petitions etc, 19 large Sanskrit books and 10 collections of Marathi poems. As the editor rightly boasts, "This work marked the revival of the national spirit in Maharashtra after the set back and despair following the disaster of 1817....A feeling of national pride was kindled. Everywhere there was awakened the desire to publish old historical works and letters".

Dr. Ramkrishna Gopal Bhandarkar, a very sober and fastidious critic, gave it high praise, saying that this magazine had been a revelation to him of how vast an amount of historical material lay unknown in Maharashtra.

So also Dadoba: "The *Kavyetihas Sangraha* has died, but its spirit liveth. As Ramdas said—True my body is gone away but I still exist in the world!" Its best title to fame was the long array of its children, *e.g.*, the *Kavyamala* series of Bombay (which printed Sanskrit mss. only), the *Bharatvarsha* magazine of Parasnis (two years 1896-1897), Khare's *Aitihasik Lekh Sangraha* (1896-1930, 14 vols.), Rajwade's *Marathyanchya Itihasanchin Sadhanen* (1898-1926, 22 vols.), Vad's *Peshwas' Diaries* (11 vols.), Parasnis's *Itihas Sangraha* (6 years), *Ramdas ani Ramdasi*, and *Itihas ani Aitihasik*, besides the publications of the Poona Mandal. *

Besides the collection of Marathi historical letters (*Patren Yadi waghaire*) which he published by instalments in the *Kavyetihas Sangraha*, Sane separately printed the *Sabhasad Bakhar of Shivaji* (which went into six editions in his lifetime), the *Chitnis Bakhar* (of which the volumes dealing with Shivaji's successors were issued by him for the first time, while of the Shivaji volume of Chitnis he brought out a richly annotated second edition in 1924), *Bhau Sahib's Bakhar* (three editions), the *Panipat Bakhar*, and Ramchandra Pant Amatya's *Rajniti*. While his editions of the Sabhasad and Chitnis *bakhars* are marked by minute accuracy in giving variations of reading and scrupulous fidelity to the original, he spoiled the *Bhau Sahib's Bakhar* by modernising and simplifying the text for the benefit of schoolboy readers! This is

---

* Pancham Sammelan Britta, pp. 133 *et seq.*

opposed to the canons of scholarship. A diary which he kept in his service days, describing the topography and remains of many old places all over Maharashtra, has been published anonymously in the *Vividha-jnan-vistar*.

In his character he was an example of the best type of Chitpavan Brahmans,—as G. K. Gokhale was. A stern disciplinarian, with a strong and independent character, he was very tidy and punctual in his habits, and gave in his own life a fine illustration of that orderliness, method and minute accuracy which he insisted on in others. In reading his works, as in conversation with him, one was impressed not by the depth of his scholarship, but by his admirable precision, methodical habits and strength of mind. Indeed, Sane's sanity was a pleasing surprise among modern Marathi writers on history.

His private life was what one would expect from such a character. His grown up and distinguished son, a vakil of the Bombay High Court, died of the terrible influenza epidemic which swept over the world just after the Great War. Sane's heart was made desolate, but his back was unbent. He kept up his regular habit of taking daily exercise by a morning walk. When, in 1924, I paid a visit to Kalian solely for the purpose of seeing him again, I found the old man returning on foot from the Durgadi side, a slim, vigorous, perfectly erect figure, who struck even a stranger as a commanding personality. Indeed, he reminded one most of the late Justice Sir Chandra Madhav Ghosh, whose aged thin but stiff and dignified form could be seen taking his customary walk on the *maidan* of Calcutta every morning almost to the day of his death.

The end was worthy of the man. Sane retained his mental powers to the last. In extreme age, he began to languish, but his brain remained as fresh as ever, and he was ready to examine and accept any new idea. When doctors forbade him to leave his room, he took his customary exercise on its floor. For the last fifteen days of his life he gradually grew weaker and weaker, and at last sank peacefully to rest in full consciousness, without pain and without repining, like a ripe fruit dropping from its stalk.

XVI

V. V. KHARE

Vasudev Vaman-Shastri Khare was born on 5th August, 1858, at the village of Guhagar, in the Ratnagiri district of Bombay. He belonged to a family of learned but poor and simple Brahman teachers of Sanskrit of the good old type which is now rapidly becoming extinct. Young Vasudev, however, did not take kindly to the ancestral way of life. Though naturally very intelligent and possessed of a keen memory, he disliked regular work and loved to roam about and play with the other truant boys of the village. At this time he lost his father, and the burden of supporting the entire family fell upon the shoulders of his aged grandfather, Mahadev Appa. The young man acquired a good command of his mother-tongue, read Marathi books extensively, and even wrote some poems and dramatic pieces to be staged by the local amateurs on festive occasions.

When reproved by his grandfather, young Vasudev used often to stay away from the house for days together and range the surrounding hilly country or lounge about the adjoining beach watching the waves of the Indian Ocean. A small incident now turned his career most opportunely. While playing naughty pranks at the Shimaga festival, he was caught with other village urchins and a housewife poured a volley of abuse on his revered grandfather for letting him run wild. This set him thinking, and the boy left his village, walked eighty miles over the hills to Kolhapur, and set himself, though penniless, to learn Sanskrit in that ancient capital. A Brahman student is often given free board and lodging by orthodox Hindu families that can afford it, and Khare eked out his living by composing Marathi verses, for which he had a natural genius. After returning home, he was married in 1873.

Goaded by the increased wants of his family, the young husband of fifteen, left his village for Satara, where he joined the home-school of the famous scholar Anant Acharya Gajendragad-kar and devoted himself to Sanskrit studies, earning his bread by writing for the local Marathi newspaper, the *Maharashtra Mitra*. In three years he mastered Sanskrit grammar, literature and logic. Next he migrated to Poona in search of work, and was taken into the New English School recently started. Bal Gangadhar Tilak, one of the founders of the school, became his friend for life, and in 1880 secured for Khare the post of Sanskrit teacher in the High School of Miraj.

It was at Miraj that Khare's life's work was done. Here he lived till death, serving the school on a monthly salary of Rs. 30, which rose to Rs. 45 after 32 years of service. One of his former pupils thus writes his impressions about him:

"As a teacher, his impressive personality and erudition at once commanded the respect of his students. His manner, though outwardly strict, was characterised by that milk of human kindness which is found typified in the Village Schoolmaster of Oliver Goldsmith's poem. The prescribed lesson, in Sanskrit or Marathi, was supplemented and diversified by his witty remarks, choice quotations and apt illustrations. He explained the famous poets with a natural zest. Very often the students glowed with enthusiasm caught from him or were convulsed with laughter at his comic sallies. Many of his old pupils are now well placed in life and they retain the highest esteem for their beloved *Shastriboa*, as he was lovingly called."

At the Miraj High School he keenly felt how his ignorance of English placed him on a lower footing than the other teachers. Kharc at once set himself to the task of learning this foreign tongue with his characteristic vigour and perseverance. Within one year he picked up so much knowledge of it that the Educational Inspector of Dharwar, who had found him entirely innocent of English at his previous annual visit, was surprised to see him using English correctly and freely next year. Khare kept up his English studies and widened his mental outlook by reading a number of works on history and literature in that language.

To the Maratha public he was best known as a poet and dramatist of rare power. He broke away from the conventions of the old school of poets, by choosing new themes, such as the ocean, patriotism, &c., and using blank verse. All his poetical works were popular, especially *Samudra, Yashawant Rao Mahakavya* (epic), *Phutkal Chutke* (stray poems, 1881-1888),—the second of which is now a text-book for the B. A. students of the Bombay University.

Vasudev Vaman Khare's dramas brought him fame and some amount of money. *Gunotkarsha* (1880), which brings the great Shivaji on the stage, passed through five editions in the author's life-time. After 33 years of silence, he resumed this class of compositions in 1913 and produced *Taramandal, Chitra-vanchana, Krishna-Kanchan, Shiva-Sambhav* (the birth of Shivaji), and *Ugra-Mangal.* In several of these pieces, songs set to various tunes enchant the audience. The public patronage of the dramatist enabled the historian to meet in part the heavy cost of his twelve large volumes of historical records, which have not paid their way.

Popular as Khare the dramatist and nationalist poet was and still continues to be, his title to the remembrance and gratitude of posterity is his service to Maratha history. When he first went to Poona as a young school pandit, he was thrown into the company of Sane and Modak and helped them in editing their historical magazine *Kavy-etihas Sangraha* at its start. In 1888 he published a life of Nana Fadnis, in which, however, he could not utilise unpublished records. But at Miraj his attention was drawn to the vast and unimpaired collection of old historical documents in the possession of the nobles of the Patwardhan family who had occupied places of great importance in the Maratha State in the Peshwa period. Of this family 13 members had been slain and 16 wounded in the wars of the Marathas, and many others had distinguished themselves in the civil service as well. The letters they wrote from the scenes of their operations or the Poona Court, to their masters or to their relatives, form a priceless treasury of the raw materials of Maratha history.

The Patwardhan family is now divided into many branches, having their fiefs in the South Maratha country, —at Miraj (two houses, senior and junior), Kurundwad, Tasgaon, Jamkhandi. Their geographical position on the road from Mysore (under British occupation after the fall of Tipu Sultan in 1799)—as well as Baji Rao II's foolish hostility to his vassals,—made the Patwardhans court British protection for saving their patrimony. A Patwardhan was in command of the Maratha army that co-operated with the English in Cornwallis's war with Tipu. (See Moor's *Operations of Little's Detachment* for many interesting details.) The Patwardhans assisted the English in the operations following the treaty of Bassein, as readers of Sir Arthur Wellesley's despatches know. Thus, their homes were saved from war and ravage, and their records have remained intact.

Napoleon has truly remarked that in war it is not men that count but *the* man. The same truth was now illustrated in the domain of history. Khare's employment at Miraj and settlement in that town was a divine dispensation to all lovers of Maratha history. Here was the work and here was *the man*.

Khare obtained permission from the Miraj Junior State (and afterwards from the Inchalkaranji Chief) to read their papers, and seriously applied himself to the task which was destined to be his life's work. With tireless patience he made his way through these mouldy masses of old paper written in the difficult cursive Modi hand, and picked out the writings of the makers of Maratha history,—State-papers, despatches, reports, private letters and accounts,—letters from the Peshwas or the Patwardhan officials. Khare selected the really valuable documents, transcribed them in Deva-nagari for the press, chronologically arranged them and wrote historical notes to serve as the connecting tissue and necessary introduction,—and then went to publish them.

The prospect was at first hopeless. As his old pupil writes: " He had so many other obstacles in the way of publishing this material that a man of lesser stuff would have given up the attempt in despair. At that time very few of our people recognised the importance of history, much less that of historical letters. The educated men disdained vernacular publications. The author lived at a place without a printing press and remote from the world of letters; for the sake of his daily bread he had to spend the greater part of the day in drilling dull boys in Sanskrit grammatical forms. Then, there was the official opposition to the publication of these papers. He had none to help and few to sympathise with him. Above all, money was a factor too significant to be ignored. "

Still, with the courage and confidence of a religious

devotee, he began the publication of these select historical documents in June 1897, in a monthly magazine named *Aitihasik Lekh Sangraha* or Collection of Historical Letters (printed at Kurundwad.) After the fourth year, issue in monthly parts was discontinued and only complete volumes of 500 to 600 pages each were issued at intervals of one, two and even three years, according to the state of his private income, because the support of the public (and even that of the Patwardhan Chiefs) was extremely slow and meagre. The author had to meet the printer's bill for the preceding volume from his own pocket before sending a fresh volume to the press!

However, the perseverance of this poor school pandit —whose salary never rose above Rs. 45 a month— triumphed. Before his death in June 1924, he had completed 12 volumes covering 6,843 pages. And after his death, his son Yashawant has published two more volumes, bringing the collection up to 7,976 pages.

The letters begin in 1739 and become most copious from 1761, the fatal year of Panipat. It was Khare's desire to carry them on to 1802, when Maratha independence ceased in all but the name. In the twelfth volume, the actual publication of which was preceded by his death by a few months, he had reached November 1800, and his son has now brought the records down to July 1804.

Khare's most striking characteristics were his systematic arrangement, judicious spirit or strong common sense, and terseness,—in all of which he presents a pleasing contrast to V. K. Rajwade. His *Lekh Sangraha* will stand as a model for other workers among historical archives and editors of documents. His introductions are most helpful to the reader and admirably concise and free from irrelevant digressions.

He retired from his school in 1913 and lived for eleven years more. But his originally robust constitution was broken by poverty, household worries and overwork. On 11th June 1924, he breathed his last, after two years' suffering from dysentery. The Poona Itihas Mandal had elected him its President for one year, and a building has been erected at Miraj in his memory.

Among his other works are the *Harivamsha Bakhar, Inchal-karanji Samsthanancha Itihas, Maloji wa Shahji* and *Adhikar Yoga.* As a man he was truly adorable. His loving pupil writes :—

"Though for the greater part of his life he was forced to live in poverty, what Fortune denied to him was supplied by his innate contentment and simplicity. A self-respecting man, he would never stoop to abject means to enrich himself. Gifted with high brain power as he was, he never shunned hard work. He preferred silent work to platform speeches. His labours at the history of the past, did not blind him to the present, and he kept himself in touch with current literature and newspapers. He was social in his manners, and never was a man more witty and humorous in private talk." *

* Based on materials supplied by Mr. T. M. Bhat, M.A., of Shahapur (Belgaum) and Vol, XII of the *Aiti. Lekh Sangraha.*

XVII

D. B. PARASNIS

His Life

The first and most indispensable condition of historical research is access to original documents. He who collects old State-papers and other sources of history, therefore, makes research possible, and he benefits unborn generations of students by saving these unique records from destruction and dispersion. If, in addition to this, he prints the records, he confers a still greater benefit and extends that benefit to a wider circle of scholars, which may embrace the whole world.

Such a benefactor of all earnest students of Maratha history was lost to us by the death of D. B. Parasnis of Satara on 31st March 1926.

Dattatreya, the son of Balawant Parasnis, was born to an ancient Maratha Brahman family on 27th November, 1870. He read up to the Matriculation standard in the Satara High School. Even in his school days he gave a foretaste of his future pursuits by not confining his studies to his text books, but reading extensively the lives of historical personages, especially those of his native land. His strong literary bent showed itself quite early, and this school-boy founded and edited a monthly magazine which called forth appreciation from some elderly men of light and leading. After leaving school without matriculating, he founded another vernacular magazine, called the *Maharashtra Kokil*, which lasted for some years. But it was with the publication of his third monthly, the *Bharatvarsha*, in 1898 that his life's work really began. Though this periodical had a brief life of two years only, yet its 24 numbers contained many original records and learned reconstructions of Maratha history. An interval of nine years followed its death, and then he founded (in 1908) another and still more valuable historical magazine of the same type under the name of *Itihas Sangraha*, which ran for seven years, but was at last discontinued through getting into very long arrears of publication.

Young Parasnis worked for a long time, under the veteran M. G. Ranade's general guidance, among the Peshwas' records (preserved in the Land Alienation Office at Poona) and prepared the materials which were published, in some cases under other and better-known peoples' names. Later he printed in his own name. selections from these and other records as independent volumes, *viz.*,

Selections from the Peshwas' Diaries: Shahu.
Do do Balaji Baji Rao, 2 vols.
Decisions from Shahu's and Peshwas' Daftars.
Sanads and Letters.
Kaifiyats, Yadis, &c.
Treaties, Agreements, and Sanads.
Life and Letters of Brahmendra Swami.

The Royal House of Tanjore.

Historical Papers relating to the Gwalior State, 5 vols..
(for private use only.)

It was a pity that Parasnis rushed into journalism too early, instead of completing even school education. For, if he had gone through a full college course, his mind would have been equipped with knowledge of the various sources of information so necessary for research workers, his mental horizon would have been widened, and he would have gained greater confidence in his own powers as a writer and boldly challenged criticism by producing scholarly works of his own. As it was, he lived and died a collector and publisher, and not a historian, nor even a reliable editor, though the texts he published will remain invaluable to *other* men who will attempt history after him.

His Published Works

Parasnis's English works may be quickly passed over, as they were of a slight, topical character. His *Mahableshwar* (1916), *Sangli State* (1917), *Poona in Bygone Days* (1921), and *Panhala* (1923)were merely presentation books and fell still-born from the press. The *History of the Maratha People*, 3 vols., which bears his name along with Mr. C. V. Kincaid's on the titlepage, is admittedly the composition of the latter gentleman and expresses his opinions only, while Parasnis merely supplied the materials to the actual writer.

It is only by his publications in the Marathi language that Parasnis wlll live as an author. These form his enduring contribution to Indian history. His first work in his mother tongue was the *Life of the Rani of Jhansi* (1894). followed a couple of years later by *The Marathas in Bundelkhand*. Later came *Brahmendra Swami's life and letters* (the second portion of it being a source of first-rate importance for the reign of Baji Rao I.), the *Life of Baiza Bai* (of Gwalior), &c. Parasnis published by instalments in his magazines several collections of State-papers of the highest value to the student of Maratha history and even of *North* Indian history. First came the bulky *Letters Memorials &c.* (*Patren Yadi bagaire*) contributed to the *Bharatvarsha* by Kashinath N. Sane. Then appeared in the *Itihas-Sangraha* under Parasnis's own editing, two thick volumes of despatches sent to Poona by the Peshwa's agents at the Court of Ahalya Bai Holkar, and two other thick volumes followed by a supplement containing the letters of the Maratha envoys (*wakil*) at the Court of Delhi, besides smaller collections of letters written by the Peshwa's agents at Calcutta, Seringapatam, Jaipur, Jodhpur, Haidarabad, &c.

HIS COLLECTION OF RECORDS

It may not be well-known that Nana Fadnis, who was the *de facto* ruler of the Maratha State for several years, had a favourite country-seat at the quiet romantic village of Menavali. Most of the despatches and other State-papers which reached Poona during his long ministry were taken away by him to this village, and therefore, the State Record Office of the Peshwas (at least the "Foreign" section of it) was not in Poona. After Nana's downfall and death, his family was ruined and these priceless records remained in neglect or under fear of dispersion; in the course of three generations much was gone beyond hope of recovery. (Khan Bahadur Israel once told me that half a century ago he had helped to recover from Manavali a portrait of Mastani ascribed to a French artist.) But when, at the beginning of the 20th century, Parasnis came on the scene he undertook to save and print what still remained.

Similarly, the decay of the Rajahs of Satara (who had been reduced by Dalhousie to the status of land-holders or rather pensioners) opened a wide door to the sale, dispersion and destruction of the valuable historical papers, old pictures, art objects and relics accumulated by the royal house of Shivaji during nearly 150 years. In the middle of the 18th century, when the Marathas dominated North Indian politics, the Mughal Emperors and nobles and the Hindu Rajahs alike sought to please the Chhatrapati by presenting him or his Peshwa with valuable pictures of the Indo-Saracen and Rajput schools, finely illuminated Sanskrit mss., decorated swords and other objects of art. These found a refuge in Satara palace, but began to be dispersed in the last two decades of the 19th century.

Just at this time D. B. Parasnis appeared on the scene. He was an ordinary middle class man, without wealth, without official power or patronage, without social influence. But his heart and brain were ceaselessly devoted to acquiring these raw materials of history, and ultimately he did acquire many of them with infinite patience and versatility in the choice of means, in concert with a Bombay capitalist (not yet broken) named P. V. Mawjee.

The greatest disappointment of Parasnis's life (as he told me) was the burning of the Holkar records at Indore: for no fault of his own he was just too late by a week to see them. After the Peshwas' records (partly preserved in the Land Alienation Office at Poona and partly at Menavali), the next in importance among Maratha historical documents were those of Indore, because the Gaekwad's Marathi State-papers are very modern, nine-tenths of them dating from 1802), and the old records of Sindhia are said to have been cleared away as waste paper by a former governor (*subah*) of Gwalior. The Indore archives, on the other hand, were full and unimpaired. Parasnis had been after these for many years, but the perverse obstructive policy of obscurantist Native State officials had baffled him. At last a British political agent then in retirement in England, heard of it and wrote strongly to the Government of India in support of Parasnis's application; the screw was put from the top, and then the Darbar gave to fear that permission which it had refused to scholarship. With this permit in his hand, Parasnis started for Indore, but while halting at Bombay to make some purchases he received a telegram from Indore stating that a fire* had broken out in the low dark *cutcha* building where the records had been stored like grain-sacks, and that many of them had perished. Such is the harvest reaped by ignorance and folly in high places.

His Book and Picture Collections

In addition to Marathi and Persian ms. records, he made a very useful collection of printed books on Indian history, by a careful and persistent purchase extended over many years. Two examples may be given here. He did not know French or German, and yet in his careful thought to provide every facility for research in India, he bought the *Lives of the Governors-general of the Dutch Indies* printed in French (1730) and a German journal containing Dr. Oskar Mann's long summary (in German) of the *Mujmil-ul-tawarikh bad Nadiriyya* which gives the best Persian account of Ahmad Shah Abdali's rise. His hope was that it would throw light on the battle of Panipat from the Afghan side, and he was sadly disappointed when I told him that that issue ended before the Abdali's coming to India.

*The fire was real and not diplomatic. Selections from the remnant have been now published in two thin volumes by Anant N. Bhagavat, the State archivist. I have examined the records at Indore and found that many of the bundles, tied between two wooden boards, are merely singed at the two edges, *i.e.*, each sheet has lost about 4 lines on each side, and that the rest of their contents is intact.

Not content with printed books in European languages, he also bought in England the entire file of private letters (all autograph) written to Sir Frederick Currie, the British Resident at Lahore, during the eventful year of the Second Sikh War, by Dalhousie, Henry Lawrence, Nicholson and other makers of Indian history, with the drafts of a few replies by Currie. We can here read Dalhousie's defence of his policy in not nipping the Multan outbreak in the bud but taking the risk of the revolt spreading to the whole Sikh population. There are also three other volumes of ms. letters written by Lords Ellenborough, Hardinge and other high officials. Parasnis also secured a fine steel engraving of Lord Clive (in full-blown obesity) by paying something like £ 20 to his Lordship's descendant.

The Mughal paintings that Parasnis rescued out of the Satara Raj collection (sent from Delhi in the 18th century) and also bought elsewhere, include some that are genuinely old and of great value. Nobody in India can hope to write a complete study of Indo-Muhammadan pictorial art unless he examines the four greatest collections of it in India, namely, the Khuda Bakhsh (Patna,) Mr. P. Manuk's (Patna), the Rampur Nawab's and Parasnis's. As late as 1924, Parasnis acquired a portfolio of the portraits of Indian celebrities of the 17th century (mostly of the Deccani Muslim States, with some of the Mughal Court, including a very fine profile of the great Sawai Jai Singh)—which had been collected by a Dutchman in India in Aurangzib's reign. A silly dealer had spoiled many of these by retouching and adding a modern varnish to them.

Financial Tangle

The most unfortunate thing about D. B. Parasnis was that he had no ostensible means of livelihood, except latterly the precarious one of a consultant on the genealogy and territorial rights of the Maratha sardars. A cloud of mystery and suspicion hung round his financial dealings throughout life, and the revelations that came to public knowledge immediately after his death only served to deepen and confirm it instead of clearing his reputation. His failure to get a proper education in boyhood rendered him unfit to enter any learned profession or public service, or maintain himself in the free competition of modern society. Nor had he the stoic fortitude of a Rajwade or a Khare, which might have enabled him to proudly bear a life of honest poverty as they had borne.

His father, Balawant Rao, worked as a Local Fund Accountant under the Revenue department on a pay which rose to Rs. 80 a month and retired on a trifling pension. (The old man survived his son by a few years.) He had no estate and no income of any kind that he could pass on to his heirs. Yet for the last twenty years of his life D. B. Parasnis lived in a most lavish style, he bought and extended a large house-property in Satara named *The Happy Vale*, and amassed collections of manuscripts and pictures like a gentleman of means. All this while his assets were invisible.

The inevitable crash came immediately after his death. Creditors became clamant on all sides. The debts he had left behind him were said to exceed two lakhs of Rupees. One Indian prince got his picture collection attached as security for his loans, exceeding a lakh and a half. Another discovered that Parasnis had taken an advance of Rs. 63,150 from his late father on condition of publishing his ancestors' records and lives but done only a quarter of the work. And there were lesser creditors, too. His children sought Government patronage on the ground of their father's "loyalty," representing themselves as penniless,—except for the house "Happy Vale."

The known facts about D. B. Parasnis's occupations are that after leaving school without matriculating, he took some sort of service under a Southern Maratha chief, and later accompanied the Maharajah of Kolhapur to London at the time of the coronation of Edward VII. Here he made a good use of his time by search among the Marathi records in the India Office Library and elsewhere and by laying the foundations of his English library by select purchase. Before this in India he had begun his collection of Marathi manuscripts and historical records,—by what means we do not know,—and gradually made himself an expert in the history and politics of the period (1782—1818) in which the relations between the British Power and the Maratha chiefs took a definite shape. Later on, Parasnis lived at Satara solely on the bounty of the Maratha chiefs, large and small, to whom he offered his assistance as a professional genealogist biographer and historian. It is a legitimate inference that they maintained him because his information and ms. collection were valuable to them in their many controversies of a political nature with the Paramount Power.

But his purchase of old pictures and other objects of art was a speculation which failed and saddened his last years with a hopeless burden of debt. He appealed to the Bombay Government for support "in the cause of Indian history", and for four years before his death that Government granted him an allowance of Rs. 306 a month (with effect from 1 August 1922). In addition Government built and furnished a fine fire-proof building, known as the Satara Historical Museum, at a cost of over a lakh and a half, for housing "the historical mss, papers, books, &c.* in the possession of Mr. Parasnis, and they are to be at the disposal of any scholar who proposes to carry on research in history," as requested and agreed to by Parasnis. (Govt. Resolution No. 6896, Genl. Dept. 29 Aug. 1914.) This Museum was opened by the Governor, Sir Leslie Wilson, on 3rd November, 1925, but before the transfer of the articles from

*In Parasnis's letter to Government, dated 5 Sep. 1913, "pictures and articles of historical value" are expressly included in the offer, though he afterwards withheld them from the Museum. The building cost Rs. 1,47,411 and the furniture Rs. 15,000, the price of the site and extensive surrounding grounds not taken into account.

Parasnis's private residence to the Museum building could be completed and a proper Board of Trustees for the Museum constituted, he died on 31st March next. His heir made the astounding claim that the Museum building and furniture were a free gift from the public purse to his late father!

We may here mention that Government had been the chief supporter of his historical magazine (*Itihas Sangraha*, running for seven years and three months), by subscribing a large number of copies of it for schools and other public institutions. They had conferred on him the title of Rao Bahadur in 1913.

How the Bombay Tax-payers were 'done'

Rao Bahadur Parasnis had drawn Rs. 12,900 in allowances from the public funds (1922-26) without giving anything tangible in return. In his petitions to Government he had uniformly begged for money help from the State on the ground that thereby "the collection [of historical materials made by him] should be preserved *intact* for the benefit of the present generation and posterity....under proper custodianship." (Statement of Parasnis to Mr. Machonochie, I.C.S., June 1914.) Again, in 1924 he wrote to Government, "During the last 30 years I have collected from various sources a large number of papers dealing with the history of the Maratha period from 1627 to 1818....There are about 20,000 documents of great historical importance....The collection that I have made at Satara and that I am now offering to the proposed Historical Museum for the use of the public is my own private property and I have spent the whole of my fortune over it." (16 Aug. and 29 Sep. 1924.)

In 1922 the Bombay Government had given him the annual subsidy of Rs. 3,600 on the written understanding that but for such help Parasnis would be compelled to sell some of his pictures and it was necessary in the interests of history to prevent any part of his collection from being dispersed. In the draft scheme of the Satara Museum submitted by Parasnis to Government in 1914, he had clearly stated that "it shall be the primary duty of the Trust to preserve the collection of historical mss, books, papers, *pictures* and articles &c. to be handed over to them." (Resolution No. 6896, Genl. Dept.)

But when at last the Museum was about to be formally opened (Nov. 1925), he declared that he would not part with the pictures unless Government purchased them, otherwise he would sell them elsewhere. Soon afterwards came his sudden death, and then followed a period of confused negotiation which was heightened by the transfer from Satara of Mr. H. D. Baskerville, I.C.S., the only officer who had fully studied the case and taken a firm stand in defence of the public funds. There was the prospect of the Satara Museum remaining vacant unless Government agreed to buy from Parasnis's heir, not only the pictures (about which there had arisen a difference of opinion just before the owner's death) but even the historical records and books that he had collected and about which no price had been asked for by him.

The evil was aggravated by the facts that Government did not consult any historical expert in the matter and that they had not secured from the Rao Bahadur any detailed list of the records &c. proposed to be housed in the Museum. When his sudden death took place, none outside his family knew the contents and relative value of the two portions of the Parasnis manuscript collection, one of which had been recently transferred to the Museum and the other, though professedly destined for the same public institution, was still stored in his private residence and inaccessible to Government officers. His eldest son, Amrit D. Parasnis, at once denied the right of Government to keep the least particle of his father's collection in the Museum unless the family was granted a perpetual pension of Rs. 6,000 a year.

The Collector of Satara discovered that "only the inferior portion of the Parasnis collection is at present housed in the Museum building, (being worth less than half a lakh), and everything that is of real value still remains with Parasnis junior at Happy Vale." The Bombay Government offered to grant the famiiy a *perpetual* hereditary pension of Rs. 2,400, a year on condition that the Rao Bahadur's *whole* collection of documents should be handed over to the Museum and that if any part of the collection was retained in Happy Vale as private property, the offer of the pension would be withdrawn.

This was quite fair and understandable. But in the confusion caused by the frequent transfer of Collectors and the negligence of their office clerks, this order of the Chief Secretary was overlooked and in the agreement actually executed between Government and Parasnis's heirs in 1928, the latter gained a perpetual pension of Rs. 2,400 a year (worth Rs. 68,300 when capitalised in 3½ p.c. Government Paper) and parted with only such of the historical documents and printed books as were entered in a typed list, which Government had not taken the care to previously scrutinise with the help of expert advice. The result is that an important part of the collection, consisting of unpublished records about Mahadji Sindhia, is still retained by Parasnis's heirs beyond the reach of the public.

How I tracked the Secretly Printed Mahadji Records

The First Maratha War of the English E. I. Co., (1775-1782) brought to the front two great personalities,—Nana Fadnis the statesman and organiser and Mahadji Sindhia the soldier and diplomat. Nana continued to rule the Poona Government as the *Peshwa's Peshwa*, for twenty years. All the despatches and other State-papers sent to the Peshwa during these long years reached Nana's hands and were kept in his own house and not in the official Record Office of the Peshwas. Hence they are not to be found among the Peshwas' archives which the English took over on the annexation of the Peshwas' dominions in 1818 and which are now preserved in the Alienation Office of Poona. The Marathi records there suddenly dry up after the year 1773.

In 1908, D. B. Parasnis started a historical monthly named the *Itihas Sangraha* in which he serially printed all that now survives of the despatches received by Nana Fadnis from the Maratha envoys at Delhi and at Ahalya Bai Holkar's Court (Maheshwar), as well as Calcutta, Haidarabad, &c. Here he also printed, in a most tantalising fashion, once in a year or two, a single despatch from Nana's agent in Mahadji's camp, but gave no inkling as to the number and range of the documents belonging to this series, nor whether the whole of them was in his hands. This was the state of knowledge that the outer public had on the subject till Parasnis's death in March 1926.

During my first visit to Parasnis, in October 1916, I noticed two clerks under him engaged in transcribing old Marathi letters, with some twenty bundles before them. He told me that these were the original letters relating to Mahadji Sindhia and that he had undertaken, on behalf of Maharajah Sir Madhav Rao Sindhia, to print them in 15 volumes. There were more bundles of them in his cupboards.

In January 1925, the Rao Bahadur found it necessary to take me to his house at Satara in order to secure my expert opinion on the age, subjects and genuineness of the "Mughal" paintings he had collected, which he was anxious to sell. I replied that I could go only on condition that he gave me a copy of the Sindhia records privately printed by him for the Gwalior Government, and he wrote back "What you have asked for will be given to you." At the end of this visit, as I was about to leave the town, he quietly put into my hands a parcel wrapped in a newspaper, which he asked me to keep secret, as the books belonged to the Gwalior Government. These, I found, were volumes II and III of a series of Marathi historical letters bearing the English title *Historical Papers relating to Gwalior State (Private and Confidential)* and a Marathi title meaning *The original correspondence of Mahadji Sindhia alias Patil Baba*.

After the death of Parasnis, I moved the Council of Regency at Gwalior and that Government, looking into its old letters, discovered that Parasnis had taken Rs. 63,150 from the late Maharajah Sindhia by promising to print ten volumes of historical letters and five volumes of biographies relating to the great kings of this dynasty. Sindhia's Government had therefore a claim to all the printed copies of these volumes, and soon secured them from his eldest son; but these were found to consist of four volumes in Marathi, numbered II-V, and one volume in English giving merely reprints from English books already available elsewhere. Hence the first volume of the Marathi records, containing letters numbered 1 to 151, was missing. Parasnis's eldest son Amrit Rao said that he had not a single copy of this volume among his father's effects nor knew where (if at all) it had been sent to be printed. The *Poona* press where the last four Marathi volumes had been printed knew nothing of such a first volume.

The matter rested in this state of baffling darkness for two years, when a private detective investigation set in train by G. S. Sardesai bore fruit. It was learnt that a certain press *in Bombay* which had gone into liquidation and whose assets had been attached by a civil court order, held unbound sheets of Marathi letters looking like the contents of our volumes II-V. The point was soon verified. Here was lurking our missing first volume of the Mahadji letters. The Gwalior Darbar was again approached by us, and on its paying Parasnis's debt to this press, it was supplied with the whole stock of this volume (curiously enough only 40 copies as against the 100 copies printed of the subsequent four volumes.) This was done in 1932, while the volume bears 1915 as the date of printing! This is an apt illustration of Rao Bahadur Parasnis's methods.

The enlightened Government of H. H. Jayaji Rao Sindhia has done another service to Indian history. All the contents of these five volumes (608 letters) have been reprinted in a single volume of 942 pages, as corrected, re-arranged and edited with an English summary of each letter and an English Index by G. S. Sardesai, and offered for sale at the ridiculous price of Rs. 2-4.

But these are only the letters that D. B. Parasnis had printed. His heir holds several bundles of the

Mahadji papers, which his father did not live to print and which he now refuses to hand over to the Gwalior Durbar except for a fancy price,—in addition to the Rs. 63,150 digested by the Rao Bahadur. Thus, Sindhia's Government, like the Bombay public, has been "done" by this family.

The residue of the Menavali daftar (as Nana Fadnis's archives are popularly called), has been sold by Parasnis's heirs to the Bombay Government, as I have narrated above. Out of these the Satara Historical Society has picked out all the remaining important papers and published them in two volumes entitled *Historical Papers of the Sindhias of Gwalior* (*Shinde-shahichin Rajkaranen*), 1934 and 1940.

Thus, except for the portion still in the clutches of Mr. A. D. Parasnis, all the Menavali daftar is now available to the public in print. It is, however, necessary to correct the dates (frequently wrong) and readings of Parasnis's printed text, collate the print with the original ms., and rearrange the letters in their proper sequence before these materials can be safely used. Parasnis's ignorance of the Persian language and limited knowledge of Mughal history left many gross errors in the edition prepared by him, and the reader ought to be warned against them.

XVIII

ADDITIONAL DOCUMENTS

[Since the preceding pages were printed, I have been able to use certain additional documents which were for various reasons (chiefly personal) not previously available for my use. These are given in this section with a view to supplementing the information already printed at the places indicated. *J. Sarkar.*]

Ch. VIII. P. 164

13 January 1661.—Farman of Ali Adil Shah II. to Chokka-linga Nayak, ruler of Madura.

"Previously my august *farman* had been issued to you informing you that the full management (*kul madar*) of the provinces of Madura and Tanjore has been entrusted to Maharaj Shahji Bhonsla and the command of the army (*sar-i-lashkari*) of that side to Hasan Ambar Khan, and that no person except these two has any power over it; it is necessary that you should consider the words of these two as equivalent to my royal command and speedily send your tribute money to my Court. But it is very strange that you are still displaying delay and negligence in this matter.

It is your duty, immediately on the arrival of this royal letter, to send your tribute money to the aforesaid two officers and thereby prove your loyalty,—and, considering their orders as verily my orders, carry them out and thus keep them always pleased with you,—which will be equivalent to your pleasing me. 22 Jam. A. 1071.

From Shahji Bhonsla to Ali Adil Shah II.

I beg with all humility and loyalty to submit the following facts to your Majesty.

The Maulvi and Ibrahim Khan, at the time of their starting [on return] to your royal Presence sent the hostage of Tanjore to me, in charge of Baru [or Naro] Pandit, telling me to realise from him four lakhs of *chakram* as a present and then set him free.

As Dik-sabak [?] was the medium of the affairs of both the *Maniwars*,* I summoned him, took the presents and demanded [money] tribute. He replied, "You must first release the son of the ruler of Tanjore, and then at the time of the interview of the two *Maniwars*, a lakh *chakram* will be paid. There should be no demand for any extra tribute over and above the four lakhs of *chakram*. We shall pay [to the Bijapur Sultan] every year that amount of money which we used to pay to the Rayal [Sriranga the last Emperor of Vijaynagar] as tribute. Excuse us any presents over and above that. Let a petition to this effect be written to his Majesty [Adil Shah]."

At that time Itimad Rai was close at hand ; he made a collusion with Dik-sabak and threw the giving of

* *Dik-sabak* (variant *Diksik*) may be a scribe's error for *Dikshit*, a class of Brahmans. Desh-lekhak ? *Maniwar* is a Tamil word meaning 'a superintendent of revenue collection' ; probably used here as equivalent to the North Indian word *Zamindar*, and a contemptuous designation of the rulers of Tanjore and Madura, who were then called *Nayaks* and not *Rais* (= Rajahs.) *Chakram* is a very small gold coin worth 2.1 Rupees.

presents into confusion. He gave Dik-sabak the advice not to offer any *nazar* of jewels and rare articles, saying "For what are you giving a lakh of *chakram*?" The two men became of one mind, and sent a petition to the Sultan, laid every sort of accusation on the Maharaj [Shahji] and prayed that the hostage might be made over to their charge. They raised such a disturbance that all the Telingas and the troops of Bahman and Akat Nayak [? Akal or Yachapa Nayak?], to the number of 40 to 50 thousand infantry and two thousand horsemen assembled together. The Bahman took 70,000 [Rupees or *chakram*?] from Dik-sabak for his expenses, and commenced hostilities against me. He sent word to me, "Join us and release the hostage without taking any present, and thereafter the disturbances in this region will cease. And then as you find opportunities you will be able to establish your own administration."

I refused to agree to this proposal. Therefore they wrote to the Sultan alleging that the Maharaj [Shahji] was taking the tribute from the hostage for his own sake. Your Majesty believing in this representation has sent a royal farman on the subject of the hostage with Maharajah Babaji Pandit ordering me "You cannot realise the tribute; hand the hostage over to the Pandit."

I am a slave of long-standing service, I have been cherished on the salt of this august dynasty for three reigns. How can I set the hostage free unless he pays the tribute money? Without being influenced by any greed for fiefs (*jagir*) I mustered all my troops and enlisted new men, fought and defeated them. But as I had confined the hostage in Devanapatan [Cuddalore], the enemy went there, invested the fort and tried hard to assault it. Hearing of it, I hastened to that place, defeated the Telingas, slew some of them, and taking the hostage out of the fort sent him to Arni fort. I pressed them so hard that no path was left for grain and other provisions to reach them. When grain absolutely reached the price level of one seer for a rupee, they had no power left for bearing the scarcity or fighting. Then they entreated Alawal Khan, offered considerations (*i.e.*, money presents) and made peace on condition of their leaving this country, paying the agreed money contribution for ensuring the liberation of the hostage,—and in future remitting the [annual] tribute the amount of which would be fixed after inquiry [as to what was paid to the Rayal.] I took from them a written bond for observing all these conditions and then opened a path for them to go away.

At this time Chokkanath [=Chokkalinga] extracted the eyes of Dik-sabak and [gave orders for] imprisoning Lingama Nayak. [Here the document ends abruptly as its concluding sheet is missing. For the history, see pages 30-31 above.] Date *c.* 1661

Ch. XII. P. 194. Accession of Shambhuji.

19 April 1680.—Nothing more worthy your Honour's notice, except to advise your Honour &c. of the death of Shivaji, whose death we fear will cause a great deal of trouble in these parts, for most of the merchants are ready to run away, and certainly should any *lashkari* come near the place, they would embark. Shambhuji Rajah has taken up his quarters at Panhala, where goes daily to him abundance of soldiers; he hath sent down and stopped all the corn that is in town, and ordered it to be sent up to him. We likewise do expect that the place will suddenly be secured by Shambhuji Rajah's party, and what we shall do in that condition we leave to your Honour &c. to judge. [Carwar factors to Surat Council.]

26 April 1680.—That which chiefly occasions this, is to acquaint you of the certain news of Shivaji's death, and that country given to Shambhuji Rajah, who hath sent down Ravji Pandit to command all these subahdars to Panhala, to give in their accounts, and it is supposed he will send Mazotto [=Moro Dado] to govern these parts, which makes us hope in a short ti e to see trade encouraged. [Carwar factors to Surat Council.]

Ch. XI. P. 188. Prince Akbar

17 February 1683.—Shaikh Abdullah, son of Shaikh Nizam, reported to the Emperor that Ahmad Khan the thanadar of Antoor has written that Krishna Pandit [a spy in Mughal service] has brought news about the *Rebel* [prince Akbar] to this effect:—

He had newly enlisted 2,000 horse and 2,000 foot to be under his own control; their salary used to be paid by the *Wretch* [Shambhuji]. The latter had presented to the *Rebel* a necklace of pearls and an elephant. The *Rebel* made a Hindu dancing-girl Muslim and kept her in his harem, and gave her the pearl necklace and other things presented to him as gift [by the Maratha king.] When the news of it reached the *Wretch* he sent to the *Rebel* to say, 'I had offered the necklace and other things for your royal paraphernalia'. The *Rebel* replied, 'I am an Emperor's son, I shall do whatever comes to my mind'. Then the *Wretch* sent him a message asking him to send away the troops under him to the former. Therefore, the *Rebel* finding himself helpless, set fire to his house, assumed the guise of a *faqir*, and started for Goa. At last the *Wretch* wrote to the Portuguese not to let the *Rebel* enter their territory. For this reason they kept him out. So, the *Rebel* has turned back, come to the *Wretch's* kingdom and taken up his abode at the place where he formerly used to remain. [Persian *akhbarat*, dated 29 Safar, regnal year 26 = 17 Feb. 1683. This place was Banda in Savant-vadi, then on the Maratha side of the Goa frontier; he soon afterwards moved to Bicholim.]

CORRECTIONS

Page 70, Line 18 *for* 1560 *read* 1660

" 73, " 28 " Nothern *read* Northern

" 141, " 16 *omit* really seven

" 158, " 8 *for* you *read* your

" 220, Line 22 and footnote.—The passage in *Jedhe S.* may also mean "nominated D. J. to command the army sent against S. G." *S. P. D.* XXXI. 68 suggests that Shanta was deprived of the chief command in 1696 or a little earlier. The original of this letter, however, has been lost, and I distrust the copy which alone survives.

" 246, Line 14 *for* reams *read* realms

History of Aurangzib, Rs. 16-8

Complete in five volumes, sold separately

This *History of Aurangzib* is based mainly on original *contemporary Persian, Marathi and European sources*: the Mughal state-papers, daily bulletins of the Mughal Court, the records of impartial non-official writers (such as two Persian memoirs by contemporary Hindu writers), the letters of Aurangzib, his father, brothers, sons, grandsons, officers and vassals, state revenue returns and other documents.

Vincent A. Smith—You are doing **first class work.** I have the highest opinion of your learning, impartiality and critical ability.

Sir William Foster—It is easily **the best authority** on the period with which it deals.

Shivaji and his Times, Rs. 5

Awarded the Gold Medal of the Bombay Br. Royal Asiatic Society

3rd ed. Revised & enlarged

A new and exhaustive study of Shivaji's life and character and the most comprehensive and correct narrative of the rise of the Marathas, based on all the available original materials—Persian, Marathi, Hindi, Dutch, French, Portuguese and English.

Shivaji's character and achievements and the Maratha institutions and system of government are discussed in two long chapters (45 pages), and the lessons taught by the rise and fall of the Marathas are clearly unfolded. A critical bibliography (of 15 pages) is appended.

Fall of the Mughal Empire, 4 Vols.

Vols. I, II and III, Rs. 5 each ; Vol. IV (in prep.)

Sir Jadunath Sarkar's *History of Aurangzib* is a history of the Mughal Empire from 1633 to 1707 ; it is continued in his edition of William Irvine's *Later Mughals*, to the invasion of Nadir Shah in 1739. The present work in 4 volumes is designed to carry the narrative to the virtual end of the Empire by the British capture of Delhi in 1803.

Times—Sir Jadunath Sarkar has undertaken a duty of real importance. His wide scholarship, his deep knowledge, his independent judgment, admirably fit him for the task.

Mughal Administration

3rd Edition, Rs. 3

A complete treatise on the administrative system and constitution of the Mughal Empire. Daily life and powers of the Emperor. Central structure. Diwan and his duties. Provincial administration. Illegal taxes, full list. The spy system. Condition of the peasants. Religious policy and ordinances. State industries. Mughal Aristocracy. Revenue Regulations (in detail). Causes of the downfall of the Mughal Empire. Legacy of Muslim rule. Bibliography (critical and descriptive).

India through the Ages, Re. 1-8

A survey of the growth of Indian life and thought from the Vedic age to our own times—with a detailed study of the contributions of the Aryans, the Buddhists, the Muslims, and the English to the growth of Indian civilization.

Times.—An excellent little compendium of the history of India.

J. R. A. S.—The causes which led to the spread of Buddhism, and to the transition from Buddhism back to Hinduism, are *clearly and interestingly sketched*, so also is the brief review of the growth of English education in Bengal. Professor Sarkar writes without partiality or bias. The book *gives an interesting and clearly written review of* the successive factors which have contributed to *the composite development of the India* of the present day.

Chaitanya

3rd ed. with a portrait, Rs. 2

Chaitanya (1415-1533), the greatest saint of Bengal, caused a complete moral revolution in Eastern India by preaching the creed of *bhakti* or devotion to God as incarnate in Krishna. His faith conquered Bengal, Orissa and Assam, and also established its strongholds in several other places, notably Brindaban.

C. F. Andrews.—Of surpassing value...... gives the clearest picture of the Saint, and his teaching, and is **full of intense human interest from beginning to end** ....The picture drawn of the Saint is one of extraordinary beauty : a truly human figure comes before us and attracts our own love, even as it attracted the love of his first disciples. (*Modern Review, Oct. 1913.*)

Printed and Published by—S. N. Sarkar at the Midland Press, 2, Gangaram Palit Lane, Calcutta.